THE
ST. PETERSBURG
CONNECTION

ALEXIS S. TROUBETZKOY

THE
ST. PETERSBURG
CONNECTION

RUSSIAN-AMERICAN
FRIENDSHIP FROM
REVOLUTION TO
REVOLUTION

DUNDURN
TORONTO

Editor: Dominic Farrell
Copy editor: Joe Zingrone
Design: Jennifer Gallinger
Cover design: Laura Boyle
Cover image: Orthodox Cathedral Temple icon: © ARCHITECTEUR/ shutterstock.com;
        Capitol building icon: © america365/ shutterstock.com
Printer: Webcom

Library and Archives Canada Cataloguing in Publication

Troubetzkoy, Alexis S., 1934-, author
    The St. Petersburg connection : Russian-American friendship from revolution to revolution / Alexis S. Troubetzkoy.

Includes bibliographical references and index.
Issued in print and electronic formats.
ISBN 978-1-4597-3148-6 (paperback).--ISBN 978-1-4597-3149-3 (pdf).--
ISBN 978-1-4597-3150-9 (epub)

    1. United States--Foreign relations--Russia. 2. Russia--Foreign relations--United States. I. Title.

E183.8.R9T76 2015   327.7304709'034   C2015-904855-9
                                         C2015-904856-7

1 2 3 4 5   19 18 17 16 15

We acknowledge the support of the Canada Council for the Arts and the Ontario Arts Council for our publishing program. We also acknowledge the financial support of the Government of Canada through the Canada Book Fund and Livres Canada Books, and the Government of Ontario through the Ontario Book Publishing Tax Credit and the Ontario Media Development Corporation.

Care has been taken to trace the ownership of copyright material used in this book. The author and the publisher welcome any information enabling them to rectify any references or credits in subsequent editions.
— J. Kirk Howard, President

The publisher is not responsible for websites or their content unless they are owned by the publisher.

Printed and bound in Canada.

VISIT US AT

Dundurn.com | @dundurnpress | Facebook.com/dundurnpress | Pinterest.com/dundurnpress

Dundurn
3 Church Street, Suite 500
Toronto, Ontario, Canada
M5E 1M2

This work is dedicated to the class of '53,
Kent School

CONTENTS

PREFACE

The aim of *The St. Petersburg Connection* is twofold: first, to trace the historical path of the amicable, supportive relations between the United States and Russia that held firm for nearly a century and a half; second, to sketch a fleeting picture of an age that made it possible. In the bygone days of my teaching career, I strove to impress upon students that the critical aspects of historical events are not primarily to do with *when* they happened or in the details of *what* transpired. The pith of history lies in an understanding of *why* they happened and what the *results* were.

Historical events do not occur in isolation — outside forces are invariably at work. The United States did not enter World War I on account of the *Lusitania*'s sinking; it declared war because of events unfolding in Europe and the Far East. Saddam Hussein was not executed because he was nasty with his own people in Iraq; he met his end because he was perceived as a threat to Arab neighbours and to the larger world. The whys and wherefores of history must therefore be examined in the broadest perspective. And so, the story of Russian–American friendship calls attention to the likes of Britain, Japan, and Spain, to Paris, Rio de Janeiro, and Honolulu.

Fundamental to any history are the personalities of the principals involved. A history of the Roman Empire can be had in the biographies of a hundred of its leading citizens. A history of the American Revolution can be had in the stories of two dozen of its leaders. A history of World War II, for example, will inevitably focus on the ambitions of Hitler and the resolve of Churchill (together with the velleity of Chamberlain), the personality of Roosevelt, the ruthlessness and wile of Stalin, the tactical skills of Eisenhower, and the decisiveness of Truman.

This narrative follows the same model, focusing on the individuals involved — not only the famous like Abraham Lincoln and Tsar Alexander I, but also less-notable figures such as William Seward and Nikolai Rezanov, as well as the likes of the virtually unknown: Nero Prince, Andrei Dashkov, and John Ledyard. Regardless of whether they were dominant or peripheral figures, all played roles in the story of Russian–American relations.

The scholastic purist may question my lack of strict adherence to contemporary academic form in this book. I make no apologies and offer no pretense that this is a scholarly treatise. *The St. Petersburg Connection* is a story … a compelling one that needs telling.

Alexis S. Troubetzkoy

Labelle, Quebec

ACKNOWLEDGEMENTS

For their assistance and unfailing courtesies during the researching and development of this book, I wish to thank the staffs of the New York City Public Library, the Robarts Library of the University of Toronto, Oxford's Bodleian Library, the George Washington University Library, the Free Library of Philadelphia, the University of British Columbia Library, as well as the British Columbia Provincial Archive.

Much of the inspiration for *The St. Petersburg Connection* came from Alexandre Tarsaidzé's *Czars and Presidents*. I am particularly grateful to Norman E. Saul of the University of Kansas for his brilliant and comprehensive studies of Russian-American relations. In this work, I have made liberal use of the references Dr. Saul cites in his two major books on the subject, *Distant Friends: The United States and Russia, 1763–1867* and *Concord and Conflict: The United States and Russia, 1867–1914*.

In addition to Dr. Saul's writings, I refer readers wishing to explore the subject more fully to the work of John F. Dulles and Frank A. Golder, whose books are listed in the bibliography.

Thank you to Dominic Farrell of Dundurn Press for his astute editing of the manuscript, and to my good friend Cameron Macleod for his map work. As always thanks to my agent and friend Bill Hanna of Acacia House Publishing Services, who offered helpful advice and encouragement as this work progressed.

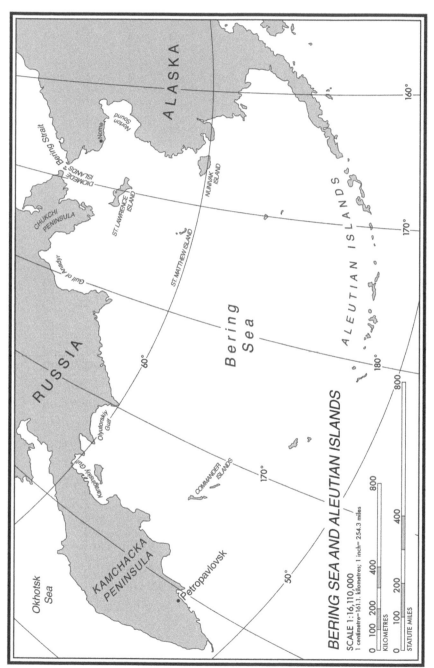

BERING SEA AND ALEUTIAN ISLANDS

SCALE 1:16,110,000
1 centimetre=161.1. kilometres; 1 inch= 254.3 miles

KILOMETRES
0   100 200   400   800

STATUTE MILES
0   100   200   400   800

RUSSIA

ALASKA

Bering
Sea

ALEUTIAN ISLANDS

KAMCHACKA
PENINSULA

Okhotsk
Sea

CHUKCHI
PENINSULA

Gulf of Anadyr

Olyutorskiy
Gulf

Karaginskiy Gulf

Petropavlovsk

Nome

Norton
Sound

Bering Strait

DIOMEDE
ISLANDS

ST. LAWRENCE
ISLAND

ST. MATTHEW ISLAND

NUNIVAK
ISLAND

COMMANDER
ISLANDS

50°

60°

160°

170°

180°

170°

Bering Sea and Aleutian Islands.

TIMELINE

1648	Semyon Dezhnev the first European to sail through the Bering Strait
1682	Peter I (The Great) proclaimed tsar at the age of ten and is forced to rule jointly with his brother Ivan under the patronage of their sister, Sophia
1703	Tsar Peter selects site for St. Petersburg
1725	Vitus Bering's first expedition Catherine I succeeds Peter and becomes the first woman to rule imperial Russia
1727	Peter II succeeds Catherine
1730	Anna succeeds Peter II
1733	Bering's second expedition
1741	Elizabeth overthrows the infant Ivan VI and the regent Anna Leopoldovna
1743	Emelian Basov voyage
1745	Yakov Chupov voyage to Aleutians
1762	Peter III formally abdicates and is then killed
1762	Catherine II (The Great) becomes empress of Russia
1778	Captain James Cook arrives in British Columbia
1781	Francis Dana becomes first U.S. envoy to St. Petersburg Northeastern Company formed
1787	U.S. explorer John Ledyard in Russia
1788	Russia attacks Turkey

	John Meares arrives in British Columbia
1789	George Washington becomes first U.S. president
1790	Washington selects District of Columbia as U.S. capital
	John Paul Jones is made commodore of U.S. fleet
	Alexander Baranov travels to Alaska to set up a Russian-American Company trading post
	Meares arrives in Nootka
1791	Captain George Vancouver arrives in British Columbia
	Robert Gray travels to the Columbia River
1792	Demetrius Gallitzen arrives in Maryland
1793	Alexander Mackenzie crosses the Rockies
1794	Spain and the United Kingdom sign the Nootka Convention, avoiding war
1796	Paul I succeeds Catherine and becomes Russian tsar
	Washington negotiates U.S. treaty with the Barbary pirates
1797	John Adams becomes U.S. president
1801	Alexander I succeeds Paul I as Russian tsar
	Thomas Jefferson becomes U.S. president
1803	Louisiana Purchase
	Fyodor Ivanovich Tolstoy, the "American" Tolstoy, sails in the Pacific
1804	Napoleon is crowned emperor
1805	Lewis and Clark's expedition
	Russian diplomat Rezanov arrives in Sitka and California
1807	Peninsular War begins
1809	James Madison becomes U.S. president
	Russia officially gives diplomatic recognition to the United States
	John Quincy Adam assumes post in St. Petersburg
1810	John Jacob Astor establishes the Astoria in Oregon
1812	Napoleon invades Moscow
	United States invades Canada (War of 1812)
	Fort Ross is founded in California
1814	Napoleon is exiled to Elba
	The British burn Washington

	Treaty of Ghent is signed
	Holy Alliance
1815	Battle of Waterloo
	Napoleon is exiled to St. Helena
	Kozlov affair
1817	James Monroe becomes U.S. president
	Russian flag flies in Hawaii
1823	Monroe Doctrine
1824	Convention of 1824
1825	Nicholas I becomes Russian tsar
	John Quincy Adams becomes U.S. president
1843	Hawaiian flag comes into being
1853	Franklin Pierce becomes U.S. president
	Crimean War
1855	Alexander II becomes Russian tsar
1861	Abraham Lincoln becomes U.S. president
	Emancipation Proclamation (Russia)
	U.S. Civil War begins at Fort Sumter
1863	Lincoln's proclamation of slavery's abolition
	Russian fleets arrive in San Francisco and New York
1865	The 13th Amendment abolishing slavery
	U.S. Civil War ends
	Russian–American Telegraph Company is formed
1867	Alaska purchased by the United States ("Seward's Folly")
1872	Grand Duke Alexis visits the United States
1881	Alexander III succeeds to the Russian throne
	Massive pogroms in Russia
1894	Nicholas II becomes Russian tsar
1897	U.S. flag is raised in Hawaii
1901	Theodore Roosevelt becomes U.S. president
1903	Kishenev massacre
1904	Japan attacks Port Arthur (Russo-Japanese War)
1905	Roosevelt organizes the Portsmouth Peace Conference
1913	Woodrow Wilson becomes U.S. president
1914	Franz Ferdinand is assassinated, triggering First World War

1915	*Lusitania* torpedoed by German submarine
1917	St. Petersburg riots take over the city
	Lenin forms Communist government
	United States declares war on Germany
	U.S. Expeditionary Forces to Russia
1918	Nicholas II and family are assassinated in July

CHAPTER 1

THE SHORTEST DISTANCE

In the summer of 1987, an extraordinary young woman from Los Alamitos, California, lowered herself gingerly into the frigid waters of the Bering Strait, some 350 miles north of Anchorage, Alaska, and set out to swim to Russia. Lynne Cox was her name. With long, persistent strokes, the stout-hearted athlete doggedly pressed forward, eventually losing sight of the United States. She wore an ordinary swimsuit and bathing cap. Incredibly, she had no wet suit — only protective grease. In those 38°F–42°F waters, hypothermia might have been expected to beset Cox, but the cold appeared to leave her unaffected. Steadily and forcefully, she propelled herself through the choppy waters dancing about her, and after what seemed an interminable time, her feet finally scraped the rocky bottom. Lynne Cox was in Russia — she had made it. That the thirty-year-old succeeded in her goal was an unbelievable feat. Warmly bundled psychologists monitoring Cox's swim from the comfort of the accompanying boat were astonished, as were the admiring publics of Russia and of the United States. In May 1990, at a White House summit conference, President Reagan and President Mikhail Gorbachev raised a toast to the indefatigable Cox who "proved by her courage how closely to each other our peoples live."

It took Cox two hours and sixteen minutes to cover the distance from Little Diomede Island in the United States to Big Diomede Island in Russia. For her, swimming in those near-freezing waters, the passage must at times have appeared endless. In reality, however, it is the shortest distance, a mere 2.7 miles. The United States nearly abuts Russia — Canada and Mexico aside, Russia is its nearest neighbour.

For over a century, this neighbourliness transcended any consideration of geographic proximity; the happy state of bilateral relations between the United States and Russia had bonded the two countries into firm friendship. From the very birth of the American nation in 1776, relations between the United States and Russia had been predicated on mutual support and respect. To this day, the two countries have never fought one another. Over the centuries, the United States has at one time or another engaged in warfare with virtually every major world power. Americans have taken up arms against the British and the French, the Germans and Spanish, the Italians and Japanese. But never the Russians. And Russia has fought with all these same powers — Spain excepted — and others, like Sweden and Turkey. But never with the United States. Even through the perilous decades of the Soviet Union, through *glasnosts* and beyond, in all the conflicts of Europe, Asia, or Africa, not a drop of blood has been shed by one of the other. The tale of how that came to be forms some of the more intriguing pages of European and American histories. Insofar as the United States and Russia are concerned, the account of early interaction is particularly compelling, and no more so than from the human interest viewpoint — the citizens of one country influencing the development of the other.

A vivid illustration of supportive action is the Russian response to American pleas for assistance in addressing the problem of Barbary pirates. For centuries, these North African brigands had engaged in high-seas extortion and raiding, at one point invading Ireland and spiriting away the entire population of the coastal town of Baltimore. Only one of the unfortunates returned home from the clutches of the Algerian raiders. The thugs considered themselves at war with any country that had failed to sign a contract guaranteeing hassle-free sailing in the western Mediterranean in return for a hefty annual fee.

In 1792 George Washington was forced to pay Tripoli a ransom fee of $56,000 to free a captured American ship and its crew. Shortly thereafter, the envious Algerians made similar demands, but for larger sums. Tripoli reacted by raising the ante. Enough was enough. Washington refused all demands, and to nobody's surprise, the pasha of Tripoli declared war against the United States. President Thomas Jefferson dispatched a fleet of four newly constructed ships to engage the Barbary *canaille*. During the ensuing battle, some American sailors were taken prisoner — naturally, a huge payment was demanded. Ransom money was out of the question, and the president turned to the Russian tsar for assistance. The response was immediate. Russia at the time had a formal alliance with the sultan of the Ottoman Empire, suzerain of the Barbary Coast, and it also had a well-armed fleet stationed in the Mediterranean. Tsar Alexander leaned heavily on the sultan, and within weeks the incarcerated seamen were released; Jefferson sent a warm letter of gratitude to St. Petersburg. Such was the cooperative relationship between both the two heads of state and also their nations.

Thomas Jefferson, as secretary of state, wrote in 1791, "Russia is the most cordially friendly nation to us of any power on earth." Tsar Alexander I — the eventual vanquisher of the indomitable Napoleon — declared, "He [Jefferson] is the only sovereign who cordially loves us." Alexander reciprocated in admiration not only of Jefferson but of the United States, particularly for its "... free and wise constitution, which assures the happiness of each and everyone." Warm words indeed. Such was the relationship in Jefferson's time and so it continued over a hundred years. By 1809, when Russia finally extended diplomatic recognition to the young American republic, the relationship between the two countries had solidified into a friendship that ended only with the fall of imperial Russia in 1917.

In Jefferson's day, the United States was in its infancy, a nation founded on the principles of equality and freedom — in the truest sense an open country with an open society. Russia, on the other hand, was an ancient country of startling inequality and, in the words of Churchill, "a riddle wrapped in a mystery inside an enigma." In one country, the democratically elected president, a zealous republican answerable to his people; in the other, a hereditary monarch, an autocrat of boundless power, answerable only to himself. "In the domain assigned to the Tsar," wrote an eighteenth-century historian, "he can, like God, create what he wills." Russia and the United States were two countries, nearly half a world apart, standing in startling contrast but regarding each other with respect and partiality.

The countries did have one element in common at that time: insofar as Europe was concerned, they were both outsiders. The United States was a newcomer to the family of nations, physically distanced by the Atlantic Ocean, and just beginning to develop muscle. It was a country where democratic ideals had rooted in revolutionary soil. Many crowned heads in Europe viewed the new nation as a novel, possibly insidious experiment — for some, bordering on anathema. Ancient country as it was, Russia remained largely unknown to the West. The tsars for the most part had not been drawn into European internal affairs. It was only with Alexander's critical participation in the Napoleonic Wars that Russia became a key player on the continental geopolitical stage. Until then, Europe viewed both Russia and the United States as potentially threatening elements in the preservation of the balance of power. That both countries were outside the European pivot no doubt helped to draw them closer — psychologically, if nothing else.

Political outsiders as America and Russia may at one time have been, trade soon propelled them to the continental fore. Something else that concurrently caused the nations to find common cause were their respective rivalries with Britain. By the second half of the nineteenth century, New York, Boston, and Philadelphia had developed into major trading centres — and the lucrative maritime trade triangle of North America, the Caribbean, and Europe had also burgeoned by then. To sustain and expand this growth, ships were required in large numbers. Enormous quantities of raw materials had to feed the shipyards: iron for anchors and chains, linen for sailcloth, hemp for ropes, wood for hulls and decks. For much of their supply, shipbuilders looked to Russia and its Baltic ports. And the tsar's domain delivered. Its vast hinterland was a trove of raw material, but above all, the country offered an inexpensive labour force. Prices were right. Additionally, there was a market for Russian linens, ironwork, and glassware. In return, quantities of tobacco, cotton, coffee, sugar, spices, and other non-indigenous goods were received in St. Petersburg. Trade between the two countries flourished. (In passing, it may be noted, the supply of these low-cost goods depended on serfdom and slavery. Legitimate argument can therefore be made that the profitable commerce between the two nations contributed to the perpetuation of these social evils within the two countries.)

The United States and Russia shared something else in common: space. Both countries had lots of it — arable lands galore, broad prairies, fertile river valleys, rich forests, and an abundance of natural resources. Frontierism helped to mould the national character of their respective peoples. While the energies of the great powers centred on empire building, Americans and Russians were also focused on the cultivation of these illimitable resources. The priority in both cases was first and foremost the exploitation of their lands' bounty, as well as the maintenance of their security. Referring to the frontier and to national character, Foster R. Dulles observed in 1954 that "Russia and America have always looked to the future, for it has always been big with promise, and their people have shared a sturdy confidence, a sense of inherent power, that have often impressed foreign visitors."[1] It was Alexis de Tocqueville, writing over a century and a half earlier, who defined it best:

> There are at present two great nations in the world, which seem to tend towards the same end, although they start from different points. I allude to the Russians and the Americans.... Their starting point is different and their courses are not the same, yet each of them appears to be marked by the will of heaven to sway the destinies of half the globe.[2]

At the turn of the nineteenth century, the tsar's domain stretched east from the Baltic Sea seemingly without end. It was the world's largest country, a vast expanse that covered nearly one-sixth of the earth's habitable surface. For over four centuries, the tsar's territory had expanded at a rate of almost twenty square miles a day. Among its extensive steppes, rich farmlands, and dense forests, and along its massive waterways, lived some forty-four million subjects of diverse ethnic and religious origin. Much of the country was unmapped and sections of it simply unexplored.

And so it was also with the United States. When the thirteen colonies came together in 1776, the united territory included 892,000 square miles of land, stretching north to south along the Atlantic seaboard. The western borders of some states were not clearly delineated and most of the enormous territories required clearing. The population at the time was just over five million inhabitants, not counting slaves and the surviving indigenous people. In 1803, a determined Thomas Jefferson persuaded the Continental Congress to purchase from France the Louisiana Territory. On April 30 of that year, the triumphant president signed the deed of sale in payment for which Napoleon received $15 million. With a single stroke of the pen, the United States doubled in size. The nation now stretched from the shores of the Atlantic, across the Mississippi River and deep into the northwest. Apart from a few forts and the occasional trading post along the waterways, however, only Natives inhabited the newly acquired land.

At the time of the American Revolution, Catherine II was on the Russian throne. The formidable ruler had been watching the unfolding events in North America with curiosity, and, as a daughter of the Enlightenment, Catherine the Great was interested in the theoretical aspect of it. How would the principles of self-government take root were the colonials to succeed? She also wondered about the impact the developing events might have on Britain, a Russian ally. A disturbing aspect to the American Revolution was this: France, their common enemy, was aiding the young nation. Moreover, it did not escape Catherine that whatever the outcome, Russia's trade with the United States would no doubt be affected. But how? Positively or negatively? And finally, she feared that the North American conflagration could draw European powers into conflict, which then might upset the delicate balance of power and in turn affect her expansionist ambitions.

Catherine observed the troublesome events as an interested bystander. From the beginning, and especially as the struggle gained momentum, she had little doubt that the British would fail, and she boldly expressed her opinion in public. Britain's George III appealed to Catherine for military support — "a few Cossack regiments" (specifically, twenty thousand soldiers). She refused the request, pleading that her forces were exhausted from the recently terminated Turkish campaign, and she said, "I am just beginning to enjoy peace." In alliance with Britain or not, the empress had little personal affection for its king and ministers, and no doubt this aversion influenced her reply. Besides, the whole matter was a hopeless case. George received her reply with profound resentment. He had, after all, supported the Russians in their recent Turkish war, and some form of reciprocation might reasonably have been expected.

As the confrontation in the American colonies went from bad to worse for the British, the king once more appealed to the tsarina, this time pleading for a force significantly greater than a few Cossacks. Before things went bad for the British, the request was as much for moral support as anything. Now it was a critical matter of maintaining the monarchical system and the status quo. Another Russian refusal, George said bluntly, would risk Britain's enmity. In presenting his request to Catherine, British ambassador James Harris asked, "Suppose the colonies were yours. Would you give them independence?" To which Catherine indignantly replied, "I would rather lose my head! But the American colonies are not mine, fortunately."

In 1779, Harris made one final, desperate appeal for Russian assistance, this time offering Catherine the island of Minorca as an enticement. If she were to decline that Mediterranean base, she might have been offered "one of the sugar islands" in the Caribbean — perhaps Jamaica. The empress would have none of that and George III was once more rebuffed. The miffed envoy in concluding his written report to the king quoted Catherine's final rejoinder: "If England desires peace she must renounce her struggle with the colonies." She did, however, offer her services as a mediator. The proposal was summarily rejected by George.

An intriguing academic question: had Catherine not steadfastly refused King George's entreaties, but instead expedited the requested twenty thousand Cossacks, might the revolution's been reversed? Imagine, then, the United States today as a Commonwealth nation, with the queen at its head ... not unlike Australia and New Zealand.

CHAPTER 2

THE DETERMINATIVE PERIOD

The capital of the United States had been moved by 1800 from Philadelphia to its present location in Washington, D.C. The new capital city, however, was more of a concept than a reality. In 1790, George Washington had selected a sixty-nine-square-mile parcel of land that he persuaded Maryland and Virginia to cede (Virginia later reclaimed its part). Through the centre of the president's dream capital flowed the Potomac River, referred to by First Nations people as "river of the swans." These waters merged with the Anacostia River and then continued out through Chesapeake Bay to the shipping lanes of the Atlantic. Washington was a judicious selection of location, being halfway between Vermont and Georgia at the geographical centre of the thirteen colonies. That the selected site was within easy reach of Mount Vernon, George Washington's beloved and impressive home, was serendipitous. Or was it?

The district was relatively unpopulated, holding just the villages of Georgetown, Carrollsburg, and Alexandria plus nineteen outlying farms belonging to wealthy landlords. "The Father of the Nation" was well pleased with the forested site and he plunged enthusiastically into planning for its future. He was determined to develop "… a federal city which is to become the capital of this vast empire, on such a scale as to leave room for that aggrandizement and embellishment which the increase of the wealth of the nation will permit it to pursue to any period however remote."

Nicholas King, 1771–1812. Watercolour. Library of Congress.

Washington, D.C., c. 1803, showing a pastoral view with the President's House, Gales' House, and the Old Patent Office (later the New Post Office & Blodget's Hotel) in the foreground.

Congress, however, was strongly divided over George Washington's choice of site. As Thomas Jefferson observed, "This measure produced the most bitter and angry contests ever known in Congress, before or since the union of States.... The Eastern [New England] members threatened a secession and dissolution." The northern states felt the location was too far south and the southern states deemed it too far north. Eventually, however, through Jefferson's forceful persuasion, the legislators acquiesced and the bill creating the new capital was approved.

At the centre of the diamond-shaped territory, called the District of Columbia, plans for the nascent metropolis of Washington were laid out. To chart a municipal plan for the site, Washington called on Major Pierre L'Enfant, a Frenchman who during the revolutionary years had served in the colonial army as an engineer. Jefferson, a self-taught city planner from his earlier days in Europe, lent a guiding hand. L'Enfant drew up an elaborate plan, one that took its inspiration from the magnificent garden layout of Louis XIV's Versailles. He envisioned broad avenues and a maze of geometrically designed streets intersecting one another at circles, where elaborate fountains and statuaries would be found.

When John Adams, the second president of the United States, took up residence in the nation's capital in 1801, it bore no resemblance to L'Enfant's plan. He and his beloved wife Abigail found the place primitive to say the least — full of tree stumps, shabby shacks, unfinished construction, and clouds of mosquitoes. The settlement numbered 3,210 inhabitants, excluding slaves.[1] Ringing the Capitol building was a handful of shops and boarding houses. In these establishments, "together around the common mess-table, kindred spirits" from the same section of country gathered — in caucus, really — to consider the bills of the day. Vice-President Jefferson moved into one such lodging and there he "lived in perfect equality with his fellow boarders and ate from a common table ... always placing himself at the lowest and coldest end of the table at which a company of more than thirty sat down."

From the Capitol, a muddy roadway ran through a thicket of trees, joining up to the White House: Pennsylvania Avenue. "The presidential palace," reported an English visitor in 1803, "is without fence but a few broken rails upon which hang his excellency's stockings and shirts to dry and his maid's blue petticoat." The residence stood in isolation, neighboured only by the Treasury, which housed various government departments. In a letter to her daughter, the first lady wrote,

> Woods are all you see, from Baltimore until you reach *the city*, which is only so in name.... The river which runs up to Alexandria is in full view of my window and I see vessels as they pass and re-pass.
>
> The House is on a grand and superb scale, requiring about thirty servants to attend and keep the apartments.... There is not a single apartment finished.... We have not the least fence, yard or other convenience, without, and the great unfinished audience-room, I make a drying room of, to hang up the clothes.[2]

In addition to the river traffic, Abigail Adams delighted in observing the grazing cattle and the occasional partridge that chanced by.[3]

A hundred years earlier in Russia, Peter the Great, journeyed to the western edge of his empire — to the mouth of the Neva River at the shores of the Baltic Sea, a flat, wild, and swampy area with a network of islands among the river's tributaries and feeding streams. But what he found pleased him. He ordered that a fortress be erected at the spot, a citadel that eventually would serve as the centrepiece of his empire's new capital. If his tradition-bound Slavophile countrymen were to be dragged into Europe, ancient Moscow would have to be forsaken in favour of a new capital, one with access to the oceans — "a window to the west." The new capital was a singularly unlikely place, in winter freezing winds blew in from the Gulf of Finland, and in spring the Neva backed up, often causing untoward floods. Thick mists habitually enshrouded the region and in summer, mosquitoes plagued the area. And to top it all off, it was uncertain whether the selected spot actually belonged to Russia or to Sweden. But none of this concerned the tsar. After all, he was "master of his country ... he creates what he wills." And so, it was done.

On May 16, 1703, Peter the Great turned the first shovel of excavation, heralding the start of the ambitious enterprise. A phalanx of carpenters and workmen scurried about to build the tsar's quarters — the fortress would follow. Within three days, a three-room log cabin, fifty-five by twenty feet, stood ready for occupancy and Peter moved in. Five months later, the massive earth, timber, and stone fortress was well under construction. To finance the grandiose scheme, Peter not too subtly persuaded a half dozen of his closest, wealthiest friends to assume the cost and the supervision of building the six massive, grim bastions that form the basis of the fortification, today's Peter and Paul Fortress.

Whereas the birthing of the U.S. capital was a painfully drawn out affair, the new Russian capital grew quickly. The fortress sprung up rapidly, and around it spread the city. That Peter's capital was located at the edge of the empire, far from the country's centre bothered him little. What mattered was its saltwater location. Within a decade, St. Petersburg had become a full-fledged city with wide boulevards and aristocratic mansions. Its population had sprung from nothing to one hundred thousand.

But to develop this unique undertaking the cost by way of human suffering and loss of lives was horrendous. Scores of thousands of peasant labourers and craftsmen were conscripted from all parts of the country to work on St. Petersburg. The conditions under which they toiled were appalling and thousands died, not only from the physical hardships of their labours but also from malaria, dysentery, and scurvy. The actual number of deaths is unknown, but some have it as high as one hundred thousand. Truly, this was "a city built on bones."

Washington and St. Petersburg — national capitals founded by two strong-willed heads of state, one answerable to the people through an elected congress, the other beholden to no one. One city endured a protracted birthing; the other became an "overnight wonder" — glaring contrasts in operational modes of democracy and autocracy.

No sooner had American independence been won than the Continental Congress set out to woo foreign states for diplomatic recognition of the newly formed nation. The first such state was Russia. In 1781, Francis Dana was dispatched to St. Petersburg to persuade Catherine — that "wise and virtuous Princess" — to recognize the republic. The Boston

Joseph-Maria Charlemagne-Baudet, 1860.

Marble Palace in St. Petersburg.

lawyer-turned-diplomat was at the time in Paris serving as secretary to John Adams, then the American envoy. An austere and puritanical individual, Dana possessed intelligence and was fervently dedicated to the advancement of his country. To accompany the envoy, Adams seconded his fourteen-year-old son, John Quincy Adams (forty years later, the sixth president of the United States). Not only was the charming, dark-eyed boy handsome and intelligent, but he was also uncommonly mature for his age. "A delightful child," beamed Abigail Adams. "Master Johnny" was fluent in French, an essential skill that Dana lacked. It was a judicious appointment and the youngster acquitted himself with aplomb in the diplomatic discussions that later took place. The unlikely couple travelled the 1,200-mile distance in a modest post-chaise to St. Petersburg, a place few Americans had ever visited. The journey took over a month.

On reaching the Russian capital, Dana and his young charge established themselves in a modestly priced inn rather than in the luxurious Hôtel de Paris that was favoured by visiting dignitaries. The two marvelled at the beauty of the elegant boulevards and squares, the colourful canals, and the imposing residences and churches. "The monumental city," reported Dana, "far exceeds all my expectations; alone it is sufficient to immortalize the memory of Peter." The two Americans were offered a tour of the Winter Palace, today's Hermitage, a massive building that dominated the banks of the Neva. Dana and young John Quincy delighted in the expansive picture galleries, assembly rooms, card-playing salons, and, above all, the winter garden. This vast, glass-covered space of sweet aromas was a symphony of lush vegetation. The profusion of flowers, shrubs, and tropical trees blended together into an exotic forest of sorts, and among its branches frolicked colourful parrots and lively canaries, chattering and singing shrilly.

Catherine's palms and parrots may have impressed Master Johnny but he was not much taken by her people. In a delightfully naive account, the fourteen-year-old records some impressions:

> Upon the whole this nation is far from being civilized. Their customs, their dress and even their amusements are yet gross and barbarous. It is said that in some parts of the

empire, the women think their husbands despise them or don't love them, if they don't thrash them now and then, but I do not give this as a fact. In St. Petersburg they have baths where they go pell-mell, men and women. They bathe themselves at first in warm water and from thence they plunge themselves into the snow and roll themselves in it. They accustom themselves to this from infancy and they think it preserves them from scurvy.

The city sported theatres, museums, a library, an art gallery, and even a zoo. Less than eighty years had passed since Peter's initial turn of the shovel and within that brief time, the capital had bloomed spectacularly — "from nothing the thing sprung up with the rapidity of a mushroom," as a Russian expression put it.

Catherine II (Catherine the Great).

Dana and the young John Quincy Adams did not travel the vast distance from Paris to St. Petersburg merely to admire Catherine's lush winter garden. They were there "to engage her Imperial Majesty to favor and support the sovereignty and independence of the United States," as the orders read. In addition, Dana was to do what he could to stimulate trade between the two countries — in the charmingly archaic wording of his instructions, to establish a base for a "good understanding between both countries and for friendly intercourse to the mutual advantage of both nations." Some historians carelessly refer to the envoy as having been America's first minister to Russia — that is not so. The first minister of the United States was not Dana, but rather the same person with whom he had travelled, John Quincy Adams. At age twenty-eight, Adams was appointed to that post following Russian recognition of the new republic. At the time that the two Americans were in the Russian capital, Dana was merely an emissary of the Continental Congress, travelling with high hopes.

In sending Dana to Russia, the American leaders had taken a somewhat pretentious, perhaps wishful step. The mission was destined for failure, as anyone schooled in the rules of diplomacy and aware of great power interchange might have foretold. To begin with, the Russian foreign office was simply uninterested in exploring diplomatic relations with the United States; it had more pressing issues on the table. And then, the Continental Congress, having given Dana the mandate, offered him little encouragement or support, as there were greater, more urgent matters requiring attention.

The congressional emissary arrived in Russia with no official status; Dana was there "as a mere private gentleman" without formal credentials. Not only was he wanting credentials, but he was also lacking substantive financial backing — Dana had a paltry, miserly allowance. He could not afford lodgings worthy of his station, engage competent staff, adequately meet everyday expenses, or offer the exchange of precious gifts — jewelled snuff boxes, for example. "The diplomatic technique of the eighteenth century," explains W.P. Cresson of the University of North Carolina, "reserved certain peculiar rewards. Accepted custom provided that costly gifts should be bestowed on foreign diplomats and the ministers of the European courts. These gratuities usually took the form of snuff boxes or *objets d'art* studded in such a manner as to make the removal of diamonds possible without difficulties." For hapless Dana, all this was out of reach. During his twenty-five-month stay in St. Petersburg, a goodly portion of his own personal capital went to paying expenses. "I am sick, sick to the heart, of the delicacies and whims of European politics," he complained bitterly.

To add to Dana's frustration, he could not communicate effectively for lack of French, the language of the court and of St. Petersburg society. At first, he had the services of young John Quincy, but the boy was soon recalled to France to resume his studies. This left Dana in the hands of professional translators who more often than not were agents of foreign powers. Such were the travails of the deprived envoy. All the while His Britannic Majesty's Ambassador to the Court of St. Petersburg, the urbane and experienced Sir James Harris, was ensconced in his lavish, well-staffed quarters, meeting brilliant successes in advancing his country's interests. (And, it may be added, stirring up every sort of mischief for the amateur American. Where a spoke could be put into Dana's wheel, it was.)

Dana's mission was doomed to failure from the moment of his arrival in Russia. Despite the vicissitudes of court life and a lack of overall success, however, Dana was bathed in admiration by St. Petersburg society — he was, after all, an American, and things American were novel and admirable. Dana formed a circle of friends from within the growing and influential opposition to autocracy, particularly from among the young crowd.

The four decades that followed the American Revolution were the determinative years in the formation of Russian-American concord. The period was one of booming commercial development both for the United States and for Russia, and within it the interests of the two countries intersected regularly. Boston at the time had not only grown into America's largest city, but it had become the country's commercial hub. The venturous merchants of Massachusetts met success after success in expanding their trade networks and rapidly acquired international reputations for astuteness, reliability, and honesty. It was Massachussetts where the great merchant families — the Peabodys, Cabots, Endicotts,

Russells, and Derbys — were founding their dynasties. These entrepreneurs moved goods along a triangular pattern of sea lanes; from Boston they sailed their vessels to the West Indies where they discharged finished goods, such as shoes, clothing, printed books, kitchenware, and household items. They then loaded up with raw sugar, coffee, rum, rice, cacao, and citrus fruit, which they transported to the Baltic, initially selling to Sweden but subsequently to Russia. In exchange, the merchants acquired hemp, tallow, cordage, linens, flax, furs, and, above all, iron. These goods, together with other raw materials, were then brought to Boston to supply the manufacturing plants of Massachusetts.

By the turn of the nineteenth century, a lively commerce had blossomed between the United States and Russia. The first American ship to enter a Russian harbour was the square-rigged trading vessel *Wolfe*, owned by a prominent Boston merchant, Nicholas Boylston, who in 1763 brought to St. Petersburg a cargo of West Indian goods, principally sugar, rum, and indigo. There followed many more ships — rough estimates have it that as many as five hundred American vessels had called at the Russian port by 1800. The growth in trade was spectacular and by 1803, fully 15 percent of all Russian exports were flowing into the United States. Between 1806 and 1811, American exports to Russia grew from $12,407 to an astonishing $6,137,657.

Even the White House relied on Russian goods. "I wish you to purchase me a piece of Russian sheeting," wrote Abigail Adams to her sister. "I have not half sheeting enough for these people, which is stout. I also want you to get me a piece of the plain Russian toweling. The sheeting and toweling take a receipt for as thus, 'for the use of the Household of the President of the U.S.'" One student of Russian-American trade relations of the time puts it thus:

> Young America, more than we have ever realized, was economically tied to Russia. By 1800, the average American blacksmith used either Swedish or Russian iron if called upon to make anything finer or stronger than horseshoes or andirons; and the American sailor, possibly the most important individual in our young economy, thought

twice — and twice, again — before he took any craft without Russian rigging, cables, and sails beyond the harbor mouth. To an appreciable extent, the American economy survived and prospered because it had access to the unending labor and rough skill of the Russian *muzhik* [serf].[4]

During the period in question, the White House was occupied by a succession of four gifted and notable presidents, each serving two terms: John Adams, Thomas Jefferson, James Madison, and James Monroe. (Our youthful John Quincy Adams, Dana's protégé in St. Petersburg, became president in 1825.) Each one in his own way was a giant in American history and each played a significant role in the moulding of the young nation.

But on the global scene, towering over them all, was a supremely illustrious icon of history — Napoleon Bonaparte, a man of unfettered ambition and a genius for action and management. Born of a humble Corsican washerwoman, this lowly corporal of the French army shot up meteorically through the ranks and beyond, with such success that in a matter of a few short years, he found himself Emperor of France. Not only was Napoleon the ruler of that great country, but he also held sway over most of Europe. Through a series of conquests, alliances, and family marriages, Napoleon had dominion over virtually the entire continent by 1811. Only Britain to the west and Russia to the east remained outside his control.

In February of that year, the emperor made an unusually frank declaration to Duke of Otranto Joseph Fouché, the man who, as minister of police, really guaranteed the tranquility of France while his sovereign waged wars. "How can I help it if a great power drives me to become dictator of the world? ... I have not yet fulfilled my mission, and I mean to end what I have begun. We need a European code of law, a European court of appeal, a uniform coinage, a common system of weights and measures. The same law must run throughout Europe. I shall fuse all nations into one.... This, my lord duke, is the only solution that pleases me." First person singular aside, it was a statement of remarkable vision and uncanny prophecy.

Napoleon's insatiable ambition plunged Europe into a series of wars and in the complex political maelstrom that resulted, Russia found itself drawn into the vortex. As for the United States, it, too, was unwillingly dragged into the fray, albeit more peripherally.

For Napoleon, dominion over the continent was one thing, but "to become dictator of the world" was quite another matter. For that to happen, Britain had to fall into his hamper, and so did Russia. The emperor at first turned his glance to the British, "this island of shopkeepers," as he disdainfully labelled them — it was the British, after all, who had consistently thwarted him as far back as the 1798 Egyptian campaign. And now, with Admiral Nelson's spectacular victory at Trafalgar, French naval power had effectively been broken. Britannia ruled the waves, as it continued to do throughout the nineteenth century. A maritime invasion of the United Kingdom was out of the question. The elaborate plans drawn up by Napoleon's engineers for the digging of a tunnel under the channel were also dismissed.

Napoleon therefore decided to throttle his arch-enemy to death. "The shopkeepers" would be had by a destruction of their commerce — curb all trade and there would be no money and no political power. A series of decrees were promulgated in what became known as the *continental system*. The decrees effectively closed European ports to the importation of British and colonial goods; there would be no more markets for the islanders. There was no objection, however, to having the British buy continental goods, but for cash only. England's gold reserves would thus be depleted and British traders and merchants would fall into ruin.

Napoleon's ambitions, war-torn Europe, the continental system — all seemingly excluded the United States and Russia, and both countries strove hard to maintain a detached, disinterested posture. All to no avail, for diverse economic and political interests would soon force their involvement and the two nations found themselves entangled before long. As the continental system took hold, a complex series of declarations, reversals of alliances, treaties, embargoes, and armed threats took place. France, Britain, the United States, Russia, and other European powers all had to cope together with the confusion and discord seeded by Napoleon's unfettered appetites. Suffice it to say that the continental system failed in its purpose, and in the events of the day Russia moved even closer to the United States. Although Tsar Alexander had not yet granted Russia's full diplomatic recognition to the young nation, he did agree to receive officially an American emissary in 1803. Levett Harris, a Philadelphian, was appointed by President Jefferson to be consul in St. Petersburg, where he was greeted enthusiastically not only by the court but also by the populace. He reported:

> The marks of friendship and attention which I received in the city were far beyond what I expected or deserved. I should say no more on this subject if I did not think that they were in many instances directed rather to the country to which I belong than to myself. At the fetes of the court I was put on a footing with the foreign ministers, and often, as an American traveler, I found myself more favored than if I had a diplomatic character.... The Emperor invited me to dine with him "en famille," placed me next to him and conversed with me some time respecting America and France.

The wheels of early-nineteenth-century diplomacy turned slowly, particularly as they were often caught in the tumultuous events of the times: wars, treaties, and changing alliances. It was a full five years after Harris's arrival in St. Petersburg that the tsar appointed an envoy to the United States. Andrei Dashkov, a bureaucrat in the Ministry of Commerce, was sent to Philadelphia as consul general with the additional and rather cumbersome title of chargé d'affaires near the Congress of the United States.

President Madison and Secretary of State Robert Smith awaited impatiently the arrival of the Russian and in 1808 received him cordially. During the meeting, Dashkov somewhat presumptuously made a request to address Congress, but it fell on deaf ears — a polite but firm no. The president, however, did take the occasion to invite him to the White House for an intimate family dinner, which the Russian accepted with alacrity. Word of the first lady's penchant for hospitality and entertainment had even reached him in St. Petersburg.

Of all first ladies, Dolly Madison is the most notable of the White House *douairières* — even Jacqueline Kennedy was a shadow at her feet.

This "fine, portly buxom dame" had laughing blue eyes, fair skin, black curls, and she radiated charm. Settling into the presidential residence was no problem for the first lady, inasmuch as she had over the years played hostess for the widowed Jefferson. At receptions, she invariably appeared dressed in an elegant, low-cut empire gown with a trademark turban headpiece, feathers and all. Her buffet tables were weighed down with elaborate dishes of every sort of food. "Lady Presidentess," as she was lovingly called behind her back, rarely failed to serve an ice cream–filled pastry for dessert, a dish that became the vogue among the discriminating hostesses of the land. Unsurprisingly, Dashkov readily fell under her enchanting spell. Later, during the British invasion of Washington in 1814, Dolly hastily fled the White House in advance of the approaching redcoats — her husband was out of town at the time.[5] To her sister, she wrote a running account of what was happening:

> The enemy seemed stronger than had at first been reported, and it might happen that they would reach the city with the intention of destroying it. I am accordingly ready for it; I have pressed as many Cabinet papers into trunks as to fill one carriage. Our private property must be sacrificed, as it is impossible to procure wagons for its transportation ... disaffection stalks around us. My friends and acquaintances are all gone ... French John [a faithful servant] with his usual activity and resolution, offers to spike the cannon at the gate and lay a train of powder which would blow up the British, should they enter our house.... Mr. Carroll has come to hasten my departure.... [but] I insisted on waiting until the large picture of General Washington is secured and it requires unscrewing from the wall. This process was found too tedious for these precious moments. I ordered the frame to be broken and the canvas to be taken out ... the precious canvas is in the hands of two gentlemen from New York.... I must leave this house or the retreating army will make me a prisoner.

George Washington's official, life-size portrait continues to hang today in the White House, in a rightful place of honour. Following the British withdrawal, Dolly Madison organized volunteers to clean the burned building and then worked for three years with Benjamin Latrobe in designing and building the residence of today.

A year after Dashkov's arrival in the United States, John Quincy Adams, made his return trip to Russia, this time as the American minister — full diplomatic recognition had at last been extended. He held the appointment for six years, during which time he had "frequent and informal conversations" with Alexander. From the start, Adams was much impressed by his Russian hosts. "One of the first things that at once delights and surprises an American traveler here," he wrote, "is the great respect entertained by the Emperor and Court for our national character."

CHAPTER 3

THE PACIFIC PASSAGES

The 1803 Louisiana Purchase opened an important chapter in the story of Russian-American friendship. By that shrewd acquisition, the United States extended its territory far into the northwest, lands that today take in all or part of twelve states. Even before the conclusion of negotiations. Thomas Jefferson had commissioned Lewis and Clark to undertake their monumental journey of exploration into that unknown hinterland. The elusive Northwest Passage, a potential trade route to Asia, had been sought for over three hundred years, and the hope of securing it continued. The formidable Rockies, however, proved to be an insurmountable obstacle — exploration abruptly stopped. Although Lewis and Clark returned home in 1806 with a trove scientific data, promise of an easy access to the Pacific had been crushed.

But the expedition by the two explorers did ignite the imagination of a singular immigrant, John Jacob Astor, a butcher's son from Waldorf, Germany. Arriving in the United States in 1784 at the age twenty to join his brother, Astor developed a fascination with furs. The young man had ample business sense, including insight, patience, perseverance, and a penchant for risk-taking. It didn't take long for him to parlay a modest New York fur shop into the American Fur Company, a vast organization that came to dominate the fur trade of central and northern United States. It was America's first monopoly. By 1808, Astor was a man of untold wealth.[1]

Early in his expansionist years, John Jacob recognized the potential offered by the Pacific coast. Not only did its shores provide easy access to the lucrative markets of the Far East, but they were also home to countless thousands of sea otters, their extraordinary glossy, rich, and soft pelts much in demand. In 1810, he travelled to those distant parts, and stopped at the mouth of the Columbia River in Oregon. There he established a trading post that he named Astoria — much credit for the American presence on the Pacific coast, therefore, belongs to that venturesome German immigrant.

The Russians, however, had already been on North American shores of the Pacific for seventy years. From the times of Ivan IV, his people had been pushing east from Moscow across the Urals into Siberia. These were mostly Cossacks, traders, and trappers, plus a handful of missionaries. By the early seventeenth century, Irkutsk in central Siberia had grown into a commercial centre for the vast hinterland. Nascent trade relations with China were proving lucrative — tea, silk, and other luxuries were acquired in exchange for furs. Merchants and trappers pressed farther and farther east until the Pacific Ocean was finally reached in 1639 — on the Sea of Okhotsk north of Japan. With expanding Asian demand for furs, Moscow sought more effective and less costly means of transport of goods — ideally an avenue through the Arctic Ocean. Since most of the great Siberian rivers flowed into those polar waters, new and rich fur-trapping grounds would open up inland as explorers continued their work.

In 1721 Peter the Great burst onto the Russian stage, a man of boundless energy, intellectual curiosity and unfettered ambition. His overriding priorities were to consolidate and expand the empire and to bring his people into the world outside their country. Like the double-headed eagle in the Russian coat of arms, Peter gazed simultaneously in both directions — a push to the east was no less important than the much-coveted "window to the west." The idea of a northeast passage, a sea lane that would connect Russia with China, intrigued him, as it would be a splendid avenue for developing the lucrative fur trade with the Far East and for expanding the empire.

Early in Peter's reign, the young tsar had travelled to Western Europe, where, among other activities, he laboured as a volunteer carpenter in the Amsterdam shipyards of the East India Company. He was fixated on mastering every aspect of warship construction.[2] During that tour, he

William Faithorne. Engraving. c. 1700. Library of Congress.

Peter the Great.

spent sixteen weeks in England, where in 1698 he met William Penn. The eccentric Quaker was not only a man of intellect and breadth of interests, but he also spoke Dutch, a language in which Peter had greater fluency than English. In his student days, Penn was much admired for his athletic ability but criticized for an exaggerated piety. He was expelled from Oxford for non-conformity; soon afterwards, Penn was imprisoned by London authorities on the same charge. But he was not held for long. Years later, Charles II awarded Penn the proprietary rights to the colony of Pennsylvania — a repayment of an enormous debt owed the father.

Not without reason, Peter was charmed by this uncommon individual, despite Penn's irritating attempts to convert him to Quakerism. The two took special delight in debating matters related to exploration and geography. It was in one of these sessions that Penn challenged Peter to determine whether North America was connected by land to Asia.[3]

And now, in 1725, at the twilight of his reign Peter set out to meet that challenge. On the recommendation of the Ministry of Marine, he appointed Captain Vitus Bering to undertake an exploration east. A Dane serving in the Russian navy, Bering was reputed to be audacious and single-minded as well as in possession of sharp seamanship skills. He had once sailed from Denmark to the East Indies — a daring voyage for those days. But the man's scientific training was sorely lacking, as well as any sense of curiosity.

The tsar commissioned him to cross Siberia to the shores of the Pacific, and from there do what was necessary to ascertain whether a physical connection existed between Siberia and North America. If not, the Dane was to carry on with the search for the elusive passage west via the Arctic Ocean. If anyone could do it, it would be the likes of Bering. Peter, however, did not live to savour the fruit of his initiative. Within six months, he died at age fifty-three — all but ten of them as autocratic sovereign of the massive Russian empire. His widow and successor, Catherine I, endorsed the commission, and urged Bering to get on with it. The instructions dictated by Peter are brilliant, as much for their brevity and as for their naiveté. In part:

I   You shall cause one or two convenient vessels to be built at Kamchatka or elsewhere.

II You shall endeavor to discover, by coasting with these vessels, whether the country towards the north, of which at present we have no knowledge, is a part of America, or not.

III If it joins to the continent of America, you shall endeavour, if possible, to reach some colony belonging to some European power. In case you meet with any European ship, you shall diligently inquire the name of the coasts, and such other circumstances as it is in your power to learn. These you will commit to writing, so that we may have some certain memoirs by which a chart may be constructed.[4]

On the morning of Sunday, January 24, 1725, twenty-five sleds pulled out from the Admiralty in St. Petersburg with an entourage of ninety-seven carpenters, blacksmiths, seamen, and support staff. Bering had begun an arduous twenty-one-month passage to the Sea of Okhotsk across seemingly endless and inhospitable stretches of Siberia. Roads for the most part were non-existent and those available were primitive. Numerous rivers had to be forded without available boats. Settlements were few and far between. Freezing temperatures and deep snows brought misery in winter; unbearable heat and clouds of mosquitoes were common in summer. Their first winter was especially harsh — "the local people who have lived here more than twenty years say that it is the worst winter in memory," one diarist noted. The passage of the resolute travellers was made all the more laborious by the immense quantity of food and equipment being hauled. Additionally, a hefty amount of iron was loaded aboard the sledges, material deemed essential for the construction of a vessel sturdy enough to battle the roughest waters. Builders on the Okhotsk normally used leather thongs to strap together a ship.

The tiny settlement of Okhotsk proved to be a miserable collection of native huts and houses belonging to a handful of Russian colonists. Since departing St. Petersburg, nearly two years had passed, and five thousand miles had been travelled. At this point, in keeping with the Russian naval tradition of consultation with subordinates, Bering summoned a conference to consider the next step. Despite their fatigue, they agreed to speed up matters, all in the interests of a rapid return home. They would now push forward to Kamchatka, another thousand miles. By the early spring of 1727, Bering's party had not only established itself on the peninsula's forlorn coastline, but the men had constructed a shipyard of sorts. A rapid start was made in the building of a vessel, and in less than three months the job was done. The iron brought from St. Petersburg was indeed an effective means of reinforcing the hull, but the caulking was primitive, made from heavy grass bonded together by a crude tar distilled from bark. On July 13, the *St. Gabriel* was launched and Bering immediately set sail on his mission. Access to the Northeast Passage would be his — if, in fact, it existed.

Winter comes early to those parts and that year the weather turned steadily foul at the start of September. Continuous fogs and drenching rains beset the tiny vessel. Frigid, depressing dampness enveloped the decks of the *St. Gabriel*. The hull's rudimentary caulking began to give way, and what started as minor seepage developed into a worrisome flow, which seemed to increase by the hour. After fifty-three days at sea, shipboard conditions had become wretched. Weather and high seas were developing into a threat. The Siberian coast seemed to go on and on — and there was no sign of a connection with America. Enough was enough. The dispirited Bering wished nothing more than to quit the inhospitable waters and return to St. Petersburg, and his colleagues agreed unanimously.

The *St. Gabriel* in its sail had all along been hugging the Russian coastline, land to port and heavy fog to starboard. In reaching 67° 18' north, Bering had in fact penetrated the Arctic Ocean, and unwittingly sailed through the very strait they were seeking. It was at this juncture that Bering came about for the return home "because the coast did not extend farther north and no land was near."

On the return passage, the fog cleared sufficiently to reveal a small, rocky island, which Bering named St. Diomede (known today as Big Diomede). Had the Dane ventured to circumnavigate the island, he would undoubtedly have spotted Little Diomede, the place where the unwavering Lynne Cox started her swim in the 1980s. But lacking the will for further exploration and because the fog closed in once more, he never laid eyes on the American shoreline. Sighting or no sighting, Bering was satisfied that the two continents were unconnected.

By March 1729 the expedition returned home after an absence of four years. The fledgling Academy of Science received Bering's comprehensive report with skepticism and no small degree of dissatisfaction. The academicians heatedly debated the data, which for the most part they judged inconclusive. Agreement was eventually reached and a report submitted to the newly enthroned Empress Anna. The sovereign concurred with the Academy of Science's recommendations and agreed to send a follow-up expedition to the Pacific. Despite the manifold criticism and rebuke that had been levelled at Bering, he successfully persuaded the authorities once more to trust him, but this time with an enlarged (and significantly more costly) enterprise.

The objective of his new commission was twofold: first, to explore a coastline east of Siberia, which charts showed was there, a land called Terra da Gama.[5] Bering and crew were to find it and proceed south as far as latitude 46° (5.5 on today's maps, a point just north of the U.S.-Canadian border); second, the expedition was to return north and continue the search for the Northeast Passage.

In the spring of 1733, the fifty-three-year-old Dane set out once more from St. Petersburg to travel the arduous trans-Siberian route to Kamchatka again. On the earlier expedition, he carried nearly a hundred men. By the time the second expedition was completed, three thousand men had been drawn into the work. The original budget for the enterprise was ten thousand rubles, but it ultimately cost over three hundred thousand rubles. It took the cumbersome enterprise eight years to cross the immense distance, to establish a base of operations on the Okhotsk and to complete the construction of two vessels. (It might be noted, however, that much of the time spent on the trans-Siberian segment had been devoted to assigned scientific studies.)

Bering christened his two new ships the *St. Peter* and the *St. Paul*. They were small double-masted riggers, approximately eighty feet in length, each carrying fourteen guns. He commanded the *St. Peter*; the sister ship was under Captain Alexei Chirikov, a veteran of the first expedition. Chirikov was much younger than the Dane, but he was well educated in the sciences and possessed a developed sense of curiosity. The vessels sailed out of Kamchatka on June 4, 1741, and headed due east to Terra da Gama, whatever it was.

The best of plans can go astray and these certainly did. Shortly after quitting Russian shores, an impenetrable fog enveloped the ships and sight of each other was lost. Days of circling and searching for the other came to naught. In exasperation, the two frustrated captains, each on his own, gave up the exercise and continued on solo.

A fortnight later, Chirikov was making slow but steady progress south, confident that the elusive shore lay just ahead. Then, on July 26, through the gloom of lingering fog, a flock of forest birds were heard and then sighted. They hovered over the ship, circled a couple of times, and landed on the *St. Paul*'s yardarms. This was clear evidence that land was nearby.

Two days later, the vessel dropped anchor just off the shore, in a wide basin of still water. The shoreline seemed to blend neatly into the woodland, which rose vertically into sharp mountains. Latitude 55° 21' had been reached, just south of Sitka, midway down the Alaskan panhandle. Delighted with the prospect of replenishing the ship's supply of freshwater and the larder with meat, Chirikov dispatched a party of crew members to feel out the prospects. Hours passed with no return of the men — then more hours passed. The worried captain sent out more crew to search for the missing party, and these men also failed to return.

Eight anxiety-filled days passed. Then, at a distance, two dugouts of Natives were spotted paddling toward the ship. When they came within hailing distance, one of the Natives stood up and, gesticulating angrily with his arms, let fly with an unintelligible stream of words. The perplexing message delivered, the two little boats paddled away speedily. Chirikov notes dryly in his diary, "Some misfortune had happened to our men.... The fact that the Americans did not dare to approach our ship leads us to believe that they have either killed or detained our men." Whatever happened, his crew had vanished, as though swallowed up by the eerie silence that now resounded all about.

The lengthy passage to American shores in untenable conditions was bad enough. The disappearance of fellow crew members, plus the unfriendly encounter with the Natives, was even more unsettling for those remaining on board the *St. Paul*. The men petitioned Chirikov to quit the terrible place for a prompt return home. As he thought about the idea, the situation grew worse — mutiny was in the air. With little to gain by remaining where they were, he gave in. Anchor was weighed and sails were raised for a return to Kamchatka, despite the nearly empty water casks and sparse larder.

On October 19, the battered *St. Paul* at last reached its destination. The crossing had been anything but smooth — appalling weather, high seas, privation of every sort, and illness plus torn sails and a leaking hull all played havoc with the voyage. For a significant portion of the trip, the captain had been bedridden with an unidentified illness.

Days after their arrival in Kamchatka, Chirikov died.

While Chirikov had been following his path, Bering — chagrined over having lost the *St. Paul* — continued on his own way. But everything changed for Bering and his crew on July 6. The fog unexpectedly cleared and skies opened up into dazzling blue. Ahead of him, a brilliant congregation of snow-covered peaks came into view, soaring almost vertically — the range that stands on the Alaskan-Canadian border, with mountains exceeding eighteen thousand feet. Bering named the tallest one Mount St. Elias. Today's visitors to the area are no less awed by the sight of it all than were those early Russian explorers. For them, however, it was not simply dazzling nature; it was justification for years of gruelling search. The American continent had been found, unconnected to Siberia.

As suddenly as the skies had cleared for the *St. Peter*, they became thick again; the ship once more found itself in dense fog. Bering couldn't wait to quit the place — enough of rain and fog, of fickle sea, and volatile winds. He was satisfied that his commission had been executed — they had actually seen the separate continent, and that was sufficient, so it was time to turn about and head for home. After a steady month at sea, however, his shipmates were unready for an immediate departure; they yearned to stretch their legs and run about. The scientists on board particularly objected — the new land promised to be a trove for discovery. Only upon the strongest persuasion of his senior officers and the scientists did Bering grudgingly acquiesce and permit a ten-hour shore leave. He himself did not go ashore — the discoverer of Alaska never set foot on it.

With shore leave over, the impatient Bering turned the *St. Peter* about, and made sail for Kamchatka. The story of that return journey is a lamentable saga. Shortly after quitting Alaskan waters, a wave of much-dreaded scurvy struck the unfortunate crew — eleven men eventually died and virtually everyone else became incapacitated to some extent. Weeks later, when they were at the farthest point of the Aleutian archipelago, a violent gale struck with overwhelming force. Try as they did, the decimated crew was unable to cope with the frightful situation. Bering decided that their only salvation was to beach the ship on one of the nearby islands. The *St. Peter* was steered ashore, beached, and in the process wrecked. The stranded crew camped over the long, dark, and frigid winter months in conditions beyond the pale.

Their island was teeming with foxes, and their curiosity was aroused since they never had encountered humans. Initially, they circled the encampment cautiously, but with each ensuing visit they became increasingly bold and more aggressive. So close did the fearless foxes approach that the men were forced to beat them off with clubs — scores were thus killed and skinned. The pelts were bountiful enough for fur coats to be stitched for each crew member. Fox pelts were also used for caulking the makeshift cabins the group had built.

With the passing of time, illness — scurvy above all — took its toll on the men and many lives were lost. The frozen ground made proper burial impossible. The deceased, therefore, were dragged away distantly, but insufficiently far to prevent the spectacle of foxes fighting over and playing with the cadavers.

As critical as conditions were during those months, most of the crew survived principally because of the abundant animal life. Slowly over time, a small, rudimentary vessel was ingeniously constructed from the wreckage of the *St. Peter*. In spring, surviving crew members managed to raise sail and reach home base on Kamchatka. Among those welcoming the returnees were a handful of colleagues — the survivors of the ill-fated *St. Paul*.

What a curious spectacle it must have been: a bearded, bedraggled bevy of wild-looking individuals garbed from head to toe in fox furs. (Vitus Bering was not among them. At age sixty, the expedition leader had quietly died of scurvy months earlier.)

The discovery that Asia and America were unconnected ultimately proved to be an unimportant one. Nothing really came of the Northeast Passage — nor, for that matter, of the Northwest Passage — and the rich benefits Peter had envisioned accruing to Russia were illusory. And poor Bering. What he did not know was that Europeans had long before found the strait that eventually came to bear his name. In 1648, an adventurous Cossack, Semyon Dezhnev, had sailed a flimsy boat from the mouth of the Kolyma River at the eastern reaches of the Arctic Ocean south through the strait. The record of that particular exploit, however, was uncovered only in 1736, at the very time that Bering was at sea carrying out his explorations.

Northeast Passage or not, a successful offshoot of Bering's expeditions was the greatly expanded knowledge not only of Siberia's Pacific coast but also of its interior. But above all, through the discovery of Alaska and northern American territories, the Dane brought to Russia and Europe a clear understanding of the immense potential of the Pacific fur trade. The Asiatic and American shores teemed with fur-bearing animals, all there pretty much for the taking. At no time was this more graphically illustrated than when Bering's bedraggled, fur-clad crew stepped ashore on Kamchatka lugging bundles of high-quality pelts — seal, sea otter, and blue fox, in particular.

By the time John Jacob Astor made his venturous move in establishing his Oregon trading post on the Columbia, enterprising Russians had long been reaping rich harvests from the craggy shores and the boundless northern forests. Northeast of Astor's outpost, inland within the British territory of western Canada, the Hudson's Bay Company and the North West Company were prospering mightily in the fur trade.

Eleven years before Lewis and Clark began their effort to search out an overland passage to the Pacific, an employee of the North West Company in Canada successfully achieved precisely that. Setting out from the inner part of the continent, Alexander Mackenzie and his party of nine crossed the Rockies in 1793 and made it to the Pacific Ocean.

They did it in just over a hundred days. The nine-member party travelled in three birch bark canoes, carrying limited supplies. The expedition commissioned by Thomas Jefferson, on the other hand, was staffed by a well-equipped force of forty-five trained soldiers travelling in sturdy vessels, fully equipped.

On a boulder in Bella Coola, the Canadians inscribed in vermilion and bear grease the words "Alex Mackenzie from Canada by land, 22nd July 1793." Years later, a similar inscription was carved on a tree: "Capt William Clark December 3rd 1805 by land. U. States in 1804–1805."

Alexander Mackenzie, a Canadian hero who showed that the impossible was possible ... and in the process indirectly helped to send off Lewis and Clark on their mission.

CHAPTER 4

ALEXANDER I

By the time the twenty-three-year-old Alexander I was catapulted onto the throne in 1801, St. Petersburg's population had grown to over three hundred thousand, overtaking that of eight-hundred-year-old Moscow. The newly enthroned emperor came from a mixed and complicated lineage of rulers: on the one hand, a number were intelligent and determined; on the other, some were unstable, even mentally deranged. Alexander's father was the bitter and unpredictable Paul, son of the formidable and enlightened Catherine. In 1762, following the murder of Paul's father, the sickly and slow-witted Peter III, Catherine simply assumed the throne, leaving her son standing on the sidelines of government and power for thirty-four years, harbouring resentment and hatred of his usurping mother.

When Catherine died unexpectedly in 1796, Paul gleefully took possession of his rightful inheritance and immediately proceeded to reverse his mother's enlightened domestic and foreign policies. Bitter years of maternal neglect and frustration had further deteriorated his warped mind. Imagined danger, shadowy conspiracy, and ruthless enemies lurked everywhere — nobody was to be trusted. "In Russia," he declared, "the only person of importance is the one with whom I speak — and then only for the duration of the conversation." It wasn't long before the country was on its knees before the paranoid and unpredictable emperor. It cried for deliverance, and delivered it was on the night of March 11, 1801. A group of conspirators, fortified by generous quantities of brandy, broke into Mikhailovsky Castle where Paul had secluded himself behind moats and stout walls. A tumultuous confrontation took place, followed by a scuffle during which the tsar was struck on the forehead with a gold snuffbox — a mortal blow. An anguished Alexander was informed of his father's death ("a fit of apoplexy," he was told) and with no small degree of reluctance, the young man assumed the throne.

The newly anointed tsar brought together his closest, like-minded friends to form an advisory group called the Committee of Friends. This select body of young men consisted of liberal, reform-minded thinkers whose primary focus was on constitutionalism and serfdom. They were well familiar with the French Declaration of the Rights of Man and of the Citizen, and, drawing from the example of the United States, a constitution was deemed desirable, one that would give a voice to the people. As for the serfs — by far the largest segment of the population, accounting for 90 percent of the country's gross national product — they required emancipation. Serfs were not slaves, yet they were not free agents. They were permanently attached to the land, and a nobleman's wealth was measured not in terms of the acreage he possessed but in the number of "souls" he owned. Serfs enjoyed certain rights and protection of the law, but at the same time they were entirely at the discretion of the owner. Some proprietors were benign and caring while others were ruthless and cruel, and there certainly was much abuse of the system.

On the issue of a constitution, the young idealists heartily agreed that it was needed, but that there was no way of framing it without encroaching on the emperor's autocratic power. As for emancipation, the Committee of Friends concluded that serfdom was evil, but the group reckoned little could be done about it for fear of alienating the nobility. Alexander and his short-lived committee talked the talk, but weren't prepared to walk the walk.

During the course of the early deliberations and those that followed, Alexander corresponded with Thomas Jefferson, whom he held in high regard. "I would be extremely grateful to you," he wrote to his former tutor, Frédéric-César de La Harpe, "if you would be helpful to make my closest acquaintance with Jefferson." As a youth, he had read the Declaration of Independence and he knew that the singular document came from the pen of this one man. In June 1776, the thirty-three-year-old Virginian had been in Philadelphia to attend the fateful Continental Congress and

Alexander I.

Stefan Semjonovitsj Stjukin. Oil. 1808. Museum of Pavlovsk, Russia.

rented the two second-floor rooms of a modest home belonging to a bricklayer, on the corner of Market and Seventh Streets. And there, at the urging of his congressional colleagues, Jefferson isolated himself for ten hot summer days, working and reworking the reverberating words that came to affect the world so profoundly. "When in the course of human events it becomes necessary for one people to dissolve the political bonds which have connected them with another ..."

Alexander I and Thomas Jefferson made an interesting pair. One of them was a youthful, idealistic, and naive autocrat, newly come to the throne; the other was an elderly, pragmatic, and experienced republican with decades of service to his country. They were two visionaries from radically dissimilar worlds. Jefferson's devotion to a constitution and democratic principles was as firmly fixed as his abhorrence of slavery (although he, himself, owned slaves). What was good for him was equally good for his friends, and he considered the tsar a friend. "A more virtuous man, I believe, does not exist," he wrote. "Nor one who is more enthusiastically devoted to better the condition of mankind." The elderly statesman was paternalistically solicitous of the young sovereign and he sought to encourage him. To the American representative in St. Petersburg, Jefferson wrote, "The Emperor entertained a wish to know something of our Constitution. I have therefore selected the two best works we have on the subject for which I pray you to ask for a place in his library." Deep down, however, Jefferson harboured grave doubts that a constitution could be had in Russia — the populace simply was not prepared for it. It would be "an Herculean task," he wrote to a friend, to attend "to those who are not capable of taking care of themselves. Some preparation seems necessary to qualify the body of a nation for self-government." This was vintage Jefferson, and words that resonate today around the world.

Gilbert Stuart, c. 1898. Oil. Library of Congress.

Thomas Jefferson.

The young Alexander was indeed the virtuous man Jefferson said he was, and without a doubt he embraced the idea of "bettering the condition of man." Emotionally and psychologically, however, he was a person of contradictions: complex and elusive — "the sphinx," he was called, or "the enigmatic tsar" — he often seemed not to know his own mind. "Something is missing in his character," commented Napoleon, "but I find it impossible to discover what it is." One of his more conspicuous shortcomings was indecisiveness, especially with respect to controversial or unpopular issues. Emancipation and constitutional talk were indeed controversial and unpopular — certainly among the wealthy and influential. All such discussions came to naught. The emancipation of the serfs had to wait until 1861. A constitution with any degree of credibility was not produced until after perestroika took hold in the 1980s and '90s.

The Committee of Friends, as well as similar groups in the imperial reigns that followed, clearly identified Russia's problems, but they lacked the capacity or the will to address them except under extreme pressure. Alexander and his successors were well aware not only of the issues at hand but also of the solutions. Furthermore, this line of autocrats possessed the power to force solutions, but the fibre to do so simply was missing. The tragedy of that massive and magnificent country was that it lacked the collective will to tackle such reform challenges head on.

During Alexander's twenty-four-year reign, the benign and supportive relationship between Russia and the United States blossomed and held for a century thereafter.

CHAPTER 5

THE ADMIRAL AND THE PRINCE

It would be proper at this juncture to deviate somewhat from the principal thread of our narrative to consider the intriguing stories of two colourful individuals who unquestionably are part of the overall fabric. One was an American in the service of Russia and the other a Russian in the development of the United States.

In the summer of 1788, the fourth of the century's Russo-Turkish wars began with Catherine's attack of Ochakov, a strategically situated fortress on the Black Sea that controlled the mouths of the Dnieper and Bug Rivers, the key to the Crimea. The fort had been lost earlier to the Ottomans and the empress now sought to regain it.

As the Russian forces engaged the Turks, King Gustav III of Sweden grasped the moment to launch an attack against Russia through Finland, and he was soon predicting the imminent capture of St. Petersburg, what with the Russians fighting a war in the south and a war in the north. Catherine found her military resources were being stretched to their limits, and the navy's in particular. It was clear that that the fleets had to be strengthened, especially the Baltic Sea fleet. To assist in the work, she invited a noted Dutch naval officer, Admiral Jonkeer Jan Hendrick van Kinsbergen, to enter her service, but he graciously declined. The empress then turned to her second choice: Admiral John Paul Jones, the celebrated American hero who in time came to be known as the "founder of the United States Navy."

The compelling story of this singular individual is as inspiring as it is pathetic. Jones's naval career had been brilliant, but his personal life was punctuated with difficulties and disappointments. John Paul (the Jones would come later) came from Kirkbean, Scotland, on England's border, where his father served as a landscape gardener to a nobleman. At age twelve in 1759, he entered the British merchant navy as cabin boy and within seven brief years found himself the chief mate of a slave ship operating out of Jamaica. By 1770, he was master of his own vessel making several voyages to Tobago, and it was on the final run that he suffered the greatest misfortune of his life. While anchored in a West Indian port, a mutinous crew member engaged him in a deadly contre temps, insisting on a denied shore leave. In the course of the blistering exchange that took place on deck, the hot-headed sailor raised a threatening bludgeon against his superior, which Captain Paul thwarted by running the attacker through with a sword. Self-defence or not, the sensational death called for an arrest and a hearing. Rather than risk facing an admiralty court, John Paul fled to North America, to Fredericksburg, Virginia, where his brother had a small estate. He was now a fugitive from justice, a wanted man, and in an effort to conceal his identity he assumed the surname of Jones.

With the outbreak of the American Revolution, John Paul Jones travelled to Philadelphia, where friends in the Continental Congress secured for him a commission as senior lieutenant in the continental navy. The term *navy* is perhaps a misnomer — what later developed into a proper navy was in Jones's time simply a small collection of lightly armed vessels whose role was to harass British shipping. It was George Washington who recognized the need for a bona fide fleet and it was he who effectively pushed the Continental Congress into such investment; the country's first president was also the founder of the United States Navy.

In 1776, Jones took command of the *Providence*, a 110-foot sloop of twelve guns. He first sailed to Bermuda, where he inflicted extensive damage on the ships in harbour, and then moved on to Nova Scotia. At Canso and Arichat Harbours, Jones effectively destroyed the English fishing industry, taking sixteen British vessels as prizes of war. Canso suffered such devastation that the population virtually abandoned it. What was at one time the seat of the Nova Scotia government and an important commercial centre became a deserted village — by 1812, only five families remained.

Harris & Ewing, 1936. Engraving. Library of Congress.

John-Paul Jones.

In the period that followed, Jones sailed the Scottish and English coasts and terrorized the populations with his daring and effective raids on port towns and merchants. In between two such forays, he put another of his ships, the *Ranger*, into the French port of Quiberon and on entering the harbour, he fired the customary gun salute to the receiving admiral — France and the United States were allied. The entry of Jones's warship into French territorial water on that Valentine's Day of 1777 was a notable occasion for the United States — Admiral La Motte-Piquet returned the salute, the first time the Stars and Stripes was formally recognized by a foreign power.

By 1779, Jones had been promoted to commodore in command of a squadron of American and French ships. On September 23, a spectacular confrontation with the British took place, this time between his vessel and two of the enemy. At the Battle of Flamborough Head, Jones out-manoeuvred the twenty-two-gun *Countess of Scarborough* and took on the fifty-gun *Serapis*. With clever tacking, he brought his own ship, the *Bonhomme Richard*,[1] alongside the larger British vessel, which he then managed to grapple and lash together with his. The two adversaries now found their gun muzzles virtually touching each other at point-blank range, spitting fire point into one another's hulls in a murderous melee. With Jones's smaller vessel ablaze and sinking, the British demanded surrender and it was here that the valorous American made his celebrated reply: "I have not yet begun to fight!" Samuel Eliot Morrison, the noted naval historian, describes the scene:

> The British frigate was in a deplorable condition; the spars and rigging were cut away and dead and dying men lay about her decks. But the state of the *Richard* was even more frightful. Her rudder was hanging by one pintle, her stern frames and transoms were almost entirely shot away, the quarterdeck was about to fall into the gunroom, at least five feet of water were in the hold, and it was gaining from holes below the waterline ... and her topsails were open to the moonlight.[2]

Against all odds, John Paul Jones prevailed, and within three and a half hours of the battle's start, the *Serapis* surrendered. The victor moved his flag from his own doomed *Richard* and raised it aboard his prize of war. The impressive triumph was a climactic moment in Jones's career — he entered the realm of legend. Within weeks, he was the subject of toasts and ballads in stately drawing rooms and in lowly taverns throughout France, America, and Holland. Ambassador Benjamin Franklin wrote to Jones, "Scarce anything was talked of at Paris and Versailles but your cool conduct and persevering bravery during the terrible conflict." Even in England, where the British defeat was a shameful blot on the naval escutcheon, ordinary folk stood in admiration of the daring American. "Paul Jones," declared the London *Morning Post*, "resembles a Jack o' Lantern, to mislead our marines and terrify our coasts ... he is no sooner seen than lost." On his arrival in France, he was received by King Louis XVI and was presented to Queen Marie Antoinette, whom he found "a sweet girl." The king awarded the hero a gold sword.

The Treaty of Ghent in 1783 brought a formal close to the American Revolution and the United States received recognition as an independent nation. The Continental Congress began a slow demobilization of its armed forces, rewarding its hard-fought veterans with parcels of land. Jones, however, was unready to settle down into the sedentary life of a country squire and he set about exploring the possibility of a command abroad. It was at this point that Catherine persuaded him to enter the service of Russia, largely on the recommendation of Thomas Jefferson, then the U.S. ambassador to France. By that time, Catherine had begun to disassociate herself from the British and was cozying up with the French. That Jones was anti-British and a friend of France suited her well and she appointed him rear admiral. "Jones," she confidently predicted, "will get us to Constantinople."

Kontradmiral Pavel Ivanovich, as he was now called, arrived in St. Petersburg in May 1788 and was well pleased with the reception he received from Catherine. "The Empress," he declared, "with the character of a very great man, will always be adored as the most amiable and captivating of the fair sex." Within weeks of arriving, he was dispatched to the Black Sea with orders to take command of a flotilla of ships and engage the Turks. He was further ordered to put himself under the direction of the brilliant but capricious Prince Potemkin, commander of all Russian forces in the south — and Catherine's lover.

Jones's new assignment was beset with difficulties from the start. In the first place, he found himself junior to another mercenary, Prince Karl Heinrich von Nassau-Siegen, with whom he had been associated earlier during their joint service with the French. A strong enmity existed between the two men stemming from an incident in which Jones at one point refused to follow certain orders from Nassau-Siegen. But an even greater burden for Jones was Potemkin's attitude toward the fleet — the prince viewed the navy as a mere adjunct to land forces and, much to Jones's chagrin, he used it thus in coastal campaigns. And finally, Jones was appalled at the poor physical state of the ships he commanded. Would they be effective in action?

Dispirited or not, Kontradmiral Pavel rapidly established himself in the eyes of his crew as an admired leader and a brilliant tactician. On the eve of encountering the enemy at the Battle of Liman, he mustered his men and urged them to victory. "I see in your eyes the souls of heroes," he declared. "We shall all learn together to conquer or to die for the country!" (Note: *the* country, not *our* country.) Were it not for the prospect of imminent battle, there was something droll about it all. An American commanding officer was extolling Russian naval officers to victory against the Turks, addressing them in the French language. With the successful outcome of that particular engagement, Jones's stock increased even further.

In time, the endless and tiresome feuding between Nassau-Siegen and Jones became so serious that Potemkin could no longer bear it. He requested the recall of Jones to St. Petersburg. Returned to the capital in early 1789, the unhappy but relieved Jones plunged himself into a variety of schemes to strengthen Russian-American maritime cooperation. Proposals were drawn up for the suppression of the Barbary pirates, for direct naval alliances between the two countries, for joint partnerships in shipbuilding, and for bilateral naval action in the Black Sea. As he awaited government reaction to these initiatives, the unfortunate man became embroiled in a scandal so dire that by the year's end he had to exit the country. A twelve-year-old delivery girl reported that the kontradmiral had attempted to rape her, a charge Jones heatedly denied. "The charge against me is an ignoble fraud," he wrote to Potemkin. "I love women, I confess, and the pleasures which one enjoys only with their sex, but any enjoyments which it would be necessary to take by compulsion are horror to me.... I give you my word as a soldier and as an honest man that, if the girl in question has not at all passed through other hands than mine, she must still have her virginity."

Unsurprisingly, the sensational accusation became the focus of much whispered gossip in the city, with John Paul indignantly claiming that the whole matter was the perfidious intrigue of his archrival, Nassau-Siegen. Formal charges were laid, but the matter never reached the justice courts and the case against him remained inconclusive. The court and St. Petersburg society, however, effectively washed their hands of Jones — he was a thorough embarrassment and ostracized. The French ambassador at the time commented in his memoir, "The enemies of Paul Jones, not being able to endure the triumph of a man whom they looked upon as an adventurer, rebel and corsair, determined to destroy him."

By December 1789, Catherine had given him permission to retire from Russia, which he did in humiliation, but he did carry away with him the Order of St. Anna. On his way home to Paris, he passed through Warsaw and called on Tadeusz Kosciuszko, the volunteer hero of the American Revolution. Jones tried unsuccessfully to have the Pole intercede on his behalf to King Gustav IV of Sweden for an appointment to the Swedish navy — which was continuing to be at war with Russia. Interesting times, those were.

Jones returned to Paris, impecunious, embittered, and broken physically as well as in spirit. Apart from a few supporters, he was all but forgotten in the United States. On July 18, 1792, he died with his face down on the bed but feet firmly planted on the floor. In the words of one historian, "It must have been simply his nature to confront the one inevitable defeat in a posture which symbolized the spirit of, 'I have not yet begun to fight.'"

The admiral's body was conveyed through the hot, dusty streets of Paris to the cemetery. A detachment of uniformed gendarmerie and a tiny entourage of servants and faithful tradesmen accompanied the remains to the Protestant cemetery of Saint Louis. An admiring Frenchman graciously provided funds for a lead coffin and alcohol to preserve the body in case the Americans ever wished to reclaim the remains of their forgotten hero.

Over a century later, Horace Porter took up his post as U.S. ambassador to France. A fervent admirer of John Paul Jones, Porter was determined to secure for the admiral a rightful place in the pantheon of American heroes, and to this end he petitioned President Theodore Roosevelt for assistance. Languishing in an unknown grave across the ocean was a fighting hero of the American Revolution — a man of action, a man of daring, characterized by Benjamin Franklin as "sturdy, cool and [possessing] determined bravery." A man, in other words, like Roosevelt himself. The media-savvy president was easily persuaded, and he allocated $35,000 dollars to help conduct a search for the remains of "The Father of the American Navy." The public-relations outcome of such an undertaking was not to be missed.

After extensive explorations, the body was eventually found and exhumed in 1905. The 113-year-old corpse was perfectly preserved, and in such fine shape that a meaningful autopsy was possible. The final diagnosis stated that cause of death was end-stage kidney failure as a result of viral or bacterial infection, coupled with pneumonia.

John Paul Jones's body was transferred to a fresh coffin and draped with the Stars and Stripes — the first instance of such honour. It was then formally paraded through the city's boulevards out of Paris to Cherbourg and placed on board the U.S.S. *Brooklyn*, one of four cruisers sent by Roosevelt to convey the remains to American shores. The remains of the great admiral today lie in the crypt of the imposing chapel of the United States Naval Academy at Annapolis. In front of the sarcophagus are the words "He gave our navy its earliest traditions of heroism and victory."

The appalling humiliation John Paul Jones suffered and the unhappy conclusion to his brilliant career was, in his own words, through "the meanness and absurdity of the intrigues that were practiced for my persecution in St. Petersburg." A poignant ending of the remarkable Kontradmiral Pavel Ivanovich Jones.

An equally engaging and out-of-the-ordinary tale may be had of a Russian aristocrat in the United States, in the wilds of the country's frontier.

In 1792, there stepped ashore in Baltimore a nobleman, Prince Dimitri Dimitrievich Gallitzin. He came as a visitor but stayed as a resident, the first notable permanent emigrant from Russia to the United States. Today, in the village of Loretto, Pennsylvania, ninety miles east of Pittsburgh, his remains lie in the Church of St. Michael.

Dimitri Dimitrievich came from one of the noblest families in Russia, one of ancient lineage. The Gallitzin estate outside Moscow was considered to be among the finest private homes in the country, much admired by Alexander I. (Much later, Stalin took it for his country residence.) Over the centuries, members of the family unfailingly played leading roles in government, in the military, and in Russia's social and cultural life. So distinguished was the name, that the prophetic story is told of one very young family member who, in being told about Jesus, innocently inquired, "Was he also a Gallitzen?"

Dimitri's father was a diplomat, for many years serving as Russia's ambassador to Holland. A wise, witty, worldly man, the prince was a product of the Enlightenment. Among his vast circle of friends were Voltaire and Diderot; the foremost thinkers of the time frequented his embassy in The Hague. It was in this residence that Empress Catherine at one time bounced the young Dimitri on her knee. So charmed was she by the delightful three-year-old, that she commissioned him an officer in the Guards Regiment.

The boy's mother was Countess Adelheid Amalie von Schmettau, the daughter of a Prussian field marshal. In her earlier years of marriage to the prince, she was, for lack of better word, a flower child; Rousseau's noble savage was her inspiration. The young, irrepressible Amelia persuaded her husband to permit her to move to the couple's country estate some miles outside The Hague — it was called *Niethuis*, or "nobody home." Once installed there, she cut off her long locks and donned the plainest of clothes, giving her time over to the study of Plato and Aristotle and to the care of her children, each of whom she addressed as "our dear Socrates." The unfortunate children were subject to cold baths and pitch-dark bedrooms. Whenever they cried — and cry they did, despite mother's exhortations to the contrary — Amelia comforted them with Socratic dialogue.

In 1783, when young Dimitri was a lad of thirteen years, his mother fell seriously ill, so ill that the boy's headmaster counselled her to receive his own confessor. Although Amelia had been born a Roman Catholic, the church had meant little to her. Nevertheless, she agreed to meet the priest and in the days that followed as the sickness progressed, she promised herself and the confessor that if God spared her, she would seriously study religion. Amelia survived her illness, made good on her promise and two years later was received into the Church as a full communicant. At age seventeen, Dimitri followed suit and converted to Catholicism, forsaking the Orthodox Church into which he was born.

Prince Gallitzin did not take seriously either his wife's conversion — which he deemed another capricious phase, similar to her Socratic period — or that of his son. He did, however, feel that it was time for the boy to enter military service and, through Amelia's Germanic connections, young Dimitri was duly appointed as aide-de-camp to General von Lillien, commander of the Austrian troops in Brabant. Dimitri served two years at that posting. Amelia then determined that her son would best be served by travel and, on the suggestion of her father, she persuaded her husband to endorse the idea of having their son spend time in America. The prince, a keen admirer of George Washington and the American Constitution, thought this an excellent idea, and thus it was that young Dimitri came ashore in Maryland in October 1792.

The new arrival carried a letter of introduction to Bishop John Carroll of Baltimore, the first Roman Catholic bishop in the United States. Here he found a cordial welcome and was soon quite at home in his new surroundings. Dimitri took up serious study of the church and within two years, he was determined to become ordained. The good bishop deemed the decision precipitous and he urged the young man to consult with his parents. Amelia, who by then had lost all interest in her conversion, received Dimitri's news with horror and was appalled by the idea that her boy should become a priest. At first these developments were kept secret from the prince, but it did not take long for him to discover his son's stunning intentions. That a scion of the Gallitzin family, traditional pillars of orthodoxy, would convert to Catholicism was bad enough; an ordination into that alien church was unthinkable. The desperate prince wrote to his wife, "Above all, I beg you to discuss that which is properly our common trouble and to seek some means of solving it. I do not know what to write to my son."

At this stage, serendipity came into play. Notice was received from Russia that the commission bestowed by Catherine years earlier upon the infant child had now come due. Dimitri was ordered to return to Russia to join the guards regiment. But the young man, having received the summons together with pleading letters from his parents, remained adamant. Nothing would dissuade him from his declared intention. On

March 18, 1795, he kneeled before Bishop Carroll to be ordained and tonsured. Prince Dimitri Dimitrievich Gallitzin became Father Dimitri.

At the time, there was a shortage of priests in the Maryland parishes, particularly in Baltimore, but Father Dimitri's calling was for missionary work. He successfully persuaded Bishop Carroll to assign him deep into the distant countryside, over a week's journey west, beyond the crest of the Allegheny Mountains. Here in the forests and mountains of the remote wilderness, the young priest made his home for over forty years, building a church here, converting there, "labouring in God's vineyards." He purchased twenty thousand acres of land in the greater the Loretto area, which he then sold for one quarter the price to impoverished settlers. In the village itself, he built a church at his expense, plus a grist mill and a sawmill — all to enable his parishioners to cope better with the vicissitudes of frontier life.

In 1808, Dimitri's father died and he received notice that the tsar had disinherited him, "by reason of your Catholic faith and your ecclesiastical profession." It was devastating news, for he had borrowed heavily in expectation of the inheritance. Now without funds, good Father Dimitri nevertheless pursued his initiatives, soon falling into greater and greater debt. He occasionally received small sums from his sister. King William V of Holland once sent Dimitri $2,000 dollars under the pretext that it was a payment for some insignificant items left behind at the royal palace from the days when the two were boys together at play. Another time, in desperation the priest travelled to Washington to seek assistance from the Russian ambassador to whom he owed money. Historian Alexander Tarsaidze picks up the story:

> The minister suggested that the discussion of financial matters be postponed until after dinner. Present at dinner were Henry Clay and the Dutch Envoy. After the plates had been removed, a servant brought in a candle to be used by the gentlemen in lighting their cigars. The Russian Minister rolled a spill, thrust it into the flame of the candle, lighted his cigar leisurely and smiled. A black ash was all that remained of the $5,000 bond.[3]

Dimitri struggled on, never out of debt but always confident that somehow God would provide. His fiscal irresponsibility provoked more than one tempest with the presiding bishops, but ultimately they appeared accepting of the situation and often came to the rescue.

Gallitzin was more than once proposed for a bishopric: in Bardstown, Kentucky; Philadelphia; Pittsburgh; and Cincinnati. All these he declined in favour of continuing his rural work in the verdant hills of western Pennsylvania. At the time of his death, there were an estimated ten thousand parishioners within his church's district. The turnout for his funeral was massive and as the remains were being lowered into the crypt the choir intoned, *I will lift up mine eyes unto the hills from whence cometh my strength.*

CHAPTER 6

THE PACIFIC FRONTIER

By the mid-eighteenth century, the Spanish had taken possession of the Pacific coast, from Mexico north to San Francisco. The lands north of San Francisco's Bay area, up through Oregon, Washington, and British Columbia, remained largely virgin territories open for exploration and development.

The Aleutians and Alaska, however, had long been strong drawing cards for Russian traders. The forests along the shores teemed with foxes, and shoal areas abounded with millions of sea otters. (That the waters were also home to an abundance of whales was initially unappreciated.) It was furs, furs, furs that propelled the initial Russian forays into the distant northwest Pacific regions. They thought little of crossing vast Siberian distances, embarking on vessels built in Kamchatka shipyards, and then sailing east to America.

The first to make a mark in the region was a barely literate Cossack sergeant from the Kamchatka garrison, a man whose name does not stand out among the giants of fur traders. Emelian Basov witnessed with interest the return home of Vitus Bering's fur-clad crew, and he cast a particularly covetous eye the bales of furs they lugged ashore. If they could do it, so could he. Mustering all his persuasive powers, Basov talked a wealthy trader, a certain Andre Serebrenikov, into financing the construction of a small vessel for a fur-gathering expedition. He planned to sail the 115 miles to Bering Island where, he was confident, plenty of sea otters romped. In the summer of 1743, the tiny *Kapiton*, a two-masted, flat-bottomed riverboat, departed from Kamchatka and within weeks returned home, laden with furs. Basov made three subsequent voyages, the second one of which records a detailed inventory, including 1,600 otter pelts, 2,000 fur seals, and 2,000 blue fox, for a value of 200,000 rubles — an astronomical sum in those days. Basov certainly made it rich, and in the process precipitated what can only be called a "fur rush."

The first to join the rush was Yakov Chuprov who in 1745 made his way to Attu, one of the westernmost Aleutian Islands, aboard the *Eudoxia*, a vessel similar in design to Basov's but larger. The expedition was notable not so much for the success it met, but rather for the first contact that Russians had with North American Natives. Having one dark evening dropped anchor at Agattu, an island adjacent to Attu, the expedition awaited morning's daylight. Dawn revealed scores of excited Aleuts dancing about on the shore, brandishing spears and other weapons. Was this an act of hostility or an indication of welcome? To test the waters, Chuprov catapulted to the shore bundles of manufactured goods: pots, knives, tin mirrors, and so on. In return, the Natives tossed to the *Eudoxia* freshly killed birds and small game. It was all non-threatening, and with his men on deck at the ready with muskets, Chuprov went ashore with a small party in the ship's utility boat.

Initially, all progressed well amid a friendly atmosphere. The inquisitive Aleuts displayed unfettered curiosity, poking at this and that. Items of one sort or another were exchanged, including an offering by Chuprov of a pipe and pouch of tobacco. This bewildered the Aleuts, who were at a loss as to what to do with the strange gift, but, nevertheless, they politely accepted it. In return, they presented the Russians with a bone sculpture. At this point, the principal among the Natives indicated his desire for one of the muskets carried by the sailors. Chuprov refused curtly.

The positive atmosphere soured immediately and became charged. Faces initially radiating goodwill turned bitter, and some Natives moved threateningly toward the *Eudoxia*'s utility boat. A scuffle ensued on the water in which one Aleut was shot, but the ship's crew returned safely to their vessel. Anchor was raised and Chuprov made for a return to Attu.

Word of the unfortunate events on Agattu preceded Chuprov's arrival at Attu, and by the time the *Eudoxia* dropped anchor, the locals had fled into the hinterland. After gentle coaxing and patience, however, rapport with the Aleuts was eventually re-established, and the hunt for sea otter resumed. With the onset of winter, the men took to the comfortable quarters they had erected for themselves and adapted to Native ways. They dressed in the same sort of skins and assumed the local diet of fish, meat, and even blubber.

In their dealings with the Aleuts, every effort was made to show courteousness and friendliness. The unfortunate incident at Agattu was soon forgotten and harmony once again prevailed among the lot. Attu Natives were persuaded to enter the service of the Russians — the men to hunt sea otter and the women to tend to the kitchens. In fact, Russians arriving in those parts encountered little opposition in their expansionary initiatives, certain isolated indigenous tribes excepted. They met far more success in coexisting with the Natives than did the Americans or British.

The Basov and Chuprov expeditions ignited ambitions — scores of fur traders trod off to suffer hardships in favour of profit. Fridtjof Nansen, the twentieth-century arctic explorer and Nobel laureate paints the scene: "An unending stream of straggling, struggling, frostbitten men bundled in heavy clothing, some erect and powerful, some so skinny and bent that they could hardly drag themselves or their sleds; wasted, starved, plagued with scurvy, but all gazing forward into the unknown, beyond the edge of the northern sun toward the dream which they sought."

Mounting success came to these entrepreneurs as they pushed further south along the continent's coastline. Financing the ventures, however, grew in complexity — the problem of supply in particular. Ever larger sums were required for financing expeditions; individual traders had difficulty in raising capital. A score of small fur companies thus came into being, which in time merged to form the Northeastern Company. The new entity was forced to operate exclusively on its own, without any form of government subvention or protection. Trans-Pacific imperialism was not for Empress Catherine. From the outset, she declared that "it was for the fur traders to traffic where they please.… I will furnish neither men, ships nor money. I renounce forever all possessions in America."

Subsequently, as an afterthought, she added, "England's experience with the American colonies should be a warning to other nations to abstain from such efforts." However, after Ivan Golikov, the co-owner of the Northeastern Company, presented the empress with a handsome gift of costly furs, Catherine looked more benignly on the developments in the Pacific. She granted the company tax-free status, and also ordered the company "to treat your new brothers, the aborigines of those lands, with gentleness, neither oppressing nor cheating them."

With Russians in the north and Spaniards in the south, the territories between the two powers drew the interest of Britain and the United States. Before long, their explorers and settlers were making way to those shores.

Among the first of these explorers was Captain James Cook, an Englishman who in his early years set the goal for himself of going not only "farther than any man has been before me, but as far as I think it possible for man to go." In his continuing search for the elusive Northwest Passage, Cook took his ship, HMS *Resolution*[1] and the collier HMS *Discovery* around the Cape of Good Hope into the Pacific — his third such venture.

He eventually reached Nootka Sound, midway up Vancouver Island's west coast. It became instantly clear that this was not the entrance to the Northwest Passage. It did offer, however, a well-protected anchorage — and it was home to uncharacteristically friendly Natives, the Mowachahts. Cook stopped there for a spell to give his crew a rest.

Chief Maquinna appeared unperturbed by the appearance of these unusual strangers aboard the formidable-looking vessel. He encouraged his awestruck people to put aside anxieties and to welcome the new arrivals. Thirty-two war canoes embarked from shore and were soon circling the *Resolution* in ceremonial greeting with flourishing strokes of the paddles. All the while the lead stroke chanted, one officer writes, "a single note in which they all join, swelling it out in the middle and letting the sound die away in the calm of the hills around us ... the effect was by no means unpleasant to the ear.... One young man with a remarkable soft effeminate voice afterwards sang by himself, but he ended so suddenly and abruptly, which being accompanied by a peculiar gesture, made us all laugh. He, finding that we were not ill pleased repeated his song several times."

The amused sailors reciprocated by bringing out their fifes and drums, which they played at length and with gusto. The trilling sounds of British military marches were not exactly familiar to the Mowachahts, and the audience floating on the waters below received the musical offering with "the profoundest silence." Lieutenant James King concludes his journal entries with the reflection that through all the encounters Cook's ships ever experienced with indigenous people anywhere, "these were the only people we had seen that ever paid the smallest attention to any of our musical instruments, if we except the drum."

Cook notes that the amicable cultural exchanges resulted in "a trade commenced betwixt us and them, which was carried on with the strictest honesty on both sides. Their articles were foxes, deer, raccoons, polecats, martins and in peculiar, the sea beaver [sea otter], the same as is found on the coast of Kamchatka."

Mowachahts and English were soon totally at ease with one another, so much so that the unrestrained Natives began to help themselves to various bits and pieces of the ship's ironware. Cook's gold watch was whisked away from his cabin under the nose of the posted guard. "They made no scruples when stealing," observed Cook, "but upon being detected they would immediately return whatever they had taken and laugh in our faces, as they considered it as a piece of dexterity that did them credit rather than dishonor."

The Mowachahts welcomed the visitors into their village where they offered generous entertainment. Chief Maquinna beckoned the officers to his cedar-planked house. Vast drying racks were suspended from the ceilings for the curing of herring and salmon; cooking utensils and varied baskets lay scattered about the place. Exquisitely carved corner posts with figures of birds and animals stood in shocking contrast to the overall mess. A banquet was laid out with a variety of foods, both cooked and raw.

One clearly identifiable dish from which all refrained was a roasted human arm.

Time came to leave Nootka Sound, so there was an exchange of gifts. Cook received a full-length beaver cloak, in return for which he presented to Chief Maquinna a choice sword with a brass hilt. The chief "importuned us to return to them again and by way of encouragement promised to lay in a good stock of skins for us." Final farewells were had, and the ships sailed away to continue the voyage. "Our friends the

Indians attended upon us till we were almost out of the Sound, some on board the ships and others in canoes."

(En route home, the expedition stopped in Hawaii, where it was greeted with hostility by the Natives. A number of tense encounters were had, and in one punishing skirmish, Cook was killed — a particularly tragic end to one of history's notable explorers.)

When the *Resolution* reached Macau months later, word spread of the successes with the Mowachahts. The cargo of luxuriant furs in the holds was sold for handsome sums, further fuelling the fur rush.

On board the *Discovery* on that fateful voyage was the twenty-two-year-old George Vancouver, who would eventually join his commanding officer in the pantheon of notable explorers. Some years earlier, as Cook prepared his ship for the second voyage of exploration, he had been persuaded by Vancouver's father to take on the fifteen-year-old boy as a supernumerary. George thus received a thorough training in seamanship, navigation, and surveying. Subsequently, he entered the navy, was commissioned, and before long came to command his own ship. In 1791, he was sent by the British government to make a detailed survey of the entire northwest coast, and to continue the search for the elusive Northwest Passage. Vancouver spent three years in those waters, meticulously charting and surveying the coastline as far north as Cook Inlet in upper Alaska. Before it was over, he had circumnavigated Vancouver Island, passed by the mouth of the Fraser River without recognizing it, and moved south as far as the mouth of the Columbia River at latitude 46° 25' — his discovery, he thought, but not so. Five months earlier, another explorer — Captain Robert Gray, the first American to appear in the Pacific Northwest — had arrived and laid claim to it for the United States.

The Rhode Islander Gray had served in the Continental Navy during the American Revolution and subsequently joined a Boston merchant house. In 1792, he sailed the *Columbia* into the far north of the Pacific coastline, well into Russian territory. His unwelcome arrival was viewed with displeasure by the unhappy authorities, who viewed it as an unlawful incursion. But they lacked the means to expel the American. Instructions, however, were issue to the Natives not to trade with him or render any form of assistance. Gray did not linger where he clearly was not wanted. He left and eventually came to the mouth of the Columbia River, and adroitly established friendly relations with the Natives — soon beads, buttons, cloth, knives, and other manufactured items were being traded for pelts of sea otter.

Its holds brimming with valued cargo, the *Columbia* sailed on to China where the pelts were exchanged for silk, spices, and tea. With this fresh cargo, Gray made for home by sailing west around the Cape of Good Hope, thus becoming the first American to circumnavigate the globe. Inspired by Gray's successes, other New Englanders followed suit, and by the end of the century came to control the otter trade of a large part of the region. The presence of U.S. ships on the Pacific coast solidified and soon the Stars and Stripes flew over the Oregon Territory.

It would be well to note here the story of another American who sailed those Pacific waters. John Ledyard's brief lifetime had no impact on the events of the day; his legacy merely rests in the journals he kept. His story may be nothing more than a footnote in the pages of U.S. history, but it is one that's so original and reflective of the fearless American frontier spirit, that it begs our attention. Thomas Jefferson was an admirer of the adventurous young Ledyard, calling him "a man of genius, of some science and of fearless courage and enterprise."

Ledyard was born in Groton, Connecticut, where he received his early education. At age twenty-one, he entered the newly founded Dartmouth, then called the "Indian Charity School." The school had been provided with land by the governor of the Royal Province of New Hampshire, and its charter stipulated that the place was "for the education and instruction of youth of the Indian tribes of this land — and also for English youth and any other." John was from among the handful of "English youth and any others." He soon decided that the quality of instruction was uninspiring and boring — not for him — so he decided to escape the place.

Among his friends, one stood particularly close, a "youth of the Indian tribes of this land." This Iroquois friend assisted John in felling a large white pine on the banks of the Connecticut River from which the young men hacked out a thirty-foot-long dugout canoe. Equipped with essentials — including the New Testament and a book by Ovid — Ledyard shoved off to begin a life of extraordinary adventure. He left behind a cryptic note to the Reverend Eleazar Wheelock, the school's founder: "Farewell, dear Dartmouth, may you flourish like the greenbay tree."

Ledyard travelled to London where he signed on as a seaman on a West Indian trading ship. During the course of his brief service under Captain Richard Deshon, he visited a number of ports in the Caribbean and plied the shores of the Barbary Coast. Three years later, John joined the Royal Navy and was seconded to Captain Cook. With this admired explorer, he visited the Canary and Cape Verde Islands, the Cape of Good Hope, Tasmania, New Zealand, Tahiti, California, and Oregon. Ledyard was on board the HMS *Resolution* when that ship's crew exchanged musical offerings with the Mowachahts — he was one of the drummers. (It was he, incidentally, who noted the human delicacy offered at Chief Maquinna's banquet.)

The *Resolution* sailed on to the Orient, Ledyard continuing all the time to keep a journal (it's the only account by an eyewitness of Cook's death in Hawaii). In 1782, he jumped ship in New York, and took up residence in the eastern extremity of Long Island. But resting feet developed an itch. Memories were ingrained of the Pacific Northwest, particularly of his exchanges with indigenous peoples and meetings with Russians. Ledyard left Long Island to return to Europe where he set about organizing a fur-trading expedition to the Pacific Northwest.

Ledyard's valiant efforts to obtain financial backing came to naught. In desperation, he approached John Paul Jones, who at the time was residing in Paris, then the Marquis de Lafayette, and finally Ambassador Thomas Jefferson. Jefferson writes that Ledyard "was disappointed in [not raising capital], and being out of business and of a roaming, restless character. I suggested to him the enterprise of exploring the western part of our continent by passing through St. Petersburg to Kamchatka and procuring a passage thence in some of the Russian vessels to Nootka Sound, whence he might make his way across the continent to the United States."

Ledyard eagerly accepted the proposal, and wasted little time in laying out plans. It was straightforward: he would travel to Stockholm and then walk across the frozen Baltic to St. Petersburg, where he would secure the permission of the empress to carry out his further travel arrangements. He would then continue by foot through Russia, across the Urals and traverse Siberia all the way to Kamchatka. Per Jefferson's suggestion, he would then seek passage to Alaska on a Russian vessel and, once on North American shores, he would continue his solo trek down the coast to Oregon. He then planned to walk east, cross the Mississippi and terminate the journey at home on Long Island. He would thus become the first American to cross the North American continent on foot.

Jefferson forewarned Ledyard — "the roaming restless character" — that Empress Catherine's permission for the project was absolutely essential, and he suggested that the impatient man bide his time in Paris until such was received. Furthermore, the ambassador offered to set the process into motion by meeting with his Russian counterpart with whom he was on excellent terms. "Ledyard would not relinquish [his determination to press forward] … persuading himself that by proceeding to St. Petersburg he could satisfy the Empress of its practicability and obtain her permission."

And so John set off. He made his way by boat to Stockholm, and on arrival was devastated by the magnitude of problems related to his hike across a frozen Baltic. Undaunted, Ledyard trekked around Stockholm, crossed the frozen Gulf of Bothnia into Finland, and after an arduous winter passage reached St. Petersburg in March 1787.

The empress at the time was away from the capital on an extended visit to the Crimea — her sanction was not to be had. Our hero was unprepared to dally, and he attached himself to a certain Dr. Brown, one of many Scottish physicians working in Russia at the time, who was journeying to Siberia. Brown's journey terminated at Barnaul in central Siberia, and there Ledyard left him to continue his solo hike to Tomsk and Irkutsk — a distance of twelve hundred miles.

In Irkutsk, the long arm of Her Imperial Majesty's police reached out and plucked up luckless Ledyard. Suspicion had been aroused that this unknown, unregistered foreigner was a spy. He was arrested, transported back to Russia, escorted to the Polish border and banished forever from the country. Ledyard's grand plan of being the first American to cross the North American continent was shattered — at least for the moment.

On reaching London, he busied himself in the study of Asian and American indigenous people. Was there a relationship between them? At this point, fortune smiled on him. A certain British eccentric, Sir Joseph

Banks, engaged Ledyard on behalf of the African Association to explore overland routes from Alexandria to Niger. Our hero put aside his ruminations on indigenous peoples, and set off for Egypt. After an uneventful first leg of his journey, he reached Cairo, where, alas, he took sick and died, succumbing to an overdose of "vitriolic acid."

Ledyard was a unique and possessed individual. And legitimate claim can be made that it was John Ledyard of Long Island — on board a British vessel commanded by Englishman James Cook — who was the first American to make contact with Russians on the continent's Pacific shores.

Widespread publicity resulting from Cook's explorations kindled English interest in the commercial possibilities of northwestern shores. One of these people was John Meares, who upon retiring from the Royal Navy had founded a thriving trading station in Macau. To help feed this far-off station, Meares decided that furs were a good bet. So he sailed off to Alaska and made his way in 1786 to Nootka Sound, where he wintered, made friends with the Natives, and established a trading post.

Fourteen years earlier, the Spanish had sailed up and down the British Columbia coastline. Although they recognized the fur opportunities of the area, they neglected to exploit them. On the basis of that foray, they now laid claim to virtually all of that coastline, contending that they had been awarded these lands by the papal grant of 1493. To enforce Spain's claim, a patrol of ships was dispatched from the naval base at San Blas, Mexico. It entered Nootka Sound, and Meares's trading post was seized along with four of his ships. The Spanish flag was unfurled.

Meares appealed to Britain for redress. London responded by commissioning George Vancouver to regain the seized property as part of his 1791 voyage. The discussions Vancouver eventually had with the Spanish commandant of Mexico, Juan Francisco de la Bodega y Quadra Mollinedo, came to an impasse and the matter was referred to their home governments. The subsequent exchange between the foreign offices of Britain and Spain was bellicose and the sound of rattling sabres began to resonate in the capitals. At one point, war between the two nations appeared imminent.

The unfolding revolution in France, however, with its turmoil and anxieties, eclipsed the relatively insignificant discord in the obscure Pacific corner. Diplomacy won the day and the conflict was peacefully defused by the Nootka Sound Convention.

The treaty between the two belligerents, signed on January 11, 1794, delineated each nation's sphere of operation and made Nootka Sound a free port, with both nations agreeing to abandon the place. Flags were ceremoniously lowered, ships sailed out to sea, and the land was left to the Mowachahts. The Natives wasted no time in demolishing Meares's village and the Spanish fortification, taking with them every bit of iron they could salvage, including much-valued nails. (Subsequently, they even raided the cemetery and dug up coffins to salvage the nails.) Nootka Sound had reverted to the look it had twenty-one years earlier when the first white men arrived. As one Canadian historian put it, "a tide of empire had come and gone."

By the Nootka Sound Convention, Spain effectively dropped claims to lands north of forty-two degress, California's northern boundary, thereby ceasing as a player in the Pacific Northwest. Any territorial claim, the treaty stipulated, had to be backed by physical presence.

With Spain's northern limits set by the treaty and Russia's recognized southern limits at the sixtieth parallel, the lands in between now became a tussle between Britain and the United States — with Russia continuing to play a peripheral role.

The years following 1794, then, were particularly active for the British and Americans in the Pacific Northwest. Explorers were uncovering more and more of the vast, irregular coastline — its bays, channels, feeding rivers, and numerous islands. As noted earlier, Alexander Mackenzie had crossed the Rockies and reached the Pacific. British North America had thus been traversed from the Atlantic to the Pacific; the future opened for what was to become Canada.

By 1794, traders in increasing numbers plied the waters in their quest for sea otter. That year, twenty-one vessels are said to have entered British Columbian waters, more than half arriving from Britain. The numbers increased in the following season, but this time the majority were American ships that had departed from Boston.

CHAPTER 7

SUPPLY FOR ALASKA

By 1812 much of the coastline from the Aleutians down the Alaskan panhandle and into northern California was dotted with Russian trading posts, missionary stations, and settlements. The Russian-American Company, founded in 1799, held overall sway over the region. Based in Sitka, its arm reached as far south as California, to Fort Ross, just north of today's San Francisco. It had developed into a sizable fortress with a population of some two hundred and fifty Russians, Métis, and Natives.[1]

Living conditions in North America were gruelling, the critical problem being logistics. Virtually everything had to be imported from home, and Sitka was halfway around the world from St. Petersburg. A distance of four thousand miles separated the two capitals if travelled across Siberia and the Okhotsk. By oceanic passage from the Baltic, around Europe, Africa, Southeast Asia, and north, it was five times as far. Either way, communication between Sitka and St. Petersburg was painfully slow. As late as the 1850s, it took a letter over two years to travel between the two cities. (In contrast, mail from California to Madrid took a month.)

It was Alexander Baranov, the so-called Lord of Alaska, who partially came to terms with the hardships and multiplicity of problems besetting the company. The son of a storekeeper who as a youth apprenticed as a shopkeeper to a German merchant in Moscow, he moved to Irkutsk in central Siberia and established a glass factory. The enterprise was sufficiently successful to enable him to start up as a fur trader.

He joined what was to become the Russian-American Company and was sent to Kodiak as supervisor of operations — the top manager of the colonial territory. It was he who established New Archangel on Baranov Island as the capital of Russian America — later renamed Sitka. A rough and practically minded individual, he ruled his fiefdom with an iron fist, and as manager and territorial governor, he came to be the company's life and soul. Successful in most things, Baranov's principal achievement was the astronomical quantity of furs shipped home. It was through his efforts that scores of trading posts were established along the American coastline, and that a certain harmony prevailed with the Native populations.

Emperor Paul I came to the throne in 1796, viewing with suspicion Russian thrusts into North America. In his paranoia, his countrymen were denied permission to travel abroad lest they be subverted by alien ideas — dreaded republicanism above all. Licences given the fur merchants by Empress Catherine were reigned in. But by that time, the Russian-American Company had passed into the hands of the capable Count Nikolai Petrovich Rezanov, a brilliant organizer and a persuasive individual. Through his court connections and well-placed friends, he

G. von Langsdorff, 1812. Engraving. Library of Congress.

Russian fort, harbour, and ships, Sitka, Alaska, 1812.

managed to catch the tsar's ear. The merchant successfully argued that it was the country's obligation "to soften the manners of the savages by bringing them into contact with Russians." It was essential, he maintained, that the indigenous peoples of North America be imbued with monarchical ideals lest "the gullible natives" be led astray into republicanism. Furthermore, argued Rezanov, the trading nations "envious of us ... which often peep into these regions" can only bring harm to Russia. His arguments did not fall on deaf ears — Paul relented.

By 1830, the population of Russian America was over ten thousand, and to supply its needs was a gargantuan problem. That year, for example, the populace consumed 80 tons of flour, 27 tons of salt, 23 tons of sugar, 18 tons of rice, 6 tons of salted beef, 3.5 tons of tea, and, it might be noted, 3,600 gallons of rum — everything imported. In addition to food, nearly all manufactured goods had to be brought in: ammunition, tools, nails, cloth, tobacco, medical supplies, and so on. To transport these items over land to the Pacific meant surmounting obstacles of every imaginable sort. Unreliable roads; stony, potholed ground; torrential river crossings and miring bogs; lack of forage for the thousands of horses involved; summer heat and winter cold; thick bush and dense forests; steep slopes and snowy summits; predatory animals and mosquitoes; disease and sickness; and corrupt officials. And then, arriving at the Okhotsk required a sea voyage to Alaska — uncharted waters, changeable and unpredictable currents, thick fogs, alternating high winds, ice flows in spring, gales in the fall, ice most of the year, frequent groundings and floundering. All this was part of supplying strongholds in North America.

In addition, the ships they sailed were unsound and the seamen for the most part were poorly trained. Rezanov writes: "Over there [Okhotsk] the ignorance of the shipbuilders and robbery without shame by men representing the company produce worthless ships that cost more than ships built anywhere else." To maintain Russian America certainly took strong will and determination. And lots and lots of money.

State councillor Sergei Kostlivtsev, an inspector for the Ministry of Finance, stood in despair of the overall situation:

Who can ever have a mind to settle in that country, where permanent fogs and dampness of atmosphere and want of solar heat and light, leaving out of the question anything like agriculture, made impossible to provide even a sufficient supply of hay for cattle, and where man from want of bread, salt, and meat to escape scurvy must constantly live upon fish, berries, shellfish, sea cabbages and other products of the sea, soaking them profusely with the grease of sea beasts.[2]

Rezanov, "Imperial Inspector and Plenipotentiary of the Russian–American Company," arrived in Sitka in March 1805 and found the colony in pitiful state. Men, women, and children were starving, food stores were rotting, and the place was plagued with every sort of disease — smallpox, scurvy, and dysentery being the prime concerns. The condition of the Alaskan settlement was so dire that he determined to seek relief by sailing to Spanish California in order to procure medicines and provisions. On April 8, his ship, the *Juno*, passed through the Golden Gate strait and, under the watchful guns of Spain, entered San Francisco.

Rezanov made his way to the Presidio of San Francisco, the principal fortress, where he was confident of persuading the governor to relax the prohibition of trade imposed by the Spanish government. Commandant Argüello was absent at the time, but his son Don Luis, willingly welcomed the visiting Russians. Initially, language proved to be a barrier, but fortunately the *Juno*'s doctor, Georg von Langsdorff, and a Franciscan friar of the Presidio both spoke Latin and after that, no problem. In time, Spaniards and Russians found themselves quite comfortable with one another.

The bay area with its open seas and rolling hills enchanted the Russians. Von Langsdorff writes of it in his diary: "[San Francisco is a] country which is blessed with so mild a climate ... where there is plenty of wood and water, with so many means for the support of life." The visitors were equally taken by their Spanish hosts. "Their simple, natural cordiality captivated us to such a degree that we forthwith desired to become acquainted with each individual member of the family, and to learn the name of each one, having at once formed a strong attachment to them."

But it was the commandat's charming fifteen-year-old daughter who captivated the hearts of the Russians — she was the "acknowledged beauty of California." Doña Concepcion, in the words of von Langsdroff, "was distinguished for her vivacity and cheerfulness, love-inspiring and brilliant eyes and exceedingly beautiful teeth, her expressive features, shapeliness of figure and for a thousand other charms besides an artless natural demeanor."

The thirty-two-year-old Rezanov, a widower, succumbed immediately to her spell. "The sparkling eyes of Doña Concepcion had made upon him a deep impression and pierced his inmost soul." And on her part, the girl fell under Rezanov's Russian charm. All too soon, affection blossomed into friendship, and then into love. The two spent days and weeks together exploring; they seemed inseparable. "I was in Argüello's home from morning until evening and officers observed that I was becoming half Spanish," Rezanov later wrote.

Before long, the smitten Russian proposed to Doña Concepcion, a proposal he himself notes "that shocked her parents, raised in fanaticism." Marriage to anyone other than a Catholic was an absurdity. In addition, a "separation from their daughter [was] like a thunder clap to them." Eventually, however, the commandant acquiesced, and it was agreed that Rezanov would return to St. Petersburg to secure the emperor's consent and seek the pope's benediction to a mixed Catholic and Orthodox wedding.

On May 21, the *Juno* passed again through the Golden Gate, this time on its return passage to Sitka. Fond farewells had been exchanged between Spanish soldiers and Russian sailors. Rezanov and Doña Concepcion tearfully embraced, and he promised to return soon in order to take her hand in marriage.

The Russian sojourn in San Francisco lasted six weeks, and in that period Rezanov and Argüello managed to reach a successful trade agreement. In quitting the bay area, the *Juno* hold was full of grain, garden produce, salted meat, poultry, butter, and other foodstuffs. In return, the Spaniards received linen, iron tools, and other manufactured goods. That everything turned out so satisfactorily on the business side of things was largely due to Doña Concepcion. As the trade discussions moved forward, the girl kept her lover informed as to her father's negotiating strategy. Were it not for that shared intelligence, the Russians might well have returned home empty-handed.

Von Langsdroff explains Rezanov's marriage proposal in cynical terms: "A close bond would be formed for future business intercourse between the Russian-American Company and the provincia of Nueva California. He [Rezanov] therefore decided to bind in friendly alliance Spain and Russia." It is true that the two countries were in competition for ascendancy over the northwest coast. Rezanov's proposed marriage to the commandant's daughter might have had strategic value. One would like to believe, however, that it was entirely a matter of the heart.

Doña Concepcion waited and waited for the return of her lover. But it was all in vain. Like Pinkerton in *Madama Butterfly*, there was no return to a Cio-Cio-San. During his passage back to St. Petersburg, Rezanov caught pneumonia in Krasnoyarsk and died. For five years, the pathetic Doña Concepcion continued her vigil, patiently counting the days, panting for the return of her lover — no doubt struggling with thoughts of tragedy or unfaithfulness. In 1812, one of Rezanov's officers returned to San Francisco and explained to the heartbroken girl that her lover was dead. He returned to her a locket she had once presented to her lover. Doña Concepcion was inconsolable. She eventually bade farewell to her parents and withdrew from the world by joining a Dominican nunnery. She died as Sister Mary in 1857.

When in 1798 Rezanov spoke to the emperor of certain trading nations "envious of us" that "peeped" into Pacific North America, he was referring first and foremost to Britain and Spain. But the United States was rapidly developing into "a peeper." Within a couple of decades of Rezanov's meeting with Emperor Paul I, these countries were no longer peeping — they were undeniably present and actively engaged. Explorers, traders, and missionaries of varied ilk had by then penetrated the various nooks and crannies of the irregular coastline, some having arrived long before Paul came to the throne.

From his headquarters at Sitka, Baranov observed American pervasiveness with alarm and anger. He was alone. Support from home was non-existent and St. Petersburg appeared genuinely uninterested in the American Pacific. In time, however, his attitude toward "the American curse" altered as he came to realize first, that there was nothing he could do about it and second, that here were opportunities for advantageous trade — even if such trade contravened St. Petersburg's prohibition. As Bostonians journeyed to the northwest, they bypassed San Francisco and the other California ports because of Spain's rigid refusal to allow foreign trade in their colonies. Because of this, Baranov's company soon found itself cheerfully bargaining and trading with the New Englanders. He contentedly drank and caroused with his new-found friends. The Yankee political maxim had been fully embraced: "If you can't fight 'em, join 'em." By 1805, Russian trade with Americans was well established from Sitka all the way south. In the words of Baranov's superiors some years later,

> This trade with foreigners was a most beneficial event for the company.... On the one hand it spared the company the necessity of sending all essentials to the colonies at great expense and difficulty via Okhotsk and around the world. On the other hand it facilitated the local sale of those surplus furs that could not be marketed in Russia.... Baranov bought from the foreigners not only everything necessary for provisioning of the colonies but even of their ships.

Within a few years, this trade was such an open fact of life and had so spectacularly developed, that Russia's consul general in New York, Andrey Dashkov, was ordered to regularize it. More specifically, his instructions read in part "to provide our settlements with necessities in the most profitable way and to avoid the harm done locally to hunting and trading by republicans through improper commerce with the savages on the northwestern shores and islands of America." With this fresh mandate, Dashkov approached John Jacob Astor, who, as noted earlier, had become the single most important figure in the fur rush. The wily German instantly recognized the advantage of an alliance with the Russians. If his American Fur Company was permitted to penetrate north in exchange for the right of the Russian-American Company to move south, the expansionary designs of the intrusive British, his archrivals, would be thwarted.

In May 1812, the two companies signed an agreement of cooperation. They bound themselves to respect each other's hunting grounds above and below the fifty-fifth parallel. In addition, they agreed not to trade weapons and ammunition with the Natives and to offer one another support in conveying furs to markets. They agreed, furthermore, to supply one another with whatever was required at uninflated prices. Alas, within months, the War of 1812 brought all this to naught with the appearance of the Royal Navy. Astor was forced to close down his trading station on the Columbia River. The Dashkov-Astor accord, however, is illustrative of the generally friendly and cooperative spirit that prevailed between Russia and the United States in the Pacific during those times.

The Russian advance into North America had been driven by furs and by the time the rush ended, the Alaskan coast and lands to the south were dotted with Russian settlements. Arriving with the profit-driven traders were devout missionaries and by the time of Alaska's sale in 1867, the vast territory was within the fold of the Russian Orthodox Church. On September 24, 1794, a vessel of the Northeastern Company, the *Three Saints*, sailed into St. Paul Harbor in Kodiak, Alaska. Among other passengers were eight Orthodox monks from Valaam Monastery on Lake Lagoda, north of St. Petersburg. Together with two novices who accompanied them, their purpose was to establish missions for the conversion of pagan Natives. Previous expeditions had frequently included priests, but these served only the ships' crews and Russian settlers. Now, with the arrival of the *Three Saints*, the Orthodox Church was launching a missionary initiative.

Kodiak at the time numbered 225 Russians and 8,000 Aleuts, and on the adjacent islands there were more settlements. The good clergymen spread out in different directions, more fully to reach out to the Natives, and they went about their business with driven energy in preparing the Natives for baptism. The Northeastern Company looked after the missionaries generously, supplying them with all that was required, "not only for the church but also for the support of the mission, that they might have enough for three years." The monks were particularly taken by the beauty of the rugged wilderness about them. Father Herman — canonized in 1970 as the first saint of the Orthodox Church in America — wrote in a heartfelt manner:

> Although traveling by water was a joy, traveling by horse-back was even better. In the forests, mountains and ravines we saw everything ... the season was joyous. It was May, June and July but only bears grazed. They are specialists in frightening horses. What I never even heard about, God had given me the possibility to see: sea otter, beaver, whales coming near our ship, swimming and playing.

Father Herman was equally impressed by the Aleuts who "showed a desire to be baptized, surprising us immensely." Within a year, Archimandrite Joasaph, head of the religious mission, was able to report that among the Kodiak and Natives from nearby islands, 6,740 were baptized and 1,573 weddings were celebrated. Additional priests arrived from Russia, churches were constructed, and eventually the scriptures were translated into Aleut. Within six years of the arrival of the *Three Saints* to Kodiak, Orthodox Christianity had become firmly implanted on American soil.

The problem of supply for the Russians in Sitka and other parts of Alaska failed to diminish. In fact, the more the area's population expanded, the greater grew the needs, particularly for food. Although the overland route across Siberia and the Okhotsk slowly developed in sophistication, costs of transportation continued to be unbearably high. So Baranov and Rezanov both strove to develop every possible local agricultural opportunity. From earliest days, kitchen gardens were encouraged and in this regard, Grigory Shelikhov, a Russian trader, was particularly enthusiastic. He offered the following upbeat, if perhaps unrealistic assessment:

> The islands lying near the American coast and stretching from Kodiak toward the eastern side and to northwestern America are stonier and mountainous, but there

is good, suitable land for grain cultivation, to which
I attest with my own experience, having sown barley,
millet, peas, beans, pumpkins, carrots, mustard, beets,
potatoes, turnips and rhubarb. All grew in the best way,
except that millet, peas, beans and pumpkins did not
bear fruit, and then only because the time at which they
should have been sown was missed. For haymaking
there are suitable meadowy places and fairly suitable
grasses, and in places livestock can live all winter without hay.

One of the vessels arriving earliest at Kodiak unloaded livestock,
including year-old steers, calves, pigs, and goats — in equal proportion
male and female. In 1794, twenty-five peasants arrived fully equipped
with seeds, implements, and other supplies in order to start up farms.
Try hard as these early settlers did, the rewards of their efforts were
disappointingly meagre and the results of their labours did not meet
Shelikhov's optimistic expectations. The growing season proved short
and exceedingly wet; the frost-free period was barely long enough for the
maturing of vegetables, the rugged terrain offered mediocre soil conditions, and the labour force to deal with it all was insufficient. The livestock
did not prosper, mostly because of disease and predatory animals (and
large birds that carried away chickens). And, complained Rezanov, "hunting and fishing occupy everyone from spring until fall — sick oldsters,
wives, and children remain so that the land is never plowed." In short,
the company realized that its aspirations for agricultural self-sufficiency
in Alaska were not entirely realistic. It began to consider prospects of the
more clement climes of California and Hawaii.

En route back to Sitka from San Francisco after farewells to Doña
Concepcion, Rezanov determined he was going to establish a colony in
an unoccupied area of New Albion, a coastal area north of San Francisco,
"which is blessed with so mild a climate ... with so many means for the
support of life." What Alaska failed to provide, these new lands would.
And New Albion was literally awash with reserves of sea otter.

Rezanov sent an assistant, Ivan Kuskov, to scout out the area, to find

[a] more suitable and more advantageous place for a colony, which throughout its region would control hunting and trade with the Indians, open new hunting benefits for the company and avoid the current difficulties in the delivery to our colonies of vital provisions and heavy ship material, which the company now gets by virtue of the long, difficult and often unprofitable route to Okhotsk, and which are constantly becoming more expensive to convey.[3]

Kuskov set off on his assignment, terminating reconnaissance up the coast from San Francisco at a site on Bodega Bay. It immediately became clear, however, that the building of a fortified town at that location wasn't practical for lack of timber. They made a change of plans and a fresh site was selected a few miles farther north on a bluff some one hundred feet above the ocean. Kuskov oversaw the construction of sufficient buildings to accommodate his party of ninety-five for the winter. In spring, work resumed in earnest on attending to the remainder of requirements — including an encircling stockade planted deep enough into the ground to prevent Natives from burrowing underneath. With stout walls and bastions commanding a view to the west of the rugged coastal range, Fort Ross came to be. An Orthodox priest blessed walls and buildings and prayers were intoned for God's blessing on the place: "may He hold it forever in his view."

Society of California Pioneers, c. 1873. Drawing. Library of Congress.

Fort Ross.

The Spaniards situated just a few miles to the south initially resented the Russian intrusion, but before long developed a friendly rapport with the new arrivals — sufficient for the two sides to engage in clandestine trade. The first Russian settlement in the lower latitudes of the Pacific coast, nascent Russian California, was thus established.

Within a quarter century, the colony had prospered and grown substantially in population and geographic size. As noted, the population of Russian America had grown to nearly eleven thousand by 1833, half being Russian and the other either Native or Métis. Fort Ross itself, covering less than one square mile, had grown to 253 inhabitants. No description of the quarter-century-old place is likely more apt than that of Ferdinand Wrangel, director of the Russian-American Company:

On a flat, clayey ground atop a hill slopping steeply to the sea has been erected a palisade along the edges of a fairly extensive area forming a regular square. At two diagonally opposite corners in connection with the palisade have been erected two watchtowers with cannons defending all sides of this so-called fortress, which in the eyes of the Indians and local Spaniards, however, seems very strong and perhaps unconquerable. Within this enclosure by the palisade itself stand the company buildings: the house of the Manager of the Factory, barracks, magazines, a storehouse, and a chapel, all kept in cleanliness and order, conveniently and even prettily situated. However, almost all the buildings and the palisade itself with the watchtowers are so old and dilapidated that they need repairs or they will have to be replaced by new structures. On this hill, outside the fortress, facing and paralleling its sides, are located two company cattle barns with pens, spacious and kept in excellent cleanliness, a small building for storing milk and making butter, a shed for Indians, a threshing floor and two rows of small company and private houses with gardens and orchards, occupied by employees of the company.

On a cleared spot beyond this outskirts stands as wind-
mill. Below the hill, by a landing for *baidarkas* [a type
of fishing vessel], have been built a spacious shed and a
cooperage, a blacksmithy, a tannery and a bathhouse.[4]

A small port accommodated storehouses for furs, grain-storage facilities, corrals, and houses for Russians and Natives. A modest shipbuilding
enterprise briefly blossomed but then fizzled when it became clear that
California oak was unsuitable for ship construction. On a nearby cluster
of rocky islands lived a group of Aleut hunters and a Russian foreman
who were employed in the hunt for sea otters, seals, and sea bird eggs.

Although otter and seal hunting greatly occupied the inhabitants,
land cultivation and farming were the dominant concern, and this, of
course, was Rezanov's original intent for the colony. Fields were cleared
for the growing of wheat, barley, and corn. Other fields were fenced as
pasturelands for cattle and sheep. Vegetable gardens were seeded and
two crops were raised each year. Grapes were planted for vineyards as
were fruit trees. The "country which is blessed with so mild a climate"
produced and it promised to meet the company's expectations. The
outcomes were positive, as one illustrative statistic shows: in 1813, no
wheat was harvested; by 1823, 1,114 bushels were taken in; by 1833, it
was 3,080 bushels. Captain Vasily Golovnin, a company inspector, was
clearly impressed with what he saw at Fort Ross in 1819:

> Here the land produces many crops in abundance: cab-
> bage, lettuce, pumpkins, horseradish, carrots, turnips,
> beets, onions and potatoes now grow in Kuskov's gar-
> dens. Watermelons, muskmelons and grapes, which
> he has recently cultivated, even ripen in the air. The
> garden vegetables are very pleasant in taste and some-
> times reach an extraordinary size. For example, one
> horseradish weighed 48 pounds, and 36-pounders are
> often obtained. Here pumpkins are 54 pounds and one
> turnip weighed 12 pounds. The potato is especially pro-
> ductive. At Ross one potato usually yields one hundred

and at Port Rumiantzev one potato sometimes yields 180 or 200, and besides they plant it twice each year. Sowings of the first half of February are reaped at the approach of May, and in October ripen those that were planted in June.[5]

No matter how much was produced at Fort Ross, it was insufficient to meet fully the needs of Alaskans. However impressive the statistics, there was an insufficiency; harvests of wheat and barley in particular proved disappointing. By 1833, for example, New Archangel's annual requirement for these grains was 180 tons but only thirteen tons were supplied from Fort Ross. To meet the needs of Fort Ross itself and half those of Alaska, at least seventeen hundred head of cattle had to be slaughtered each year — and additional cattle was required to avoid depleting the herds. Fort Ross simply was unable to cope with such demands. In the first place, despite original aspiration of founding the colony as an agricultural centre, the place in time had developed a multiplicity of purposes. Agriculture became but one facet of its existence — hunting, shipbuilding, trade, and even manufacturing were in competition. This diversity of interests required a large labour force, but such was not available. And those actually involved with agriculture — for the most part local Natives or imported Creoles and Aleuts — proved inept in growing crops and tending to livestock. Lastly, it became evident the terrain and soil conditions immediately around Fort Ross were not ideal. The site had been selected on the basis of strategic considerations and defensibility rather than agricultural potential. Sandy tableland, wooded forests, and the steep precipice to the ocean were no assets for the raising of crops or animal husbandry. Hard as they tried, the problems of supply for the growing Alaska settlements remained insufficient.

Baranov turned his gaze to Hawaii. A decade earlier his colleague Rezanov had visited the islands and had reported favourably on them — particularly on the archipelago's agricultural potential. The Sandwich Islands, reckoned Baranov, were a promising alternative to New Albion for meeting the company's kitchen requirements.

CHAPTER 8

PACIFIC MISADVENTURES

In the summer of 1803, two sturdy ex-British frigates, the *Nadezda* and the *Neva*, set sail from St. Petersburg for Cape Horn and the Pacific on the initial leg of Russia's first circumnavigation of the globe. Scientific research was as much a purpose of the expedition as were fresh trading opportunities. Commanding the expedition was Captain Ivan Krusenstern, a distinguished naval officer who had once visited China. The expedition's central figure, however, was Rezanov.

Rezanov's ship, the *Nadezda*, carried fifty-five people: crew and scientists, plus one individual with no official duties, the twenty-one-year-old Count Feodor Tolstoy. Nicknamed the "American" Tolstoy, he was uncle to the iconic author and social activist Leo Tolstoy. Although he isn't central to this narrative, his extravagant story should not be left untold.

Feodor received the finest schooling in his early years, and in his late teens was enrolled in the elite Preobrazhensky Guards regiment. Intelligent, handsome, and strongly built, he was a womanizer, a card sharp, and, above all a bon vivant, famous for his humour and mischief making. Among his other talents, Feodor was a gourmet cook, and in later life a musician of sorts, occasionally known to conduct orchestras (once using an enormous candlestick in lieu of baton). He was also an accomplished duellist, an expert shot, and a master with the foil and sabre. It was for having dispatched a fellow noble in a duel that Tolstoy was sent by the tsar into temporary exile, away from St. Petersburg. So it was that he found himself on board the *Nadezda* with Rezanov in the Pacific.

By May 1804, the two ships had rounded Cape Horn and had anchored at Nuku Hiva in the Marquesas archipelago. The travellers were greeted by welcoming natives bearing baskets of exotic fruit. In due course, King Tanega made his appearance — a handsome man in his fifties, every inch of his stark naked body tattooed with intricate designs. Tolstoy was greatly amused with this apparition and in no time struck up an intimacy with the royal visitor whom he successfully charmed. Soon, the ship's company was regaled with the grotesque spectacle of a naked king stroking out to sea to retrieve a stick that Tolstoy hurled out with the gleeful exhortation, "Fetch! Fetch!" Not very dignified, but a jolly time was had by all, including the beaming king. So impressed and taken was Tolstoy by the king's body art that he arranged to have his own chest, back, legs, and arms tattooed in the same manner — artwork which later caused a sensation in St. Petersburg. At fashionable dinner parties, Feodor was renowned, upon request, for exposing his decorated chest and arms, much to the delight of admiring ladies.

Tolstoy had no function at sea; he had been registered in the ship's roster simply as supernumerary, "a young, well-brought-up man." As the expedition made way, the bored passenger became increasingly restless and mischievous. One prank followed another, to the appreciation of the crew but to the dismay of unsuspecting victims. On one occasion, for example, he encouraged the ship's priest, an elderly and frail individual, to overindulge in drink. When the poor cleric collapsed in a stupor, Tolstoy sealed the priest's beard onto the wooden deck with copious quantities of hot wax. As an added touch, the seal he used was Kruzenshtern's official instrument which the perpetrator had temporarily "borrowed" from the captain's quarters. One can only imagine the excitement that must have resulted when the plight of the pinned cleric was discovered. To liberate the priest from his ignominious situation, the poor man's cherished beard had to be shorn.

The final straw for the captain was Feodor's persuasion of Kruzenshtern's pet orangutan to partake in activities of unpardonable rascality. The ape was a quick learner and a happy bond had developed between the animal and Tolstoy. Once, when the captain went ashore on some errand, Feodor brought the tethered animal into the master's cabin and, arranging all of Kruzenshtern's notes and documents on the writing table, he placed a blank sheet of paper onto the pile. He then proceeded to sprinkle ink on it, and messily to spread it throughout the clean page. The orangutan observed the proceedings with interest, and soon there was little of the white remaining on the sheet. Tolstoy then folded the soiled paper into his pocket, freed his friend and withdrew from the cabin. The talented ape wasted no time in taking the baton. Before long, the entire writing table — papers, documents, and so on — was awash with ink, as was a good portion of the animal itself. All of Kruzenshtern's writings were effectively destroyed.

The infuriated captain quickly pieced together the sequence of events that had transpired in his absence. Enough was enough: Tolstoy had to go. The *Nadezda* had to be freed of its nuisance passenger. When their ship next made landfall, the "young, well-brought-up man" was rowed ashore accompanied by the offending ape.

With no further ado, they were deposited on the sandy beach, along with a supply of provisions. The ship's anchor was raised, sails hoisted, and the vessel began slowly to move out to sea. As it made way, those gathered on deck observed a nonplussed Tolstoy gradually fading from sight, gallantly bowing and waving his massive hat in adieu.

Tolstoy had been left stranded somewhere on Kamchatka, not far from Petropavlovsk. We know little of his movements in the months that followed, although the young adventurer claimed to have spent time living with the Natives. Suffice it to say that our hero eventually made his way back to St. Petersburg, travelling a goodly part of Siberia by foot. In later life, he spoke little of his marooning experience, although he did tell of having eaten his friend the orangutan.

How precisely the American Tolstoy passed his time on those lonely Pacific shores is not known. It is, however, a celebrated story of an eccentric member of one of Russia's most notable families. Leo Tolstoy described his uncle as an "unusual, nefarious and attractive person."

Much to society's chagrin, Feodor married a cabaret singer, and shortly thereafter took up with a gypsy girl. He fathered thirteen children, eleven of whom died in childhood. In time, he became quite convinced that the deaths were God's retribution for the eleven men he had killed in duels over the years. He carried on his person a well-worn list of the names of his victims, and upon the succeeding death of each child, he crossed out a victim's name and inscribed the word, "even."

Rezanov and the Russian expedition, having completed the visit in the Marquesas archipelago, continued sailing west in 1804. The *Nadejda* and *Neva* soon reached the Hawaiian archipelago, where they anchored for twelve days.

Two chieftains at the time were vying for control of the entire island chain: King Tamuri (a.k.a. Kaumualii) and King Kamehameha (a.k.a. Tamiomio). The former controlled four of the major islands and the latter ruled seven — in addition to which he possessed a number of ships and a troop of British mercenaries. Tamuri, clearly the underdog, appealed to the visiting Russians for guns and ammunition and for assistance against his rival. "Should that savage Tomiomio seize my lands," he pleaded, "he will assuredly put me and my entire family to death in a horrible manner." In return for the requested aid, Tamuri offered "to come with his islands under Russian domination." A seductive offer, indeed.

The archipelago was a veritable larder, with a variety and an abundance of every sort of produce: pigs, bananas, coconut, yams, sweet potatoes, watermelons, and so on. Also, there was a plentiful supply of sandalwood, a yellowish, fragrant wood that was greatly in demand by cabinetmakers. "These islands, which do not belong to any European power," one of the ship's officers argued, "must belong to Russia. In addition, being half-way between Asia and America, they are of strategic importance."

But after much discussion, Kruzenshtern declined Tamuri's offer. He could not in good faith commit to a military intervention without Rezanov's personal approval, and alas, the commander-in-chief had departed the islands two days earlier for Kamchatka. Kruzenshtern, therefore, ordered the *Nadezda*'s sails hoisted and the ship left Hawaii to develop on its own as an independent monarchy. (The archipelago remained such until 1897 when the United States raised its flag over the capital.)

What, it may be asked, if Rezanov, the dedicated imperialist, had not sailed away as he did? Tamuri's proposal might well have been accepted, and today the Russian flag would be flying over what became the forty-ninth American state.

During their sojourn in the Sandwich Islands (so named by Cook when he first arrived in Hawaii), the Russians not only came fully to appreciate the potential agricultural and strategic value of the place, but they also learned to understand the Natives who "differ in many respects from American savages. Energetic and good laborers, they are docile, obedient and willing to work on any European vessel." From the journal of Lieutenant Berkh, an officer from the *Nadezda*: "The local women, who so enchanted [a crew of one visiting American vessel] that, when it was time to put to sea again, less than half the original crew of eighteen were available." Hawaii offered docile men and seductive women, Berkh goes on to note. But he condemns the laws of the land, writing,

> In one of the families was a boy everyone liked. The boy's father argued with the mother and decided to divorce her. There was then the contention as to who would keep the boy. The father absolutely maintained that he remain with him, and the mother wanted to take him away with her. In the end the father grabbed the boy by the neck and by the leg and broke his back over his knee. The unfortunate child died in consequence. Hearing of this barbarous deed, [a European visitor] complained to the king and sought punishment for the murderer. The king asked the European whose son the boy was. Hearing that he belonged to his murderer, the king said, "As the father harmed nobody else, on killing his own son, he was not liable to punishment."

Aspects of the Native religion were also cause for indignant comment by Yuri Lisiansky, the captain of the *Neva*. The Russian prefaces his remarks by observing that the "natives of the Sandwich Islands recognize the existence of good and evil. They believe that after death they will have a better life." He then he goes on to describe the practice of human sacrifice:

These islanders bring disturbers of the peace and prisoners to their idols as sacrifices. This barbarous offering of sacrifices takes the following form: if the victim is of high birth, between six and twenty of his confederates are killed with him, depending on rank. A special altar is prepared for the occasion in the large temple and is covered with coconut, plantains and tubers. The corpses are scorched, then placed on the foodstuffs, the principle victim in the center and his comrades and assistants on both sides of him, feet toward the chief god of war, a little distance apart from each other. Swine and dogs are then placed in the gaps. So they remain until such time as the flesh is rotted. Then the heads are put on the temple palisade.

Such were the impressions of a couple of visiting Russians. Bidding farewell to a thoroughly unhappy Tamuri, the *Nadezda* sailed away.

Eventually, Kamehameha overcame all political opposition, and Tamuri, escaping the anticipated "death in a horrible manner," was forced to accept his new status as a vassal. Kamehameha had himself crowned king of Hawaii, the first of a five-generation dynasty. His name meant "The One Set Apart." And set apart he seemed truly to be. He is considered to have been a judicious and inspired ruler, and an astute businessman who brought prosperity to his people.

As noted, Hawaii at the time had not yet fallen under foreign domination and the archipelago continued as an independent monarchy. The maintenance of the kingdom's independence from external control was the most notable of Kamehameha's achievements. This being said, it was universally recognized that the islands enjoyed a special relationship with Britain. Kamehameha was an unabashed anglophile, and he was perfectly happy to show a degree of subservience to King George III. In a letter to the king, he spoke of himself as being "subject to" the British monarch, to which London responded with words of cordiality, but made no reciprocal comment. Visiting English traders and naval officers, however, understood fully that they held a favoured position in Hawaii.

In addition to the influential presence of English traders on the islands, there were growing numbers of Americans arriving — scores of missionaries from New England and the middle states in particular came to take up the work of conversion. A fertile soil it was for their work — Hawaiians had long been gravitating away from their own religion. In addition to traders and missionaries, increasing numbers of whalers established bases of operations on the islands. By the middle of the nineteenth century, pervasive British and American influences dominated the islands so much that when it came time to design a distinctive Hawaiian flag, the Union Jack and the Stars and Stripes were featured in the design.

But the enterprising natives welcomed everyone, and cheerfully traded with anyone who was interested. Kamehameha was particularly intrigued by Russians. He wrote to Baranov "that he understood from persons trading to that coast how much the Russian establishment had sometimes suffered in winter from the scarcity of provisions; that he would therefore gladly send a ship every year with swine, salt, *batatas* [yams] and other articles of food if they would in exchange let him have sea otter skins at a fair price." (One might legitimately ask why on earth King Kamehameha, virtually naked in a hot climate, might wish to have quantities of otter pelts.)

In reply to the invitation, Baranov dispatched a small vessel to Hawaii with a cargo of furs; it returned to Sitka awash with foodstuffs. The exchange was so successful that in the ensuing months, more Russian vessels arrived at the islands. By 1808, it seemed that Baranov was toying with the idea of establishing a permanent colony on the islands. One Scotsman observed that "it would appear that the Russians had determined to form a settlement upon these islands; at least, preparations were made for the purpose." But there is nothing on record declaring such intention. The reality was that Baranov at the time was focused on the development of Russian California; that's where his energies were directed.

A decade passed, and with Fort Ross firmly established and the needs of Alaskan food supply as critical as ever, Baranov once more turned to Hawaii. He dispatched the *Bering* to the archipelago to survey possibilities and to take on a cargo of foodstuffs. As the ship approached Kauai, a severe gale developed causing it to run aground and break up. The island was in Tamuri's territory, and the delighted king lost no time in declaring that the wreckage and cargo was legally his, in accordance with long-standing laws of the area. When word of this action reached Baranov, he was beside himself with rage.

To secure justice from the Hawaiians, Baranov commissioned the *Bering*'s ship doctor, Captain Georg Anton Schaeffer as his envoy. The physician was charged with securing payment for the lost cargo and salvaging whatever he could from the wreckage. If force was required, he was to await the arrival of naval reinforcements — another Russian round-the-world sailing enterprise was under way, expected to reach Hawaii shortly. By launching this mission under Schaeffer, an irrepressible surgeon, Baranov initiated one of the most bizarre imperialistic ventures of the nineteenth century — it had the makings of a Gilbert and Sullivan opus.

Schaeffer, in the words of one historian, was "a fast-working interloper," a man as devious as he was talented, an adventurer with chutzpah. He signed on with the Russian-American Company as a surgeon on board the *Suvorov*, a company vessel that took him to Alaska. There he brought himself to Baranov's attention and was appointed to the *Bering*. After the shipwreck disaster, Schaeffer made his way back to Sitka, only to be returned to Hawaii to seek restitution.

Kamehameha greeted Schaeffer cordially, but all too soon that warmth dissipated. The sovereign's English advisors and many of the American residents, fearing Russian encroachment, warned the king of the dangerous designs of the newly arrived foreigners. Undaunted, Schaeffer went quietly about his business, and through persistent personal assurances was able eventually to solidify his standing in court. The king's principal wife, Queen Kaahumanu fell ill with a high fever and the doctor volunteered to attend her. He did so, the fever abated, and the king was delighted. So pleased was the monarch that he asked the good doctor see what he could do with the dropsy from which he suffered. Schaeffer obliged and although he did not entirely cure the king's condition, the patient did feel himself much improved. The grateful Kamehameha elevated Schaeffer to physician-to-the-crown and by way of reward, he constructed for him a spacious residence. In addition, the ruler allocated lands for the Russian-American Company and granted a permit to establish a factory in Oahu. The queen also rewarded Schaeffer with a gift of forty goats, ten sheep, and rights to miles of shoreline fishing grounds.

Within three months of his arrival, Schaeffer was well ensconced both in material comfort and in favour of the court. All the while, he projected himself as being nothing more than a physician and a botanist — with no agenda other than scientific research.

In May 1816, two Russian vessels, the *Otkrgytie* and the *Il'mena*, arrived in Hawaii, both ships sent by Baranov with orders to render all possible assistance to his envoy in his mission. The time was ripe, Schaeffer decided, to confront Tamuri — redress for the *Bering* fiasco.

Tamuri greeted Schaeffer with enthusiasm and informed him that, in the spirit of goodwill, he had already written Baranov agreeing to return the expropriated cargo and the looted remains of the ship. Russia, he assured the physician, was his best ally. Tamuri then went on again to complain of Kamehameha's belligerent intentions, and he repeated his long-standing offer of pledging allegiance to the Russian tsar. If the Russians would assist with the overthrow of his archrival, he was prepared to swear allegiance to the emperor.

Schaeffer was thrilled with the apparently simple elements of the *Bering* issue — it was a great opportunity for the Russian-American Company ... and for himself. Not only was Tamuri offering a momentous alliance, but he also agreed to grant the Russian-American Company exclusive trading rights in the islands, particularly in the greatly valued sandalwood. He furthermore agreed to permit the company to establish factories at will and he volunteered to supply labour for the construction of buildings and plantations. This was a tantalizingly seductive package, and Schaeffer entertained visions of himself as viceroy of Russia's new Pacific dominion.

The overzealous physician agreed to the proposal, promising Tamuri the full protection of the Russian Empire. An armed vessel, he assured the king, would be put at the king's disposition, as soon as the first cargo of sandalwood was ready for export. Tamuri put his X to a treaty of allegiance:

> His Majesty, Kaumualii [Tamuri], the king of the Sandwich
> Islands in the North Pacific Ocean, Kauai and Niihau and
> the hereditary prince of the islands of Oahu, Lanai and
> Maui, asks His Majesty, Sovereign Emperor Alexander
> Pavlovich, Autocrat of All the Russias, etc., etc., etc., to
> accept under his protection the above-mentioned islands.
> He [Tamuri], for himself and for his successors, wishes
> to profess loyalty to the Russian scepter. As a sign of his
> faithfulness and devotion he [Tamuri] accepts the Russian
> flag from the ship *Otkrytie*, which belongs to the Russian-
> American Company.[1]

The document was countersigned by Schaeffer, "Russian Imperial
Collegiate Assessor, Commissioner of the Russian American Company,
Doctor of Medicine and Surgery." To mark the occasion, Schaeffer
bestowed upon the delighted king a dazzling silver medal, "to be worn
on all occasions of visit by foreign and Russian ships and at all assem-
blies." As a further visible acknowledgement of the pact, the Russian
Imperial Collegiate Assessor awarded the king a commission in the
Russian Imperial Navy and presented him with what passed as a complete full-dress officer's uniform.

Within a fortnight, a supplementary agreement was had. Tamuri
now put an army of five hundred warriors under Schaeffer's command
to enable him to reconquer the territories held by his rival. The king
furthermore agreed to assist in building Russian forts on the islands
and to "refuse to trade with the citizens of the United States." Schaeffer
in return agreed to supply ships, arms, and ammunition for the pro-
spective confrontation, and also to supply the king with timber and
fish from Alaska. He further promised "to introduce a better economy,
which will make the natives educated and prosperous." The physician
signed a document to this effect and the king placed his mark upon it.
The paper was dispatched to St. Petersburg on a Russian trading vessel
heading for Kamchatka. In the accompanying report, Schaeffer noted
that "the king asked for the Russian flag which he hoisted over his
house." He concluded his report by bluntly stating that with minimal

military support, he could easily bring the Hawaiian Islands into the Russian Empire.

Schaeffer had been progressing brilliantly well in the forging of his colonial initiatives. All of this was being done, however, without the sanction or approbation of St. Petersburg. He seemed not in the least concerned that unauthorized alliances were being made and debts incurred, nor was he worried that the tsar had accepted Hawaii as a protectorate of Britain. That country's sole interest in the islands, Schaeffer reasoned, was "to the maintenance of peaceful commercial relations."

Schaeffer pressed on, deciding to construct a proper fortification on Kauai. It was built some three acres in size, complete with magazines and barracks. When finished, it was a sight to behold, with its tall, thick walls of lava blocks making the fortress virtually impregnable. He named it Fort Elizabeth, in honour of the empress, and from the uppermost height, the Russian flag was raised. Buoyed by this achievement, he ordered three more fortresses, albeit more modestly designed than Fort Elizabeth. When Tamuri expressed reservations on the actual need for the fortifications — after all, the battles against Kamehameha would be fought in Oahu, not on Kauai — Schaeffer assured him that this was the invariable tactical practice of European rulers before commencing any military expedition.

In early October, 1816, Schaeffer toured his territories and raised the Russian flag in a number of strategic spots. Tamuri requested, he writes in his diary, that Russian names be given not only to island's prominent geographic features, but also to the local chiefs. Thus, the Hanalei Valley became "Schaefferthal," Chief Taera became "Vorontsov," a deputy, Obana Tupigea, became "Platov," and so on. The two additional fortifications he ordered built were named Fort Alexander and Fort Barclay (after General Barclay de Tolly of Napoleonic War's fame).

In early December, the long-awaited *Rurik*, under Lieutenant Otto von Kotzebue, arrived in Honolulu — it had been expected six months earlier. Delighted as Schaeffer was with the shipload of supplies, he was equally pleased with the appearance of Kotzebue, as the officer's moral support was much needed. By then, there had been a acute falling out with Baranov, and the governor was recalling Schaeffer — Baranov had

had enough of Schaeffer's adventurism. Baranov was also demanding the return of the shipwrecked capital he had been seeking at the mission's start.

Kotzebue, however, was in no mood to offer any form of succour to the ambitious physician. En route to Kauai, he had stopped over in Hawaii, where he learned from an angry Kamehameha of the "devious machinations and villainy of that German, who came as a botanist and turned militarist." The king was enraged that after he had treated Schaeffer with consideration and trust, "he repaid my kindness with ingratitude which I bore patiently." And then, continued the king, having settled on Oahu, Schaeffer "proved himself to be my most inveterate enemy … exciting against me King Tamuri, who had submitted to my powers years ago." He added that "Schaeffer is there at this very moment and threatens my islands."

Kotzebue, ever the diplomat, calmed the ruler. He assured Kamehameha "that the bad conduct of Russians here must not be ascribed to the will of our emperor." He promised that as soon as the tsar would be apprised of the unfortunate situation, Schaeffer would be punished. The distraught king was placated, and before long the two men were communicating amicably as old friends. "The king seemed very much pleased on my assuring him that the emperor never intended to conquer his islands," he noted.

Kotzebue spent a few days with Kamehameha as an official guest, and his journal provides us with colourful vignettes of life in the Hawaiian royal court. One evening, for example, the king took the captain to visit his son and since the young man was considered sacred, "nobody is allowed to see him by day. If any person is so unfortunate, he must expiate his transgression by death." Entering the home of Liholiho (translation: "Dog of All Dogs") he found

> a tall, corpulent and naked figure, stretched out on his stomach and just indolently raised his head to look at his guests. Near him sat several naked soldiers armed with muskets who guarded the monster. A handsome young native with a tuft of red feathers drove away the flies from him…. The Dog of All Dogs at last rose very lazily and gaped upon us with a stupid vacant

countenance. My embroidered uniform seemed to meet his approbation for he held a long conversation about it with a couple of naked chamberlains.... I guess his age to be twenty-two years and am of the opinion that his enormous corpulency is occasioned by his constant lying on the ground.[2]

On the final evening in Honolulu, the king and several of the court were invited on board the *Rurik* — this was reciprocation of the host's hospitality. Regrets were received from one chieftain whose wife was too inebriated to be left on her own. Another of the distinguished guests arrived sporting a tall silk top hat, which he declined to shed throughout the evening. Dinner progressed well until a commotion arose on the starboard side of the ship. The king sprung to his feet and scurried to the guardrails to see what was happening. It turned out that two naked women were swimming in the waters at the base of the gangway and the sailors were doing their best to encourage them to come aboard. One of the women was Kaahumanu, queen of Hawaii, and the other was a lady in waiting. The king exchanged pleasantries with them and the two, having given a friendly wave, turned about and headed back to the shore. Kamehameha seemed amused with it all. He shrugged and exclaimed, "The curiosity of women!"

Schaeffer's originally reasonable mandate had been taken to alarming extremes. As the Hawaiian events unfolded, neither Sitka nor St. Petersburg offered encouragement. In fact, Russian officialdom repudiated him. Especially irritating for the Russians was his having consorted with Tamuri, thus infuriating King Kamehameha, the archipelago's supreme ruler. Schaeffer now found himself a *persona non grata* in that court. The envoy's machinations had effectively thrown the island chain into turmoil.

For Kotzebue, he would not even consider supporting Schaeffer. He had assured Kamehameha that Schaeffer would be harshly dealt with by the tsar for treacherous manoeuvrings. Most importantly, he assured the king that the integrity of the island chain as an indigenous monarchy had to be maintained, under his rule. "The Sandwich Islands," he subsequently wrote, "will remain what they are — the free port and staple of all navigators of the seas. But should any foreign power conceive the foolish idea of taking possession of them the jealous vigilance of the Americans, who possess the almost exclusive commerce of these seas, and the secure protection of England, would not be wanting to frustrate the undertaking." Kotzebue reviewed the lamentable situation with Schaeffer and then sailed away, giving no support or encouragement.

In the weeks that followed, the storm clouds broke. On returning home to Kauai, Schaeffer was chagrined to find that the customary Russian flag was not raised in his honour and that the seven-gun salute was not fired. More upsetting still was the evidence that Tamuri had blatantly stolen from the company's warehouse, including the stock of sandalwood.

On May 8, 1816 Schaeffer set off to demand of the king that the purloined sandalwood be immediately loaded onto the Russian ships. He encountered the monarch on the seashore in company with a number of his ministers and a sizable group of warriors. "I made my request to the king, who agreed," Schaeffer writes, "and when I walked away about one hundred feet, one Indian and six American sailors seized me and sent me to the [*Kod'iak*] in a badly leaking canoe, with orders not to return to shore. I could hardly keep the leakage down long enough to reach the ship."

After nine long weeks, the anchored *Kod'iak* quit Tamuri's territories to return to an unknown sanctuary in Honolulu. Broken and disappointed as he was, the stubborn Schaeffer continued in trying to carry out his vision of incorporating the island chain into the tsar's empire. He vowed to return.

Upon entering Honolulu, the centre of Kamehameha's domain, Schaeffer ordered the Russian flag to be hoisted upside down — a signal of distress, all in hope of a sympathetic reception. The king, however, was distinctly unamused at the appearance of the Russian vessel; permission to come ashore was refused. Schaeffer, captive on his own vessel, was furious about the ignoble treatment and lack of respect shown, first by Tamuri and now by Kamehameha.

He complained bitterly to Baranov, concluding his report with bombast:

Send me as soon as possible a few hundred Russian Aleuts, two or three ships, Captains Podushkin and Young, a few twelve and eighteen pounders, and as much fish as possible to feed the Aleuts. When you send me to St. Petersburg, I can assure you that all the Sandwich Islands will be Russian ... do not worry. When we get help, the Russians will be on top again and everything will be settled.[3]

To his men, Schaeffer addressed a declaration of intention. No way was he going to depart from the islands in defeat and with a whimper.

I intend to show these Indian bandits what Russian honor is and that it cannot be treated lightly. The Russian flag is not a toy and the name of our great sovereign is not to be scorned. I will show these barbarians that a Russian staff officer can put down a rebellion.... Be assured that I shall always be with you and leading you.[4]

Brave words indeed — ones that came to naught. The Hawaiians continued steadfastly in refusing Schaeffer permission to come ashore, and he continued to languish on board the dilapidated ship. A message to Baranov was penned in a temperate mode: "There is nothing left for me to do.... [The Americans] plan to put the Sandwich Islands under the American flag because everyone knows that there is no true British protectorate over Tomari.... I am reduced to nothing more than skin and bones since I assumed the service of the Company."

The standoff became an imbroglio, which was not resolved until the arrival of the American brig *Panther*. Its captain, Isaiah Lewis, had once been medically attended by Schaeffer, for which he was grateful. He now extended the desperate physician an invitation to transfer to his ship — it was due to sail to Canton on the following day. The offer was accepted.

The troop of sixty-five crew members who Schaeffer left behind "in charge of the settlement and the company's property" quit the archipelago shortly thereafter. So ended Russian presence in Hawaii.

We next hear of Schaeffer from Latvia. He writes in his notes "The Sandwich Islands are the keys to China, Japan, the Philippines, India and the Northwest coast of North America. By holding Honolulu, Russia can, with the posts she already holds at Petropavlovsk, Sitka and Fort Ross, control the entire Pacific." All of Schaeffer's exhortations fell to deaf ears; Nicholas I wished no part in his schemes. The seizure of the far-off islands would be hazardous in the extreme because of the difficulty of effectively supplying the place, and such a move would pose awkward diplomatic complications with the British.

The Schaeffer saga concludes at this point with the excitable doctor simply disappearing from the scene. Nothing is heard of him until 1832, when he emerges in Brazil as an advisor to Emperor Dom Pedro I, with a new name: Count von Frankenthal. So goes the story of the "Russian Imperial Collegiate Assessor, Commissioner of the Russian American Company, Doctor of Medicine and Surgery," who without the approval of the tsar strove mulishly to bring Hawaii into the Russian orbit.

CHAPTER 9

DIPLOMATIC TUSSLES

John Quincy Adams arrived in St. Petersburg in 1809, the first U.S. minister to visit imperial Russia. As we have seen, Adams knew the country from boyhood days, but judging by his youthful reports, he wasn't much taken by it. Once established in his new position, however, it appears that he took to the country. President Madison offered to release Adams midway through his six-year tenure, but he refused to leave. A year later, the president offered him an appointment to the U.S. Supreme Court. Adams again would not leave St. Petersburg.

Adams's passage from Massachusetts to the Russian capital was not without incident. His party sailed for Russia on board the *Horace*, a merchant trading ship out of Boston. At Kristiansand, Norway, the vessel was stopped by a Danish privateer and ordered into port for inspection. Adams was dismayed to find that his was not the only American vessel being held — thirty-eight other ships had also been summarily ordered into port to awaited "investigation."

The envoy correctly deduced that the English were behind the action, and without further ado, he went directly to the British flag officer. Admiral Sir Albemarie Bertie received the envoy disdainfully — he didn't even offer Adams a chair. The enraged American protested against the intolerable breach of convention governing diplomatic status. Unless the admiral offered an apology, and guaranteed an immediate release of the *Horace*, he would most certainly hear from higher authority and would come to rue his precipitous action. Bertie heard out Adams, and after some bluster of his own, he acquiesced and ordered the release of the envoy's vessel. The *Horace* went on to sail to St. Petersburg without further incident.

At the time of Adams's appointment, Andrey Dashkov continued as Russia's chargé d'affaires. Although the country's capital had already been moved from Philadelphia to Washington, D.C., Dashkov preferred to remain at his post in the Pennsylvania city. The prospect of relocating to the nascent capital, in all its primitive provincialism, was simply too much. Philadelphia, on the other hand, was a quiet, ordered city with institutions of higher learning and intellectual activity. Professional demands were minimal, and the social life stimulating.

John Singleton Copley. Painting. Library of Congress.

John Quincy Adams.

One relatively minor incident, however, did cause Dashkov no small amount of grief. In 1810, on the coronation anniversary of Alexander I, the envoy decided to throw a grand party, inviting to it the cream of Philadelphia society. For the occasion, he festooned his home with elaborate decorations and illuminations, the centrepiece of which was a huge representation of the imperial crown. A small crowd of curious spectators gathered outside the residence to observe the comings and goings. It grew in size, and before long became agitated by the prominent display of a crown.

An inebriated sailor upholstered his revolver and fired a couple of shots through the windows of the room in which Dashkov's distinguished guests had assembled. Mayhem briefly broke out inside, but soon all was under control. The satisfied mob made its way triumphantly down the streets, leaving behind a shaken dinner party. (It's more than likely the incident was not so much a demonstration of anti-monarchical sentiment as a reflection of the lawlessness that abounded in many American cities at the time.) But the volatile Dashkov was beside himself in anger, and briefly contemplated logging a formal protest with the police. He didn't, and the incident was soon forgotten.

For both the United States and Russia, 1812 was a momentous year. In June, President Madison, after a prolonged period of tension with Britain, declared war on that country and invaded Canada. In October, Napoleon marched an army of six hundred thousand into Russia. Washington had been set afire at the hands of the British. Moscow had been burned by the French. The war in America raged on until the signing of the Treaty of Ghent in 1814. Russia's war with France ended with Tsar Alexander's entry into Paris that same year. Two concurrent wars were happening a world apart.

These wars doubtlessly had an impact on Russian-American relations. What John Quincy Adams faced in St. Petersburg was something of a conundrum: how to maintain the friendship of Russia, now allied with Britain, while his own country was at war with the Brits. Hope as he might for Napoleon's defeat, it was clear that such a victory would free up British forces, which would then be directed against his own country.

Some of Adams's anxiety was temporarily relieved because of an initiative taken by the tsar. Communication between St. Petersburg and Washington was painfully slow. On the day that Napoleon entered Moscow, word reached Alexander of the outbreak of hostilities between the United States and Britain — the information took three months in coming. Despite the extreme pressures he himself was facing, Alexander called in Adams and offered to mediate the America's conflict with Britain.

The tsar's motives in making the offer were probably more self-serving than humanitarian. If the war in North America could be successfully brought to a close, it would free up British forces for the ongoing struggle against archenemy Napoleon. Furthermore, in the event that Britain prevailed in the United States, American commerce would be irreparably damaged and British dominance over the Caribbean would likely be re-established. None of this, he judged, was in his country's interest. A strong, independent United States was essential to the maintenance of a balance of power — a counterbalance to Britain's growing might.

President Madison readily accepted Alexander's offer. The war was beginning to drain the treasury; the economic impact of the struggle was strongly felt. Britain on the other hand, recognizing the mutuality of Russia and America, was decidedly cool to the tsar's initiative. Not wishing to offend their sole European ally, the British simply gave no immediate response to the invitation.

In Washington, Madison had been encouraged by St. Petersburg and was led to believe that the British would eventually come to the table. He assembled a team of negotiators and sent it on its way to St. Petersburg. But by the time the group arrived in the capital, the British had declined the offer of mediation. Disappointed as Alexander was, he received the American delegation with warmth. Each individual was presented with a small jewelled gift and an offer was made to assume the group's expenses as it continued to linger on in the country. When, however, the foreign office proposed that a portrait of the empress be sent to America's first lady, the tsar balked. "Entertain our guests by all means," he reportedly said, "but owing to our relations with England it is perhaps better not to present the Empress's portrait."

In 1814, despite a renewed offer by Russia to mediate — or possibly because of it — the British and Americans did come to the table, but on their own. Both sides had had enough of the ongoing struggle in North America, and both were reeling not only from the expense of the war but also from the costs of arrested commerce. On Christmas Eve, the Treaty of Ghent was finalized and lasting peace was achieved over North American boundaries between the United States and Britain.

The new year ushered in a significantly changed world. Napoleon had been vanquished and was safely tucked away in exile — at least for the moment. Russia had not only survived a baptism by fire, but had emerged from the fray as the major player on the European scene. When Alexander paraded in Paris down the Champs Élysées at the head of the victorious allied armies, he was hailed as a saviour. Spectators marvelled at the waves of Cossacks and colourful troops passing by; Europe stood in awe of the autocrat's unlimited power.

Across the Atlantic, Americans had passed through a critical point in their history. Were it not for Britain's struggle with Napoleon, the United States would certainly have had it far worse in its invasion of Canada. The United States, once more unencumbered, resumed its course on the path of its spectacular development.

As with any friendship, familial or political, the decades of harmony and mutual support between the United States and Russia did not always hold tight. Misunderstandings and irritations inevitably occurred, but the friendship held firm through the years. The most notable of such blips was the lamentable Kozlov affair.

In 1811, Andrei Dashkov had been promoted from chargé d'affaires to a full minister in Washington. To replace him as consul in Philadelphia, St. Petersburg appointed Nikolai Kozlov, a plodding bureaucrat with no great ambition, unassuming and something of a bon vivant. Under normal circumstances, the likes of Kozlov would not enter the pages of history, but in this instance he rates mention, simply because of a clumsy indiscretion he committed. Within Kozlov's household was a lovely young maid, pink-cheeked and with large doe-like eyes. In no way was her attractive, well-rounded figure that of a twelve-year-old, which in fact she happened to be. In her childish, but perhaps not so innocent way, she beguiled the diplomat who increasingly had fallen under her spell. One evening, no longer able to contain himself, Kozlov stole into her bedroom and forced himself upon her. A struggle ensued that served only to increase the intruder's ardour. As soon as the girl had freed herself, she ran to the police station to report the incident and charged the Russian consul with rape. An arrest warrant was issued. The police went to Kozlov's residence and forcibly hauled him off to the local jail, where he had to spend an uncomfortable night.

The following day, an infuriated Dashkov, who at the time was still living in Philadelphia, appeared at the precinct station, and in no uncertain terms demanded the consul's immediate release. Kozlov had diplomatic immunity, he reminded the sergeant on duty — local police held no jurisdiction over foreign diplomats. The officer, however, would have none of that. Dashkov then offered to pay a bail until such time that higher authorities would resolve the matter. The suggestion was summarily rejected — this was not a bailable offence. Further argument ensued but the stalwart officer, now quite angry with the indignant foreigner before him, held his ground. "He's raped a girl," he is alleged to have replied, "and he stays in jail until a judge lets him out. And if you keep pestering me, you'll find yourself sitting in there beside him."

The following day, an unsuspecting U.S. attorney general had the quiet of his afternoon rudely broken by the appearance of an irate Russian ambassador. Dashkov denied the ludicrous charge that had been laid against the consul and demanded Kozlov's immediate release. The attorney general, although sympathetic and understanding, explained that federal courts had no jurisdiction over crimes such as rape and that the matter had to remain with the State of Pennsylvania, by whom the arrest was made. He did suggest that Dashkov might apply for a writ of habeas corpus. This the ambassador did and the unfortunate Kozlov was forthwith brought before a judge. The justice heard the case and remanded it to the next session of court, releasing the consul in the interim.

Dashkov at this point travelled to Washington to seek out President Madison's personal intervention. He was courteously received and a sympathetic president promised to look into the matter. When in time a formal reply was delivered, Dashkov found nothing encouraging in it. According to American law, Madison wrote, federal courts could over-rule state courts only on matters of constitutional guarantees. Since this was a criminal charge, it fell entirely under the jurisdiction of the Commonwealth of Pennsylvania. Regrettably, there was nothing he could do, although he did assure the Russian that "all the rights belonging to his character as Consul General" would be guaranteed.

Five month later, the Pennsylvania court held its hearing and it conceded that Kozlov did in fact enjoy diplomatic immunity. Despite the prosecutor's apparently tight case, no judgment was passed on the charge of rape and insofar as the state was concerned, the matter was closed. But in Dashkov's mind this was not to be. He was unprepared to let matters die so easily — he now demanded that the court fully exonerate Kozlov. And furthermore, Dashkov insisted that an apology be had from the U.S. government for the breach of international law in the mistreatment of his diplomatic colleague. When neither was forthcoming, Dashkov announced that he was ceasing further communication with the U.S. government.

The State Department retaliated. It charged the Russian consul in Boston, Alexei Evstafiev, with illegally protecting British property during the recently concluded war — which, it appears, he did (and were it not for the Kozlov affair, probably would have gone unnoticed). When news of the fracas eventually reached St. Petersburg, the Russian foreign office reacted by declaring the United States consul general in St. Petersburg, Levett Harris, a *persona non grata*, thus depriving him of all social status.

The fires were further stoked by an intemperate letter Dashkov sent to the State Department, in which he accused the president of backing impertinent officials. For weeks thereafter, diplomatic notes continued to shunt back and forth between the two capitals, their contents growing in passion and fury. In some more hysterical corners of the two capitals, there was even talk of war.

An entire year had passed since Kozlov entered the bedroom of the beguiling chambermaid, and now matters were totally snarled between the two nations with few people recalling the root cause of it all. At this

point, Alexander I stepped into the melee and demanded c
ministry that an immediate close be brought to the unfort
In Washington, President Madison did likewise. And so
came to be. Dashkov and Kozlov were both recalled, and charges against
Evstafiev were conveniently forgotten. The first serious contre temps
between Russia and the United States was laid to rest.

For nearly a decade following the Kozlov affair, a few other waves
rocked Russian-American relations. In the north Pacific, the Russian-
American Company continued to develop its fur empire, and the
hubristic Georg Anton Schaeffer was deep in his Hawaiian machinations. Meanwhile, Americans furthered their own frontiers in the Pacific,
developing numerous commercial ventures. Whichever way their paths
crossed, though, the relationship generally continued to be peaceful and
cooperative — at least until 1821.

In September of that year, Alexander surprised many by issuing an
edict that caused stinging upset in the United States. The ukase provided a fresh definition of the southern boundary of Russian-American
Company's jurisdiction. The tsar now set it at fifty-one degrees north
latitude, a distance considerably farther south to the fifty-five degrees
stipulated in the company's original charter of 1799. The ukase not only
extended Russian territorial waters to a hundred miles from shore, but it
forbid foreign vessels from entering Russia's north Pacific ports.

The responding American outcry, particularly from New Englanders,
was vociferous. Russian territorial claims had been unilaterally moved
some eight hundred miles south. Although the land in question was void
of settlers, Americans insisted on the fifty-five-degree delineation. The
tsar's ukase was an encroachment on potential American lands. Many in
the United States, in fact, felt that all of North America should fall under
U.S. jurisdiction — control of the continent was their manifest destiny.

There is little doubt that the ukase was issued at the urging of the
Russian-American Company, whose charter had just been renewed.
Significantly diminished stocks of sea otter were threatening the com-
pany's welfare, and American poachers were seen as the cause. Also,
U.S. vessels calling in Russian ports engaged in illegal trade with the
Natives. Not only was the company's monopoly being broken, but also

the supply of firearms and alcohol to the Natives was jeopardizing the peace of the land.

After the instantaneous and angry American reaction, the ill-considered ukase was withdrawn by St. Petersburg. Officials of the Russian-American Company and the foreign office had failed to fully appreciate the joint interest that the United States and Britain shared in the northern Pacific. Might they join forces against Russia? Such a menacing union had to be avoided at all costs — hence the speedy withdrawal of the offending decree.

Events unfolding in South America at the time proved to be even more disturbing for Washington and St. Petersburg than the fight over the northern Pacific. In 1820, King Ferdinand VII of Spain was overthrown in a coup and made a virtual prisoner of revolutionaries. In the fallout, the country's control of its South American colonies disintegrated, giving rise to a chain of independence movements. In quick time, nascent sovereign states came to be formed, all headed by unstable and unpredictable governments. The Spanish king's arrest was short-lived, as the monarchy was restored in 1823. Efforts quickly got under way not only to re-establish domestic order, but also to bring to heel rebellious South American colonies.

The reaction of United States and Russia to these events stood in wide contrast, with both countries holding strong views on the matter. Once again, the friendship between the two nations was in jeopardy.

As Spain struggled to right itself and consolidate the re-established monarchy, the sympathetic Alexander supported its efforts. Years earlier, with Napoleon's downfall, the Congress of Vienna agreed to accept Alexander's proposed Holy Alliance. Framed in idealism and couched in spiritual language, this was really an innocuous guideline for sovereigns concerning the manner in which their subjects should be treated — and equally how they should treat one another. The basis of it all was the maintenance of monarchical legitimacy. "Consistent with the words of the Holy Scripture," read the treaty, "... the monarchs will remain united by the bonds of a true and indissoluble fraternity." Britain's foreign seceratary Lord Castlereagh refused to sign, scornfully calling it "a piece of sublime mysticism and nonsense." Initially, Prince Metternich, chancellor of Austria, called it a "loud-sounding nothing." Later, however, he involved himself in editing the wording, thus propelling it into a deeper nothing. But for Alexander, it was anything but nonsense or nothing. He took its provisions seriously.

The tsar viewed revolutionary South American states not only as a threat to the complete restoration and integrity of the Spanish throne, but more importantly, to the monarchical system. A man of order, he abhorred the sort of chaos and unpredictability that had unfolded in that part of the world, and he made no bones about it.

The United States, on the other hand, the original revolutionary power and the bastion of democracy, was in solid sympathy with the emerging South American states. It suited her to have in the backyard independent nations founded on democracy and constitutionality, rather than a single monarchical power. Additionally, concern was had that Britain might intervene in South America and capitalize on the unstable situation. At one time, there was even evidence that an Anglo-Spanish alliance was in the making, specifically to deal with the South American question. "I am now more than ever seriously apprehensive that great trouble will grow out of [the developing situation]," reported George W. Erving, James Monroe's special emissary in Europe, "for nobody 'loves us' — no, not even the Emperor of Russia, whom we have so incessantly flattered. And, an alliance with Great Britain for this, or any other purpose ... is most to be dreaded."

To resolve the volatile situation the president in his annual address to Congress took a bold initiative. He proposed a policy of non-colonization in the western hemisphere — European powers were to keep their hands off. "We owe it ... to declare [to all powers] that we should consider any attempt on their part to extend their system to any portion of the hemisphere as dangerous to our peace and safety," he declared.

The Americas would now be closed to foreign imperialistic expansion — that meant Britain, France, Spain, Portugal, and Russia. The emerging countries of South America would now become protectorates of the United States. Congress applauded the message, and on December 2,

1823, it approved what came to be called the Monroe Doctrine, a law that has served many presidents in maintaining hegemony over the Americas.

To what extent did the tsar's actions influence President Monroe's singular initiative? Historians continue to debate the point, but certainly Congress was conscious of Russian presence on the Pacific coast. There is no question that the Monroe Doctrine was precipitated by events in the Spanish colonies, but it was not framed as an anti-Russian instrument. Monroe was adamant that this be made clear to the tsar. Additionally, he insisted on a bilateral treaty by which all points of contention between the two powers would be normalized. So came to be the Convention of 1824, by which it was jointly agreed that the tsar's ukase would be formally abrogated, and that American ships would be free to enter Russian ports. The Russian boundary line was defined as 54° 40'. In return, the United States formally recognized Russia's rights in the Pacific, particularly in California. The treaty also prohibited Americans from trading in alcohol, firearms, or ammunition within Russian territories. On balance, the Americans probably gained more from it than did the Russians. Win or lose, St. Petersburg was relieved to be rid of the nagging Pacific issue, and also pleased to have preserved positive relations with the United States.

Watchdog Washington now sat at Latin America's doorstep, observing and noting the comings and goings of European activities in the southwestern hemisphere. A French fleet, for example, had taken up station at its island colony of Martinique, presumably in support of Spain. Puerto Rico and Cuba were being threatened with invasion from Mexico and Colombia. Haiti had just passed through a successful slave revolt and fears had arisen that a similar revolt might follow suit in America's own southern states.

An additional concern emanating from Haiti was Russia's apparent interest in that island. Washington learned that an enterprising Russian naval officer, Dimitri Zavalishin had advocated the establishment on the island of a Fort Ross–like base. He argued that such a settlement would provide Russia not only with a strategic stopover when en route to the Pacific, but also with a base of operations for trade within the Caribbean. It also offered a possible springboard for a future foray against Mexico.

Haiti had long fallen under French rule — its history was one of unchecked turbulence. In 1794, Toussaint Louverture followed the example of revolutionary France by successfully leading an uprising of mulattoes and blacks. By 1820, the white population had been ruthlessly decimated by successive black rulers. The French response all the while had been weak, and the island fell under the control of an ambitious mulatto leader, "General" Jean-Pierre Boyer who, despite being a dictator, eventually proved to be one of Haiti's more successful leaders.

At this point, another individual bearing the name General Boyer — Jacques, he was called — appeared on the scene. This Boyer was a genuine military leader who had served in the French army. Captured by Cossacks during the invasion of Russia, he remained in captivity until Napoleon's disastrous retreat from Moscow. Once released, he continued on in that capital, having switched allegiance to the tsar. Some years later, he joined the Russian-American Company.

With independence having been accorded Haiti by France in 1825, the tsar was determined to establish relations with the new republic. The "Russian" Boyer had by then convinced the foreign office that he not only knew Haiti from stem to stern, but he also claimed he was related to the original Boyer. In light of this, Alexander commissioned Jacques Boyer to travel to Haiti to explore possibilities for his country.

Boyer prepared to set off for the Caribbean to embrace his Haitian "cousin," and fulfill his mandate. Plans called for him to accompany Zavalishin, who at the time was proposing to leave for Haiti with a shipload of trading goods. "I will take a ship," the naval officer wrote, "and General Boyer will accompany me. I shall then lay the foundation for relations between that republic and Russia ... and while the proposals I shall be making are considered and the cargo is being sold, I shall busy myself with scientific explorations of the Antilles and will visit various island and continental ports, concurrently collecting information of articles of direct trade between Russia and the visited places."

The admiralty endorsed Zavalishin's ideas, and approval was given for the fitting out of a ship to carry out the project. (No doubt more than one seaman envisioned revelling under balmy skies in the shade of tropical palms during the dismally harsh Russian winter.)

Alas, nothing came of all this. It turned out that Zavalishin had more interests than just the Caribbean. As passionate as he was over the Haitian project, he was equally taken by the activities of the Northern Society. This underground organization had as its goal the overthrow of the government and the establishment of a constitutional monarchy. In the brief leadership vacuum that followed Alexander's death in 1825, the conspirators, including Zavalishin, sprung precipitously into action — this was the notorious Decembrist revolt. The short-lived coup was speedily suppressed and Zavalishin, together with hundreds of others, found himself lamenting his folly in Siberia. The proposed Haiti proposal died a quiet death, thus avoiding an almost certain conflict with the American watchdog.

At the time of Zavalishin's arrest, the ministry of foreign affairs was at work in newly independent Brazil developing its own schemes. The country had developed as Russia's second-largest trading partner in the Americas; the imperial embassy in Rio de Janeiro was comparable in size to the one in Washington.

The tsar's ambassador in that country was German-born Georg von Langsdorff, an ambitious, scholarly individual who at one time was connected with the Russian-American Company. Langsdorff proposed an elaborate plan for the exploration and development of Brazil's enormous interior, and he successfully persuaded Brazilian and Russian government authorities to support it.

Had the proposed undertaking come to fruition, Russian presence in that country would have magnified substantially — indubitably causing the Washington watchdog to bark hard, if not to bite. With Alexander's death, however, everything came to a halt. Nicholas I withdrew support for all long-distance imperialistic ventures. All of the Hawaiian, Haitian, and Brazilian forays terminated, the initiatives fading into history. The new tsar's interests focused unquestionably on the Dardenelles and the crumbling Ottoman Empire, Russia's long-standing *bête noire*.

So it was between the United States and Russia in the first quarter of the nineteenth century. The confrontations had been light trembles that failed to crack the foundation of Russian-American friendship — taken individually, the tussles proved inconsequential.

CHAPTER 10

THE AMBASSADORS

In the forty-five-year period following Tsar Alexander I's formal recognition of the United States in 1809, a succession of thirteen American ministers took up posts in St. Petersburg — the longest-serving one remaining in the job for ten years and the briefest for a mere twenty-six days. Two of these diplomats finished careers as president of the United States. Five ministers, however, were, as one wag put it, "neither very important in themselves nor left any worthwhile record of their experiences." The historian Norman Saul goes one step further by calling them "some of the worst appointments in the history of American relations."

The story is told of one of these lesser ministers, Charles S. Todd, a Kentuckian with no distinguished service record other than having once served in the army. At an imperial reception in the Winter Palace, he engaged loudly in conversation with a lady-in-waiting to the empress. In his strong southern drawl and incomprehensible French, he told her of his travels before arriving in St. Petersburg. The poor man so botched the word *an* ("year") that it came out sounding like *âne* ("ass"). "I was an ass in Paris, part of an ass in London, almost an ass in Germany and I am two asses here." To which the unfazed courtier replied casually, "And you will be an ass wherever you go."

The American ministers in St. Petersburg were indeed a mixed bag. In the interest of better appreciating the chemistry of the Russian-American relationship during this period, it would do well to briefly look at some of these ambassadors and their tenures.

We've already met in these pages John Quincy Adams, the United States's first minister in Russia, from 1809 to 1815. Adams was relieved by William Pinkney of Maryland who held the post for two years. A one-time senator and attorney general, Pinkney had also served as minister to Britain. He was en route to Russia when the Kozlov affair exploded, and having learned of it, he deliberately delayed his arrival until the dust had settled — he was not one for such absurdity. It was not long after assuming his St. Petersburg post, however, that he became even more nonsensically embroiled in a diplomatic incident.

A certain American, William Lewis, resided in St. Petersburg where he studied languages. One evening at an informal social occasion, he found himself in a heated discussion with John Harris, the U.S. consul. As the argument increased in fervour the onlookers were surprised to see the enraged Lewis tweaking the diplomat's nose and slapping his face.

An insult of such magnitude might normally have called for satisfaction by a duel. But Harris would have none of that. Instead he reported the matter to the police, filed a formal charge, and demanded his antagonist's arrest. Unlike the response of Philadelphia police in the Kozlov case, the St. Petersburg constabulary begged off, arguing that it was a matter between foreigners — the incident did not concern them. The matter was referred to the foreign ministry, and eventually the file found its way to the desk of Chancellor Nesselrode, who had already received a number of letters from the distraught Harris concerning the case. Like the police, Nesselrode refused to have anything to do with the complaint and he referred the matter to the newly arrived Pinkney. After all, it did involve two of his countrymen, one of whom was the minister's own consul.

Pinkney, who happened to have been present at the unfortunate argument, thought the whole thing a "ridiculous and disgusting business." Although he admired Harris — "the young and extremely intelligent and respected American" — he did not believe that a consul enjoyed diplomatic immunity, a position in direct contrast to the one taken earlier by Dashkov. So the minister refused to take any action, despite Nesselrode's assurance that the tsar wished the matter be concluded through Pinkney's office. The unresolved matter remained a problem for months to come, providing sensational grist for the St. Petersburg gossip mill — all to Pinkney's discomfort and embarrassment.

Lewis and Harris were both called home, and the feud continued to burn stateside. The resolutely aggrieved Harris petitioned the U.S. secretary of state. Legal battles were fought over alleged liable printed by Lewis in certain pamphlets, and a duel was fought on a New Jersey beach, where Harris was wounded. Nothing, however, was resolved. At last, three years after the offending tweak, a Solomonic court judgment was rendered, in which both principals claimed victory and the matter was concluded.

But poor Pinkney — he was so mortified and upset over the sensation created by the Harris-Lewis contre temps, that he requested a recall on the grounds of ill health. "I was not a little vexed to find that this mortifying affair was, after I had shaken it off, returning to me in a circle," he confided to Nesselrode at one point. Despite the dreadful commotion during his tenure, Pinkney was fond of Russia and liked its citizens. And they liked him, so much so that the empress agreed to be godmother to the minister's newborn child: "Doushka" she called her (meaning "little darling"). The disheartened diplomat departed St. Petersburg in early 1818 without even waiting for his replacement.

It was George W. Campbell who replaced Pinkney for a two-year stint. A former senator from Tennessee and one-time secretary of the treasury under President Monroe, his appointment took place at the time Russian-American diplomatic negotiations were ongoing regarding the Latin American issues discussed in the previous chapter. Since the tsar was almost constantly abroad for one reason or another, it took Campbell nearly half a year to present his credentials. In the months that followed, tragedy hit the Campbells — one after the other, their three daughters contracted typhus and died. The distraught and depressed diplomat soldiered on spiritlessly with his duties, but then requested a return home.

Henry Middleton was an urbane plantation owner from South Carolina and an internationalist who had once resided in Britain. A man of wealth, he regularly dipped into his own pocket to supplement the paltry diplomatic allowance assigned him. Upon Middleton's arrival at the capital with his family of seven and a retinue of servants, he moved into a lavish St. Petersburg home that belonged to a Russian noble. It did not take long for the Middletons to establish themselves as an engaging couple who were quickly swept into the capital's whirlwind social life.

Middleton spent ten years in St. Petersburg (1820–1830), which was a long appointment by any standard — so much so that many back home accused him of having become a Russophile and of "kissing aristocratic hems." The accusations were not groundless; the minister felt completely at home with the Russians, particularly with the nobility. (One pretentious quirk of Middleton's was that his calling card bore the ostentatious name, "Monsieur de Middleton.")

In 1826, he represented the United States at the magnificent coronation of Nicholas I in Moscow, the travel expenses of which he bore himself. However significant the event was, on this occasion he left his family behind, much to the unhappiness of one daughter. "Our most stingy … government," she huffed in a letter to a friend, "will not pay our expenses to go there and behave like decent people."

The Middletons favoured Russian society — the glitz of colourful receptions where bejewelled and bemedalled gathered frequently during long, dark winters. Middleton generally eschewed the capital's growing American colony — well-placed professionals and businessmen were the exception. This, of course, added fuel to the charges that the minister was a snob, interested only in toadying to the aristocracy.

It was during Middleton's ministry in St. Petersburg that a number of significant developments took place in the story of Russian-American relations, not the least of which was the Convention of 1824.

Through Middleton's efforts, the United States secured commercial advantages from the Ottoman Empire. The Greek War of Independence in 1827 culminated in the Battle of Navarino with the decisive destruction of the Turkish fleet by Britain, Russia, and France. During the peace negotiation that followed, Middleton successfully persuaded Russia to champion American interests, which the tsar's delegation did. Not only was a favourable commercial treaty wrested from the Turks, but the United States acquired the right of entry into the Black Sea, which until then had been closed to them.

Middleton's appointment as United States minister to Russia was the longest of any; his successor's was the shortest. John Randolph, an aging, sickly, quarrelsome eccentric, was posted by President Andrew Jackson. As one observer coyly put it, Jackson appointed Randolph "partly to pay a political debt and partly because he was advised not to."

For his travel to St. Petersburg, Randolph persuaded authorities to put at his disposal the frigate USS *Concord*. His entourage was anything but modest. Family, secretaries, and servants came on board bringing along vast quantities of baggage, including a chicken coop for the supply of fresh eggs. Ensconced in style, he proceeded to make a perfect nuisance of himself with the ship's crew and its captain, Matthew C. Perry. But that was his style, always arguing and deriding. "Randolph, called President Adams a traitor," his biographer observes, "Oliver Wendell Holmes a dangerous fool, Daniel Webster a vile slanderer, Edward Livingston unfit to touch without tongs, while to Henry Clay he addressed this classic apostrophe: 'So brilliant! So corrupt! Like a rotten mackerel in moonlight, he shines and stinks.'" Such was the American minister.

For whatever reason, Randolph laboured under the impression that the Russian court secretly laughed at American diplomats for attending formal functions dressed in black — head to toe, like undertakers. He therefore made his first appearance in court dressed in the gaudiest suit possible and carried a steel sword. The stunned gathering of people observing the entrance of the flamboyant American envoy suppressed giggles, straining hard not to laugh aloud. Randolph, oblivious to the commotion he was causing, advanced toward the tsar and greeted him loudly in English, "How are you, Emperor? How's Madam?" And when he finally spotted the empress, he plunged before her on his knees.

Nothing was ever satisfactory for Randolph — all was wrong in his life and needed to be fixed. He disliked everything about Russia. The country "is Egypt in all but fertility. The extremes of human misery and human splendor here meet." In poor health from the start, his mental state quickly came into question. St. Petersburg was convinced that the American minister quite simply was mad.

Within weeks of his arrival, Randolph fled his post — he sailed away on a departing Danish vessel. "During his short stay in St. Petersburg," one contemporary notes, "he was thought to be insane, which his speedy flight or hegira seemed to confirm."

James Buchanan, the fifteenth president of the United States, was minister to Russia from 1831 to 1833. Invited by President Jackson to succeed the cantankerous Randolph, Buchanan at first was reluctant to accept the post, pleading ignorance of the French language. He subsequently acquiesced and served two years in St. Petersburg.

The major bilateral issue during Buchanan's time centred on a commercial treaty the United States was anxious to secure: a supplement to the Convention of 1824. Discussions on the matter had been under way for a couple of years, but the Russians had been stonewalling the Americans for fear of alienating the British. The tenacious Buchanan persisted in the matter, underscoring that American ships carried nearly two-thirds of Russia's exports, and that the United States annually imported in excess of $1.5 million of goods from its trading partner. The tsar eventually relented.

Buchanan relates the amusing anecdote of how he came to learn of his victory while attending an imperial reception:

> The diplomatic corps, according to etiquette, were arranged in line to receive the Emperor and Empress. Mr. Bligh, the English Minister, occupied the station immediately below myself. You may judge my astonishment when the Emperor, accosting me in French, in a tone of voice that could be heard all around, said, "I signed the order yesterday that the Treaty should be executed according to your wishes," and immediately, turning to Mr. Bligh, asked him to be the interpreter of this information. Mr. Bligh is a most amiable man and his astonishment and embarrassment were so striking that I felt for him sincerely.[1]

Another of the more notable American ministers in Russia was George Dallas, a retired senator from Pennsylvania, who started his St. Petersburg tenure in 1837. Little time was lost in presenting his credentials, and soon thereafter the tsar tendered a dinner in honour of the newly arrived diplomat. The imperial couple took an instant liking to the American. The empress in particular found Dallas well read and engaging. The two plunged into a discussion on American novelists — the empress wished particularly to learn more of James Fenimore Cooper, her favourite author. Toward the dinner's conclusion, she lamented the rapid turnover of American ministers, and declared loudly enough be heard by the entire table, "I hope you will prove an exception to this practice and will be happy in Russia and stay long."

Dallas's two-year stint in Russia is not noted for any practical outcome. His innate skills in the job, however, bolstered St. Petersburg's respect for American diplomacy. As he was quitting his post for a return home, the emperor presented Dallas with exquisite gifts. (Additionally, he was also requested to carry a diamond-studded snuffbox, a present to J.J. Audubon, the noted ornithologist, whom the tsar admired.)

It was in Dallas's time that we have the touching story of an eighteen-year-old American boy of whom little is known other than his name was Tom. Having spent weeks travelling abroad, he arrived in St. Petersburg and managed somehow to secure an interview with the minister of war. Tom informed Count Tchernishov that he wished to arrange a meeting with the emperor. He carried a unique gift for the tsar: an acorn from the tomb of George Washington, "who was also a friend of humanity." So endearing was the youngster that Tchernishov made the appropriate arrangements, and in time, Nicholas, together with the empress, received the boy. The imperial couple was delighted with the visitor and the three remained closeted together for over an hour.

Tom made his presentation. Nicholas then and there summoned the court gardener, and ordered that the acorn be planted in the gardens of Peterhof Palace. (A plaque was subsequently erected to commemorate this singular presentation.) The elated young man quit the palace carrying a reciprocal gift: a gold watch and chain set with a ruby.

In the first forty-five years of diplomatic relations between the two countries, St. Petersburg welcomed a succession of thirteen American ministers and Russia was served in Washington by six representatives. Like certain of their American counterparts, some of these men were of backgrounds having no particular merit. Each had been appointed through a strong personal connection with the emperor or was simply seconded from the bureaucracy. But whereas certain of the American envoys developed brilliant careers after their postings, their Russian counterparts did not shine. One was promoted as minister to Switzerland, another minister to Brazil, and the remainder faded into obscurity. What was said of certain American ministers might for the most part be applied to the Russian envoys — they were "neither very important in themselves nor left any worthwhile record of their experiences."

Before Russia's diplomatic recognition of the United States, Andrei Dashkov was the country's chargé d'affaires in Philadelphia, then the country's capital. With the granting of formal diplomatic recognition in 1809, the tsar appointed Count Feodor Pahlen as Russia's first full-fledged minister.

Pahlen took an immediate dislike to Washington. He complained vociferously about everything: the provincialism, unpaved streets, impassable Pennsylvania Avenue, hot and humid summers, and lack of civilized company. He certainly was not alone in such complaints. "My God!" wrote an unhappy French minister. "What have I done to deserve having to reside in this city!" The Portuguese minister was subtler, labelling Washington "a city of magnificent distances."

So miserable was Pahlen (and well connected in St. Petersburg) that he persuaded the foreign ministry to reassign him. Months later, he found himself happily ensconced in Rio de Janeiro. During the count's brief ministry in the United States, Dashkov had remained in Philadelphia as consul, but with Pahlen's departure, the tsar elevated him to ambassadorship with orders to relocate to Washington.

Possibly the most striking ambassador to the United States during the period in question was Alexander Bodisko — the exception to the claim that no Russian diplomat left behind a notable reputation.

A legend in his own time, the widowed "Uncle Sasha," as he came to be known, was a bon vivant who enjoyed Americans and liked everything about Washington. A man of independent wealth, he invested heavily in the country and did well. Bodisko didn't hesitate to spend freely. He happily entertained at lavish parties in his stately Georgetown home, and in Newport during the summer. Not a physically striking gentleman, he painted his greying hair. In a further effort to disguise his age, Bodisko spoke of his grown-up children as being nephews and nieces— particularly when in company of delightful young women.

Uncle Sasha was popular with just about everyone except his fellow diplomats, most of whom envied him for his success, and for his sumptuous lifestyle. Here is one unflattering description, obviously coloured by jealousy:

> A dandy in dotage ... his mouth toothless, his breath horrible and the *tout ensemble* justifies the opinion of those who considered him the ugliest man in the United States ... the old fellow becomes the admiration of the Washington ballrooms and wins the love of pretty damsels of sweet sixteen.

The French emissary took particular exception to the Russian. Whereas Monsieur de Bacourt made no bones about his dislike for Americans and for Washington, Bodisko seemed ever to be championing the cause of both — this to the irritation of the other. "Everything about Americans revolts me," de Bacourt declared haughtily. "Their opinions, their manners, their habits and their character!" He complained bitterly of the city's streets, virtually barren in the daytime but crowded in the evening with every sort of *canaille* and riff-raff. He once carped on the proliferation of scavenging pigs and dogs that seemed to run rampant during the night. Bodisko, to the Frenchman's disapproval, countered that the streets at least were made more sanitary thanks to the animals' consumption of refuse. De Bacourt referred to Bodisko as a *villain vieillard* (a dirty old man) — there was little love lost between the two ministers.

On Christmas day, 1839, Bodisko threw a gala party, complete with gifts for every guest and toys for the children. The house was sumptuously decorated with wreathes, candles, and a vast tree, while in the street bonfires were thoughtfully lit for the guests' coachmen, providing protection from the unseasonable cold. Guests were grandly announced, servants in livery shuttled about with trays of drinks and canapés, and before long the revelry was under way.

Bodisko moved about the crowd, chatting, smiling, laughing, working the rooms. In one corner, the younger generation had gathered around the piano, and he gravitated toward them. His wandering eye fell on Harriet Williams, a particularly beautiful and vivacious teenager, the daughter of a clerk in the adjutant general's office. Bodisko was smitten with the attractive teenager who was "as beautiful as the devil." Before long, he was showing her about the house, and when the dancing started he whirled away the blushing Harriet.

In the following weeks, Bodisko was observed many afternoons patiently waiting at the school doors for Harriet to emerge. He delighted in accompanying the girl home and gallantly carrying her schoolbooks. What an incongruous sight it must have been … the short, stout, and homely sixty-year-old trotting alongside the tall, slim, and elegant teenager. It didn't take long for Washington to be set abuzz over this highly irregular relationship. Heads shook in disbelief and disapproving tongues clicked away.

And then Uncle Sasha proposed to her. Young Harriet accepted.

The engagement was announced and a wedding was scheduled — all within three months of the Christmas party. Every propriety, however, had been observed: Bodisko had formally called on the girl's father to ask for her hand, and as was appropriate for a diplomat, permission for the match had been requested of the tsar. President Martin van Buren had also been asked and the couple received his blessing.

In advance of the April 9 wedding, a variety of dinners and receptions were held, attended by the glitterati of the time. One such dinner included the president, vice-president, secretary of state, and chief justice of the Supreme Court together with the entire diplomatic corps and scores of other dignitaries. A few nights later, Uncle Sasha hosted a grand open house that caused one of Georgetown's first traffic jams. The gossipy *Washington Herald* reported,

> The green house was open with the orange trees, with the sweet smelling blossoms…. In one of the balcony

rooms was hung from the ceiling an enticing swing; the
seat was a soft velvet cushion, and the cords red silk.…
We hear that the new bride has forty-six new and splendid dresses, of satin, of thule, of crepe, and of muslin;
eight new bonnets, several sets of jewelry and everything that can delight a young lady.… Much champagne
was drunk in toasts to "Nicholas and Martin."[2]

Bodisko was a perfectionist and every detail of the wedding day was
meticulously planned with the ceremony being rehearsed twice. Early
on the big day, a crowd began to gather outside the residence and by
noon it was large enough substantially to block the surrounding streets.
Washington's excitement was palpable and everyone seemed caught up
in the occasion, which seemed almost imperial in style. A wedding of a
very young bride and someone who might have been her grandfather
— sensational it was. The expectant crowd was not disappointed with
the comings and goings, particularly with the spectacular arrival of the
British minister, Henry Fox. Weeks earlier, the Englishman had consented to participate in the wedding party as an attendant to Bodisko.

On the eve of the event, Fox spent most of the night at the card table,
enjoying drink and the company of friends. In the morning, he wholly
overslept, springing out bed in a panic, and while dressing ordered that
a carriage be immediately brought from the livery stable. The breathless
valet returned with the news that none was available. Fox was beside
himself and furiously ordered that any sort of conveyance be comman-
deered forthwith. The servant ran out onto the street and managed to
persuade the coachman of the first passing vehicle to stop and convey his
master to the Russian embassy.

In due course Washingtonians were treated to the spectacle of a
huge black hearse careening down the streets, funerary plumes flaying
in the wind, and perched on its roof, Her Britannic Majesty's Minister
Plenipotentiary, resplendent in full-dress scarlet uniform with plumed
hat and gold sword. From his precarious perch, the minister barked words
of encouragement at the frantic coachman who mercilessly whipped the
frothing horses. A loud cheer of amused approval greeted Fox's arrival

at the embassy. As he alit from the height, Fox saluted the crowd with a flourish of his colourful hat.

The wedding itself was "the event of the century," drawing national attention. The *New York Herald* was effusive:

> This was thought to be one of the prettiest scenes of the kind ever witnessed. The lovely bride, surrounded by her train of eight young ladies all beautiful and blushing as the roses they carried; bright eyes were flashing on fresh and blooming faces; while everyone looked happy. Mr. Bodisko wore his splendid court dress; a coat almost entirely silver, decorated with several orders. The foreign ministers [including the British ambassador!] of his train also wore their uniforms.[3]

Despite all woeful predictions to the contrary, the match proved a grand success. Bodisko was exceedingly proud of his young, attractive wife who seemed never to be without a radiant smile. Uncle Sasha treated Harriet's family as his own and was particularly attentive to his wife's young siblings and her sisters. With the passing of time, Washington society came to accept the union and even its most vociferous early critics became silenced.

A couple of years after the wedding, Bodisko took Harriet for a visit to St. Petersburg, where she caused a sensation — everyone fell under her spell. Grand Duke Michael, it is said, presented her with an extravagant ball gown in which she appeared at court. The tsar was totally enchanted by her, calling her "the American swan," and he ordered the court painter to do her portrait. The couple bore seven children, the eldest of whom had the emperor as godfather.

In the winter of 1854, Uncle Sasha, while out for his daily ride, was thrown from his horse and killed. The Washington funeral became something of a state occasion. A motion was tabled in the United States Senate to adjourn for the funeral — it was later withdrawn for fear of setting a precedent. *The National Intelligencer*, the closest thing in its day to a national newspaper, reported on the event:

The funeral of Mr. Bodisko yesterday in Georgetown furnished strong testimony of the respect and regard entertained for the deceased by all ranks and classes of persons among us. The array of carriages was unusually large even for the funeral of one of high position, and great numbers of private citizens identified themselves with the occasion. The body was conveyed in an open hearse in a coffin of the best material, but plain and unornamented. [It was] followed on foot by Mrs. Bodisko, her children and the remaining members of the family and suite of the deceased, all the way from the residence on 2nd Street to the cemetery on the heights.[4]

The couple had enjoyed fourteen happy years together and the love one had for the other is evidenced in part in Bodisko's last testament. With provisions for the disposition of his estate provided, the will's touching final paragraph reads,

As my dear wife will likely become a widow when it would still be convenient for her to marry again, I do wish with my whole heart that she makes a good choice. I reply on her prudence and flatter myself that she will take for a husband only a man worthy of her. I thank my dear wife for having embellished my life and wish with my whole heart that hers will continue without clouds until the last moment of her existence.[5]

By the time Bodisko was well into his term of office, the complexion of Russian-American relations had changed almost imperceptibly. The growth of trade hallmarking such relations in the fifty years from 1775 had diminished. America's industry no longer required imports of commodities such as iron, tallow, hemp, and inexpensive cloth, and the market for fine furs had bottomed out.

Concurrently, Russian manufacture had advanced spectacularly and the country's reliance on imported goods diminished accordingly. A certain Charles Todd from Cincinnati, an elected member of the Russian Agricultural Society, brought to Russia seeds of a variety of Virginia tobaccos, "with an explanation, as full as practicable, of the mode of cultivating of each." Soon, Russian growers were happily cultivating large crops of the leaf, and the import of Virginia tobacco dried up.

At the diplomatic New Year's levy of 1833, the tsar engaged Buchanan in a conversation that the minister later summarized:

> It is evident that he places considerable value on the good opinion of the American people. He remarked it was strange, that whilst so many of our vessels entered the ports of Russia, so few American travelers visited his dominions; twice expressed a strong desire that we should come and see them as they really were and not as they had been represented by their enemies.

The thirty-year reign of Nicholas I, particularly the last half, was one of suffocation for Russia's intellectuals and the middle class — original thought and initiative went abated. His ascension to the throne in 1825 was prefaced by the ruthless suppression of the short-lived Decembrist revolt. Never again, the new emperor vowed, would he have to confront the likes of the insidious young men of the Northern Society who had launched the revolt. He established the dreaded Third Section to deal with dissidents and political crimes.

"His system," wrote Baron Jomini, a Swiss in the imperial service, "was inflexibly logical, his convictions unshakeable." Never had the country been so thoroughly administered with Prussian military order, which permeated every department of government. Foreign travel was prohibited and extensive censorship laws were ruthlessly enforced. The word *demos* was expurgated from Greek history texts, and it was forbidden to write about Caesar's death as an assassination — he "perished." From one scientific work, the expression "forces of nature" was removed by diligent censors. Newspapers published heavily censored news and offered little or no editorial comment. Writers were muzzled and scores found themselves in Siberia, including Dostoyevsky. The individual thinker was stifled and responsibility and initiative perished. Buchanan offered Washington the following:

> We have no foreign Mission which requires so much pru-
> dence and caution on the part of the Minister as that at
> St. Petersburg. The Government is extremely jealous and
> suspicious, and in general society, no man can tell who are
> spies of the secret police. Every Minister, and especially
> the American Minister on his first arrival, is narrowly
> watched; and [he must watch what he says].… When I
> say this, I do not mean to intimate that he should ever
> utter a sentiment not truly American, but merely, that he
> ought to know when to be silent as well as when to speak.[6]

Irrespective of diminished trade and Nicholas's clampdown on freedoms, the peoples of the two countries continued to hold a certain fascination for one another. Americans did visit and work in Russia, but no great numbers of Russians appeared in the United States (forbidden by ukase to travel abroad). Russians gathered impressions of America from the printed page. Authors such as Washington Irving, James Fenimore Cooper, and Edgar Allen Poe proved immensely popular (as they continue to be to this day). Cooper's works in particular were in demand and *The Last of the Mohicans* and *The Deerslayer* were trans-lated into Russian within months of publication. In later years, American novelists and poets such as Ralph Waldo Emerson, William Longfellow, Walt Whitman, Nathaniel Hawthorne, James Russell Lowell, and Oliver Wendell Holmes were received with equal enthusiasm.

One of the more profound influences on Russian perception of America came from the pen of a Frenchman, Alexis de Tocqueville. In his *Democracy in America*, he contrasts the two nations and their peoples:

> [Both nations] have grown up unnoticed and whilst the
> attention of mankind was directed elsewhere, they have

suddenly assumed a most prominent place amongst the nations, and the world learned of their existence and their greatness at almost the same time.

All other nations seem to have nearly reached their natural limits ... but these are still in the act of growth. All the others are stopped or continue to advance with extreme difficulty, [but Russia and America] are proceeding with ease and with celerity along the path to which the human eye can assign no term.

The American struggles against natural obstacles which oppose him; the adversaries of the Russians are men. The former combats the wilderness and savage life; the latter, civilization with all its weapons and its arts. The conquests of one are therefore gained by ploughshares; those of the other by the sword. The Anglo-American relies upon personal interest to accomplish his ends and gives free scope to the unguided exertions and common sense of the citizens; the Russian centers all the authority of society in a single arm. The principle instrument of the former is freedom; of the latter servitude.

Their starting-point is different, and their courses are not the same. Yet each of them seems to be marked out by the will of Heaven to sway the destinies of half the globe.[7]

A year after de Tocqueville produced his work, Alexander Pushkin, Russia's iconic writer, composed a critical study on the United States. The poet never visited the United States, but the country was one of his abiding interests — particularly its people and its writers. His article, written under the pen name "The Reviewer," came in the guise of a review of a book, *A Narrative of the Captivity and Adventures of John Tanner during Thirty Years Residence among the Indians in the Interior of North America*, and it is a severe condemnation of "the American way." Here are two small excerpts:

The North American states have attracted the attention of the most outstanding people in Europe. America calmly

follows her destiny, secure and flourishing, made strong
by the peace that reigns there, proud of her institutions
and fortified by her geographical position. Recently,
however, a few penetrating minds began to study the
character of these institutions and their observations cast
a more doubting light on certain matters. The respect for
this new nation and its laws was greatly shaken.

To our surprise, we discovered within democracy a repul-
sive cynicism, cruel prejudices and intolerable tyrannies.
Everything noble, everything that uplifts the human soul,
is being suppressed by a kind of egotism and a passion for
comfort. The majority brazenly suppress society. Despite
the cry of liberty, the slavery of negroes continues. Not
having nobility, the snobbishness of the people is surprising. The politicians show only greed and jealousy and are
ingratiating in their efforts to please the voters. There are
contradictions to all the established rules of society. The
rich man puts on a torn coat when he goes into the street
in order not to insult the proud poor; yet he secretly
despises them and is despised by them. Such is the picture of the United States recently presented to us.[8]

Pushkin continues the article with a prophetic commentary on the
fate of Native Americans:

Chateaubriand and Fenimore Cooper have presented to
us the Indians only from the poetical point of view. The
savages in some novels resemble real savages about as
much as idyllic shepherds resemble real ones. Sooner or
later, by sword, fire, rum and chicanery, savagery must
disappear with the approach of civilization. It is inevitable. The remnants of the ancient inhabitants of America
soon will be completely exterminated. The vast plains and
boundless rivers, in which the Indians procured food with

arrows and nets, will be transformed into cultivated fields, studded with villages, and into commercial ports where the smoke of steamboats will be seen and the American flag will wave. Yet must I condemn the flagrant injustice and the heartlessness of the American Congress toward Indian tribes.[9]

Romanticize "the noble savage" as he did, Pushkin in making this attack on American democracy was really condemning the autocratic tyranny of his own country, where much of the population was treated in like manner. One must not forget that the author was writing at a time of censorship and to criticize openly the government or the country's social conditions was hazardous at best. Pity only that virtually nobody in America heard Pushkin's voice, and that in Russia it hardly rose above a whisper.

At the time that Pushkin was putting to paper his thoughts on the United States, another Russian, Platon Chikachev, was actually touring that country — how he secured permission to leave his homeland remains a mystery. The following are some observations he makes in his *On Shipping and Lakes in North America*:

During my stay in North America I often thought of my country. The wealth of resources with which each of these two states has been endowed by providence, the stability of the basic principles upon which their prosperity is built, and, finally, the youth of the population, keen-witted and full of life, often led me to compare them to each other. Long reflection has further confirmed me in my conviction.

Leaving aside their political sphere of activity, one may affirm that Russia and the United States are two states before whom there is opening up a most promising future.... Having emerged only recently into the light of history, they have already secured for themselves a place in the future, moving with a firm and stately tread toward their goal.

Whatever may be the political future of these people, who should indeed be called people rather than a state, whatever talk about slavery ... a huge field of action stretches before them.

If the New World has been blessed by heaven as regards its physical structure, if it is endowed with rivers such as the Mississippi, the Ohio, the Missouri, and the St. Lawrence, on which reign industry and the spirit of enterprise, there is another land on the other side of the globe that is no less blessed, and there can be no doubt that the Volga, with its enormous tributaries forming a chain as it were, that links the Caspian and the Baltic, the Dnieper and the Dvina, the Black Sea and Riga, the Niemen and the Vistula ... are all worthy rivals of the rivers of America. Is not our steppe the same as theirs?

Everything is identical in this geographical comparison. The same gigantic size, the same majesty in proportion, the same natural advantages for the construction of transport systems. The Allegheny Mountains and the Urals both mark the beginning of broad expanses of level land suitable for railways and farming. Everything depends only on the degree to which men are prepared to work.[10]

Awareness of Americans and Russians of one another intensified in the 1830s and '40s, be it through the likes of Pushkin, Chikachev (or even the little known Tom), or through such ministers as Middleton, Buchanan, or Bodisko. The remarkable Uncle Sasha, however, receives much of the credit for the goodwill that prevailed between the two countries in the mid-nineteenth century.

En passant, an arresting footnote to this chapter: during Ambassador Middleton's term in St. Peterburg there resided in the capital a fellow American by the name of Nancy Gardner, a charming, well-educated woman of mixed African and Native American blood. Shortly after her arrival in 1810 the enterprising woman established a thriving shop specializing in high-end baby furnishings. The "toast of the town" she soon became, as members of the imperial family, and the capital's elite flocked to her emporium. Nancy grew into an appreciated member of St. Petersburg's Anglo-American community where she was particularly active in her church. In 1833, she sold her business for health reasons and returned home to Massachusetts, leaving behind her black husband in Russia.

(In Salem, she became an organizer in the anti-slavery movement and indulged in a number of good works, including the founding of an orphanage. In time, Nancy Gardner became disillusioned with the parochial life of her surroundings and emigrated to Jamaica, where she joined a missionary group. In 1843, an ill and destitute Nancy returned to the States, settled in New York, and died there — a poignant story of a singular African American shopkeeper in St. Petersburg.)

CHAPTER 11

THE CRIMEAN WAR

Alexander I's international priorities for Russia were focused on Europe, and only passively on imperial activities in the Pacific. Nicholas I, on the other hand, resolutely looked south at Russia's historic nemesis: the crumbling Ottoman Empire. Since the days of Catherine II, Russia dreamed of fulfilling its "historic mission": to precipitate the dissolution of that empire and to gain control of Constantinople and the Dardanelles, "the gates to our house."

By the middle of the century, "the sick man of Europe" had pretty well collapsed into moral and financial bankruptcy. National aspirations permeated most corners of the sultan's domains, and local massacres, revolts, and demonstrations frequently went unsuppressed. In 1852, Montenegro rose up in rebellion against the Turks, and the sultan dispatched "the flower of the Ottoman forces" to quell the revolt. The besieged Montenegrins appealed for succour from Russia, their powerful Orthodox co-religionist.

Nicholas heard the call and concluded that the time had come to teach the "insolent Turk" not to make light of Orthodoxy. "These wretched people" had already caused manifold grief to the Orthodox in the Holy Land and enough was enough. He ordered a "demonstration of force," so a hundred and forty-five thousand troops were dispatched to the Danubian frontiers of Ottoman territory.

Meanwhile, Napoleon III had ascended the throne of France and was consolidating his tenuous position, strenuously seeking to emulate his illustrious uncle. "Napoleon," wrote Bismarck, "was vaguely aware that he needed a war," for only war could bring glory to the new empire and satisfy national vanity. He commenced rattling sabres by declaring himself champion of the threatened Turks. And it did not take long for Britain also to declare itself on the side of the Ottomans. Much of its expanding empire lay to the south or east of Russia and of Turkey. It was in Her Majesty's interest to maintain a weak Turkey, and certainly one that was free of the tsar's domination.

Suffice it to say that war did break out, the immediate causes of which arose from a seemingly haphazard series of trivial and unrelated events. "Some fateful influence seems to have been at work," lamented Prime Minister Aberdeen of Britain, shortly after the armies of Britain, France, and Turkey invaded Russia in September 1854.

The allies landed in the Crimea near Sevastopol and after nearly a year of bombardment, they successfully captured the city. And there, in its disease-ridden ruins, they remained without venturing farther into the vast spaces of country's interior. Mark Twain visited Sevastopol in 1867, twelve years post-factum, and was shocked by what he saw. "Not one solitary house had escaped unscathed, not one remained habitable even. Such utter and complete ruin one could hardly conceive."

The Crimean War drew wide interest in the United States. Actually, any nineteenth-century war involving Britain had the same effect — with the vast majority of Americans invariably cheering for Her Majesty's enemy. The burning of Washington in 1812 had left an indelible imprint on the U.S. national psyche. Additionally, thousands of anglophobic Irish had by then come to American shores in an escape from the potato famine back home. Within a decade, they had acquired substantial political influence, which they used to stoke the fire of anti-British sentiment. (One rally denouncing the king ended with three rousing cheers for the tsar.)

One wonders whether any of these Irish Catholics knew of a certain Presbyterian clergyman, the Reverend Charles Boynton of Cincinnati, who was equally fervent in supporting the Russian cause. Boynton, however, was a rabid anti-Catholic, and for him there was not the least doubt that all the evils besetting humankind, particularly the war in the Crimea, were the result of papal machinations — the French, after all, were Catholics. He had earlier justified Nicholas's suppression of the

1832 Polish rebellion by explaining that the tsar was "merely defending his home from the intrigues of a spy, the Pope." Now, on Independence Day in 1855, he thundered from his pulpit,

> What Russia is in the east, America is in the west — the dreaded foe of the Papacy. The same powers that fear the progress of Russia and seek to cripple her in war are also they who fear our rapid advance and who actually threaten it ... [the very] reason which has sent those armies and fleets into the Crimea and the Baltic may also operate to send them hither on a similar errand.

Boynton went on to urge that all Catholics be expelled from the United States. No doubting it: sympathy in the United States for the Russian cause came from diverse segments of the country.

In the earliest stage of the developing Crimean crisis, Americans were divided on the issue. Many were motivated by traditional anti-British sentiment, and by indignation over Napoleon III's autocratic airs — but more importantly, people resented the Turkish abuse of Christianity. Others condemned Russia for its blatant invasion of the Danubian provinces. New Englanders feared for the security of their region's commercial relations with Britain; Southerners sided with Russia. Not only did they share common problems of agriculture, but they both also had upheld traditional aristocratic ways of manor life.

With the commencement of hostilities, American public opinion solidified in support of the Russians. Not only was the tsar clearly the underdog against superior combined forces, but he was also defending Christian interests against the oppressive, morally decrepit Ottomans. Furthermore, the balance of power was being threatened — a defeated Russia would make imperialistic France and Britain even more intolerable. The *New York Herald* declared, "Public opinion here is undoubtedly favorable to Russia. There is no necessity for disguising the fact.... Not that we love Russia more, but we hate her less." The interest in the war was such that a sixteen-page weekly periodical made its appearance, *War News*.

Whatever public opinion, President Franklin Pierce pursued a deliberate policy of neutrality. Trading rights with the belligerents simply could not be jeopardized. "We desire most sincerely to remain neutral but God alone knows whether it is possible," he declared. *Whether it is possible*: the door to involvement in the war was left ajar ever so slightly.

The United States and Russia all along had viewed one another as counterweights to Britain, which steadfastly sought to contain the expansion of both nations. The strength and welfare of the other, therefore, was a mutual interest. Minister Alexander Bodisko received orders from St. Petersburg in 1837 to assure the State Department formally that it wished nothing more of the United States than for the country to be a strong power. Secretary of State William Marcy reflected a reciprocal attitude:

> They have shown — Great Britain particularly — too much of a disposition to be guardians of the whole world. As our policy and practice has been to let them alone in their proper sphere of action, we have the right to ask and expect that they do the same to us. Will they do so if they weaken and humble Russia?

In the April 1856 issue of the prestigious *United States Review*, a scathing article appeared concerning the Crimean War, in which the Russians were viewed as underdogs and were wished well and to have every success in the "unjust conflict." Despite the author's myopic, unbalanced view of the situation and intemperate language, it does authentically reflect American sentiment of the day:

> England, clothed in a show of sanctity and France, impelled by the domineering nature of her national character, and directed by an upstart of the darkest treachery and most shameless perjury, have at length succeeded in forcing Russia into a war, which they desire the world at large — and more especially the United States — to believe holy crusade.

But it is for power and power alone, that these two hitherto hostile nations have taken each other by the hand. They already give a foretaste of how they would exercise it, if their sway by destroying Russia should become firmly established. Let us hope that the calm, quiet, self-reliance with which Nicholas accepted the challenge of the allies, may indicate a speedy and successful termination to a war, which has been thrust upon him.[1]

It's fair to say that the bond between the two governments during the Crimean War period was as strong and warm as at anytime. "Relations with the leading Russians, from the Emperor down, were all that could be desired," wrote one American attaché in St. Petersburg. The U.S. minister Thomas Seymour called the tsar "this great sovereign" and found him "perfectly irresistible," with a handshake like "a good republican grasp." He felt that "the Autocrat of Russia had been much misrepresented."

Nicholas made known his support for American policies on South America, and he showed a sympathetic understanding of the country's tenuous interest in annexing Cuba. Brown reported, "His Majesty has as kind feelings towards the United States as he can have towards any country whose institutions are free." And in Washington, a similar congenial feeling prevailed. "The Russian diplomats," read one State Department report, "have generally been on the most friendly terms with Congressmen and citizens generally, while the Prussians and Frenchmen have been several difficulties with the Department of State and with the residents of Washington."

The Crimean conflict was called "the only perfectly useless modern war that has been waged," and indeed, few wars in history reveal greater confusion of purpose. Yet the war was one of the richest from the viewpoint of unintended consequences. It is remembered for the legendary Charge of the Light Brigade, immortalized by Tennyson.[2] The war conjures pictures of the "Lady with the Lamp," Florence Nightingale, wending her way among the sick and dying in the hospitals of Scutari. And in more than one city of the world streets bear such familiar names as Alma, Balaklava, Inkerman, and Malakoff.

What is perhaps unappreciated by many is that the gunfire and casualties of the Crimean War were not limited to the Black Sea. Battles were fought in what are today Romania and Bulgaria, in Asiatic Turkey, and on the frontiers of Persia. Major campaigns took place in the Caucasus. In Armenia, the siege of Kars, for example, with a massed attack by thirty thousand troops, surely deserves the same notoriety as the battles of Alma and Inkerman.

Nor was the war limited to Russia's southern neighbours. Some nineteen hundred miles north of Crimea, gunfire was exchanged on the White Sea, and Archangel was blockaded. On the Arctic Ocean, sixteen miles from the Norwegian frontier, Russian batteries fired on British ships. The town of Kola was attacked, the guns silenced and the settlement of one thousand was out to the torch by Her Majesty's marines. Curiously, one of the earliest recorded allied fatalities was not a white man on the Black Sea but a black man in the White Sea, a steward on board a British warship.

For two summers the British and French fleets brought war to the Baltic. At one time, there were fifty-eight allied warships sailing the waters, bearing thirty-four hundred guns and thirty thousand soldiers. Russian military authority was imposed on Estonia, Latvia, and Poland and her garrisons at Helsinki, Frederikshaven, Sveaborg, Revel, and Cronstadt were significantly reinforced. In the notable siege of Bomarsund, some twelve thousand French troops participated.

In the Pacific, war fever was as strongly felt. Australians expressed concern at the defenceless state of Sidney and Melbourne — it was known that Russian frigates were cruising in the South Pacific. The shipping interests of Calcutta submitted a petition to the government pleading for naval protection along the sea routes to China. In Hong Kong, the military authorities strengthened defences, while in Hawaii, Kamehameha IV prudently declared neutrality. As we have seen, a British naval attack was made on Kamchatka at Petropavlovsk, and repulsed.

On the northeastern shores of the Pacific, it was business as usual for the Hudson's Bay Company and the Russian-American Company. Each understood the other's difficult situation and they continued to do business amicably with one another throughout the period that their mother countries fought. The naval base at Esquimalt on Vancouver Island was reinforced and its very existence offered much comfort to the concerned citizens of Victoria and Vancouver. Taken together — the Balkans, Persia, the Baltic, and the Pacific — the Crimean War really was in the truest sense a global war.

In Canada, money was raised for the Patriotic Fund and when the twenty-thousand-pound donation for the war effort was sent off, half went to England and half to France. Napoleon III in acknowledging the gift, wrote warmly of bygone days when Canadians were French colonists. The governor general of Canada, the Earl of Elgin, transmitted to Britain "loyal addresses" from the legislative assembly, the municipal councils of some towns, the ministers and elders of the Presbyterian community, and the chiefs of six Indian nations. Similar addresses and donations to the Patriotic Fund flowed to London from New Brunswick, Newfoundland, Barbados, Grenada, Gibraltar, New South Wales, South Australia, and New Zealand.

Proclaiming neutrality, Americans were not shy in demonstrating their partiality, and few opportunities were missed to lend the Russians a helping hand. William H. Webb Shipyards of New York City executed their commission for a steamship ordered by St. Petersburg, and contrary to established rules of neutrality, the vessel was duly delivered — not without chicanery. Upon its completion, the ship was provisionally christened *America*, and with the Stars and Stripes flying from its masts, it sailed for the Pacific via Cape Horn. While en route, it stopped in Rio Janeiro where it narrowly missed seizure by a British warship, which claimed it as being a Russian vessel. Only the fast talk of an enterprising American naval officer prevented it from being captured.

There were further actions of support. Colonel Samuel Holt of Hartford, the famous arms manufacturer, supplied the country with firearms and technical advice. Individual Americans travelled to the Crimean battlefields to rally around the besieged Russians. A troop of three hundred Kentucky riflemen was assembled, and it joined the fray. Fifteen American mechanics volunteered to assist Russia in the building of railroads, and thirty physicians and surgeons ended up serving the Russian armies in Crimea — most of them medical students. When the British and

French envoys called on Secretary of State Marcy to protest the alleged fitting out of Russian privateers in the United States, he dismissed them lightly. (One of the few discordant notes was struck by the Illinois state legislature, which passed a resolution condemning the "aggressive policy of the Emperor of Russia" and requiring the governor "to forward to the aforesaid Tsar a copy of the above resolution.")

Jefferson Davis, the eminently practical secretary of war, seized the occasion to dispatch in June 1855 a commission to Russia "to survey the art of war," and in particular, "to report on clothing, transport, weapons, ordinance, fortifications and bridges." In addition, the commission was instructed to ascertain "the use of camels for transportation and their adaptation to cold and mountainous countries." (No record exists of camels ever being used in the conflict.)

The three-man commission included a cavalry officer, an engineer, and an ordinance expert. The new tsar, Alexander II, received the delegation amiably, and it was wined and dined lavishly. Graciously welcomed or not, the commissioners were denied permission to travel to the Crimean battlefields. They had to content themselves with the inspection of fortifications and military installations in northern Russia. In their reports, the observers were clearly impressed with what they saw — perhaps not entirely surprising in view of one summary: "In the organization of the Russian Empire, as you are well aware, every other interest may be considered subordinate to the military power." There was however a division of views of the ordinary soldier. The ordinance expert was clearly impressed:

> The Russian soldier is remarkable for physical qualities, well adopted to his profession an athletic form, broad shoulders, small waist, erect, muscular frame. Little encumbered with fat; accustomed to a life of labor, and to be nourished by the most simple diet. Add to these qualities and to the aptitude before mentioned, the habit of implicit obedience to superiors and the strong religious sentiment which leads to blind and enthusiastic devotion to the Emperor, as the head of both Church and State, and to unquestioning submission to the

delegated authority of the officer. Such are the principal elements of the military character of the Russian soldier.

The cavalryman, who had spent much of his visit sick in bed, was less unimpressed. He found ordinary Russian soldiers to be "vagabonds, thieves, gypsies, dissipated men ... condemned to serve. Yet mingled with these worthless characters are many good men, in fact, the latter predominate, and the influence of rigid discipline soon converts the others, at least into good soldiers, if not good men."

As the bloody struggle progressed, one major power after another broke its neutrality and sided with the allies. An outstanding example of this was opportunist Sardinia, which in the eleventh hour joined the fray. Prime Minister Camilio Cavour, this "stout, spectacled, whiskered figure, affable and fluent of speech and full primed with technicalities of every sort ... this far-reaching statesman, gambling as the greatest statesmen must often do for the highest stakes, persuaded the Turin Parliament to send a Sardinian contingent to the Crimea." In April 1855, King Victor Emmanuel waved farewell to fifteen thousand troops as they set sail for Balaklava, fifteen months after the initial allied landing. By the time the contingent returned home nine months later, twenty-eight of the gallants had been killed and a thousand had succumbed to cholera. Fortune, however, favours the brave. Seated at the postwar conference table where Europe's leaders gathered to discuss peace was the smiling Cavour. Before long, the "Italian question" was raised and ultimately resolved by the winning of Italian independence — one of the many unintended consequences of the war.

Throughout it all, the United States remained steadfastly firm in its lopsided neutrality, "the only nation in the world that was neither ashamed nor afraid to acknowledge its friendship for Russia." More than once, Nicholas, and later his successor Alexander II, sent notes of thanks to President Pierce and Secretary Marcy "for encouraging words and kindly deeds."

The Crimean War was one of notable firsts and lasts. Never again would massed formations of cavalry and infantry be employed; the "thin red line" was to disappear forever. Henceforward, armies would rely on open, flexible formations and on trench warfare. For the British in particular, it was a turning point: never again would their soldiers fight in full-dress uniform, and never again would they carry colours into battle or hear on the battlefields the stirring tunes of regimental bands.

Modern nursing came to the battlefield hospitals thanks to the inspired work of "one of the most remarkable human beings ever to have lived," Florence Nightingale. Not only did she establish an ordered system of hygienic hospital care, but she also revolutionized the treatment of the common soldier. In unspeakable conditions of filth, squalor, and privation she toiled ceaselessly, often twenty hours at a stretch, to ease the plight of the private soldier. Six months after her arrival in Crimea, the hospital death rate fell from 44 percent to 2.2 percent.

But for the military scientist, the war was especially significant and it is little wonder that the perceptive Jefferson Davis sent his investigative commission to Russia. It was here that the percussion cap rifle came to being and proved so decisive. The Minié rifle, replacing the clumsy smoothbore musket, fired a cartridge, not a ball, and its accuracy proved far superior to the old firelocks. Just as the Minié rifle and explosive shells changed the face of the army, so did the ironclad, screw-propelled warships affect the fleet. "We must not blind ourselves," cautioned *Bentley's Magazine*, "that our 'screws' are, up to this point, not a novelty in war, but an experiment." The experiment was a decisive success and for warships, it ushered in an end to the age of sail.

Submarine navigation was developed. "A curious experiment had already been made at Marseilles where Doctor Payerne, in company with three sailors, went to the bottom in the presence of hundreds of spectators, and rose a considerable distance and climbed the portholes of a man-of-war without being perceived by the crew." In England, a device known as "MacIntosh's Portable Bouyant Wave-Repressor" was publicized. The machine was "based on the cause of the generation of sea waves and the correct theory of their repression." It "subdued" storm waves and permitted the making of harbours "at places now inaccessible during storms." The light military railway was first put to use and its operation between Balaklava and the front proved invaluable to the allies.

The tsar's fleet was on the defensive and his naval engineers explored every sort of defensive weapon, the most bizarre of which was the *boulet asphyxiant.* Invented in France in 1839 by a Monsieur Fortier, the design was offered to his government, but the French authorities refused it. Fortier then offered it to the Russians. The inventor described the device as a machine that distributes "a liquid fire burning under water and destroying life by suffocation in all who happen to be within a certain distance of its explosion." The prospectus concludes that "if the Emperor of Russia is really interested in possession of this deadly element of destruction, the combined navies of the whole Universe will be powerless against him." It is unclear what came of this peculiar offer.

The new technology of the day included the electric telegraph and the word *telegram* came into being. Politicians back home were now able to exercise greater control over their generals in the battlefield.

Photography came into its own, the special results of which delighted military and naval intelligence. The *Journal of the Society of Arts* gushed, "Headlands, lines of coasts, forts, fortresses, disposition of fleets, armies, face of country and military positions, may be instantaneously taken, and, if stereoscopically, with a model-like accuracy which it would defy a verbal description to emulate." Roger Fenton accompanied the allied armies and effectively became the world's first war photographer. Working with him in the field was W.H. Russell, the first professional war correspondent, sent by *The Times*. Russell reported so accurately on the details of battles, on allied strengths and weaknesses, on casualties and the state of morale, that one Russian observed, "We have no need of spies, we have *The Times*."

With the signing of armistice on February 29, 1856, the Crimean War effectively ended. We have spoken of unintended results of the war, of which the eventual Italian independence was one. In the forty years preceding Crimea, no two of the great powers had fought one another, but in less than twenty-five years after the signing of the Peace Treaty of Paris, Europe endured five great wars: the Franco-Austrian (1859), Danish-Austro/Prussian (1864), Austro-Prussian (1866), Franco-Prussian (1870), and Russo-Turkish (1878). The lineage of each of these struggles may be traced directly to the Crimean War.

A result of the war was that it helped to bring about the International Red Cross established by the Geneva Convention in 1864. The dispatches of newspaper correspondents from the front vividly publicized the campaign in terms of death and misery. Exposure to the elements, pneumonia, typhus, gangrene, cholera, and the shameful inadequacy of everyone's medical services aroused European concern. A more developed sense of the value of human life was engendered and greater respect began to be accorded to the rights of the individual soldier.

One unexpected long-term beneficiary of the war's outcome was Cuba. Spain had offered to join the allies in return for an Anglo-French pledge to maintain the integrity of Cuba as a Spanish colony. But the United States exerted such pressure on the allies that they declined the initiative and Spain did not enter the struggle. Nicholas was so impressed by the American attitude that he pledged to Washington an unqualified support in whatever action it might take regarding Cuba, and as we shall see, this pledge was eventually honoured, and Cuba ultimately won its independence.

Perhaps the most significant unintentional result of the war was that it removed the fearsome shadow of Russian might from European affairs. In 1815, with Napoleon's exile, Russia appeared to be the single greatest power in Europe, and after the successful suppressions of the revolutions of 1830 and 1848, it was not so much a question of Russian primacy as it was of domination. But the Crimean War emasculated "the gendarme of Europe." In the two decades that followed, the empire came to be viewed as an equal among the powers, and after 1870, the newly generated German Empire gained its full supremacy. The ascendancy of 1815 was never regained by imperial Russia because of the Crimean conflict.

In early July 1856, Secretary of State Marcy offered Russia his government's services to mediate an end to the war. Forty-four years earlier, it may be recalled, Alexander I had offered President Madison to mediate the War of 1812. "Russia," declared Marcy, "rendered us the same service once and it is only just that we repay this debt." Nicholas gratefully received the offer, but declined it for fear of appearing militarily weak. He was unprepared to accept mediation until the allies had responded positively. France summarily rejected the idea. Britain, suspicious and resentful of America's open friendship with Russia, also refused the offer — it came to naught.

For over two years, the belligerents had been locked in battle. By the time it was all over, the allies lost an estimated 252,000 soldiers and the Russians lost 256,000. They were lost on the battlefields, in hospitals, at sea, and in the steppes. They died of bullet and shrapnel wounds, of cholera and other diseases, by starvation, and by freezing. Such was the Crimean tragedy and such was the toll of "the only perfectly useless modern war that has been waged." The historian H.A.L. Fisher speaks of the war as "a contest entered into without necessity, conducted without foresight, and deserving to be reckoned from its archaic arrangements and tragic mismanagement rather among medieval than modern campaigns." In the simple words of an ordinary officer of the Royal Navy, "What the Russian war was about nobody knows to this day, but we all felt very outraged at the time."

CHAPTER 12

SERFDOM AND SLAVERY

From the dawn of history, slavery, in one form or another, has been an unconscionable reality in most parts of the world, and in the twenty-first century, it is still not dead. It comes by many names: serfdom, peonage, thralldom, contract labour, bondage, indentured servitude, purchase by dowry, or simply child or prison labour.

By the mid-nineteenth century, the sweat that poured from captive backs had formed much of the wealth accumulated by European powers. France, with its Declaration of the Rights of Man and of the Citizen, was the first nation sufficiently enlightened to end the practice in 1789, followed three years later by Denmark. By 1816, slavery had disappeared in Spain and southern Italy. It was abolished throughout the British Empire in 1833, and fifteen years later the practice ceased in Germany, the Austrian Empire, and the French colonies. Eight years later, bondage had all but ended in South America, with Brazil holding out until 1881. (Incredible in all this was the unchanged practice of slavery on Liberia — an institution initiated and maintained by returning American blacks set free by their owners.) By the 1860s, the United States and Russia were the last remaining world powers to support the institution of slavery. In Russia, it was called *serfdom*.

Serfdom, as it appeared during the reign of Alexander II, had evolved over several centuries. Medieval Russia knew no serfdom. Landowners possessed the land and peasants settled on it and worked it, all in accordance with specific laws. In return for the land's use, the peasant fulfilled certain obligations to the property owner such as the grinding of corn, shoeing of horses, and repair of buildings. In addition, as a holder of land and member of a peasant community, he paid taxes. The peasant was free to move elsewhere, provided his taxes were not in arrears and that he found someone else to take over his holding. By the sixteenth century, the peasant had become legally bound to the land but was not considered personal property of the landowner. Additionally, he was free from the arbitrary increase of taxes. Over the following years, one enactment followed another by which the landowners' privileges grew and peasant liberties diminished.

By 1855, with Alexander II's succession to the throne, serfdom's evolution was complete. Twenty-two million peasants found themselves in a state akin to slavery — 45 percent of the country's male population. Serf owners exercised absolute power over their people and given liberty in the way they treated them. These "souls" were the outright property of some one hundred thousand nobles and landed gentry — tokens of wealth, treated as chattel. A landowner did not speak of his holdings in terms of acreage, but rather in the numbers of *souls* he possessed. A quarter of the serf owners possessed no more than twenty souls. But certain upper-echelon nobles owned vast numbers. Count Sheremetiev, for example, owned an incredible three hundred thousand souls. There are many examples in literature of serfs being won or lost by the turn of the cards at the gaming table, sometimes by the hundreds.

Although serfs enjoyed a degree of social and economic autonomy within their peasant communities, they had virtually no civil rights. They were at the landlord's mercy. The serf, for example, could not marry without the owner's permission and a serf family might be broken apart at the master's whim. Proprietors, especially those who actually resided on the land, generally recognized that their own prosperity largely depended on the welfare of the peasants, and they strove for a genial relationship; in many instances, the symbiosis made for almost avuncular owners. But at the same time, it was more often not the case. Since the serfs had virtually no protection under the law, the record of abuse was appalling. The one circumstance in which an owner might find himself before the courts would be for extreme brutality, but usually only if the case aroused sufficient notoriety.

In such an unhappy state, unrest and revolt hung threateningly in the air. Revolts occurred and in time they became more frequent, but they were invariably and mercilessly put down. In the decade from 1825 and onward, there were 148 revolts, but in the ten years following 1845, there were 348 peasant revolts.

The ruthlessness with which some serfs were treated is perhaps best illustrated by the example in 1825 of the serfs belonging to Count Arakcheev, a devoted friend and influential advisor to Alexander I. The abuse suffered by the serfs of his immediate household at the hands of Nastasia, his mistress and long-time companion, was legendary. The servants plotted every sort of subterfuge to ameliorate their miserable condition. Once, for example, a selection of herbs was secreted under Nastasia's mattress in an effort to mollify her character. When the grasses failed, more radical possibilities were debated, including murder.

During one of Arakcheev's frequent absences from the estate, a chambermaid named Praskovya and several others were harshly beaten on the orders of the mistress. Enough was enough. That afternoon the incensed girl and her brother — both under eighteen years of age — stole into Nastasia's bedroom as she napped and stabbed her repeatedly, plunging a kitchen knife into her chest and face. The bloody corpse was so mutilated that "her head was only hanging on by the skin."

The authorities arrested the youngsters together, along with thirty-two others who were picked arbitrarily. Since capital punishment had already been outlawed in Russia, the unfortunates were sentenced to the knout. This terrible instrument was a whip of uncanny design to inflict maximum pain — when it was used excessively, it often resulted in death. Praskovya received 125 blows of the lash, and her brother, 175. One of the other luckless ones, whose only crime was to have overheard discussion of the contemplated murder without reporting it, received ninety strokes and was exiled to Siberia for life. (It might be noted that the punishment given was unlawful — no more than thirty strokes of the knout were to be applied to minors convicted of murder.)

Even before coming to the throne, Alexander I had written, "Nothing could be more degrading and inhuman than the sale of people, and a decree is needed that will forbid this forever. To the shame of Russia, slavery still exists." In 1818, the tsar ordered that the thorny question of serfdom be resolved, but he cautioned his commissioners that whatever the resolution, the nobility should not be offended. When the nobles learned of the proposal, they of course made it clear that they would hear nothing of the matter, and it was dropped.

Nothing came of Alexander's declared intentions. His successor, Nicholas I, initially affirmed his opposition to serfdom, saying, "There is no doubt that serfdom, in its present form, is an evil obvious to all." In the same breath, however, Nicholas declared, "But to touch it now would of course be an even more ruinous evil."

Serfdom differed marginally from slavery in the United States — blacks in the States had no legal rights, but the serf had certain protections under the law, albeit a law not even-handedly applied. The serf, furthermore, lived in a peasant community that enjoyed a degree of economic independence. The fundamental difference, however, between the two environments was that the Russian system had enveloped a native population composed of people of the same colour, speaking the same language, and sharing a common religion. The American slave was an African *of* the land. The cultural heritage of the American slave differed radically from that of the master. In the one-time judgment of the U.S. Supreme Court, the slave was "an inferior being."

The clearest reflection of the prevailing attitudes toward slavery are found in the words of Alexander H. Stephens, the Confederate vice-president, as he spoke on the occasion of the adoption of the Confederacy's constitution in 1861:

> Our new government is founded.... Its cornerstone rests, upon the great truth that the Negro is not the equal of the white man: that slavery — subordination to the white man — is his natural and normal condition. This, our new government, is the first in the history of the world based upon this great physical, philosophical and moral truth. The great objectives of humanity are best attained when there is conformity to the Creator's laws and decrees.[1]

* * *

The first cargo of twenty slaves was brought to America in 1619. These arrivals and those unloaded soon thereafter were considered indentured servants with specified terms of service. Blacks who had served their terms became freedmen — free to own property and cultivate it. Over the years however, as in Russia, practices and laws governing slaves changed and Africans ceased being considered indentured servants — they were now chattel. By the time of Thomas Jefferson's presidential inauguration in 1801, slaves had become the outright property of their owners — with no rights. The system had firmly rooted.

By the end of eighteenth century, America's African population had grown dramatically as slave ships, one after another, arrived at colonial ports to discharge their miserable prisoners. In 1725, the estimated slave population was seventy-five thousand. Twenty-five years later, it had reached two hundred and fifty thousand, and that figure had doubled by 1775.

In his early writings, Jefferson clearly condemns the institution of slavery, to which he repeatedly applies adjectives such as "infamous" and "abominable." A decade before his election, he had argued before the courts that "under the law, all men are born free, and every creature comes into the world with a right to his own person, which includes the liberty of moving and using it at his own will." As a member of Congress, Jefferson introduced a bill requiring that after 1800 "neither slavery nor involuntary servitude" would be permitted within any new state joining the union.[2] After a raucous debate, the vote was taken. Predictably the southern delegates stood firmly against the motion, whereas the northerners voted in favour of the bill. As fate would have it, one of New Jersey's two representatives was ill that day, unable to attend the session, and because of this, his state's vote was not counted — the motion was defeated. "The voice of a single individual," Jefferson subsequently lamented bitterly, "would have prevented the abominable crime from spreading itself over the new country. Thus we see the fate of millions of unborn hanging on the tongue of one man." (The absence of the one New Jersey representative was a cruel quirk of history. Had his state's voice been heard, it is conceivable that the Civil War might not have been fought.)

Elated as the southern delegation was with its victory, the members were outraged that the anti-slavery bill was tabled by one of their own. At the very time that Jefferson tabled the bill, he, as a Virginia plantation owner, possessed over two hundred slaves. A slave owner was seeking to arrest slavery — an unfathomable contradiction. In the years that followed, Jefferson even took one of his slaves, Sally Hemings, as his mistress and by her, reportedly fathered six illegitimate children.

And herein lies one of the greater paradoxes in American history: How could such an enlightened man — so passionately devoted to human freedom — have willingly tolerated involuntary servitude with few signs of guilt? In 1814, Jefferson bends further by declaring that "the amalgamation of whites with blacks produces a degradation to which no lover of his country, no lover of excellence in the human character, can innocently consent." There was an incredible dichotomy in Jefferson — a long-time lover of a black woman, someone who was the mother of his children, yet Jefferson in essence embraced segregation.

Alexander I in Russia and Thomas Jefferson in the United States were both interesting cases. Initially, each of them in his own way condemned the practice of one human being owning and holding another in servile labour, and each professed a desire to eradicate the practice. But like one, so the other — each had to work with a large population of influential and intransigent landowners. The Russian landowning nobility and the American plantation owners were unwavering in their entrenched support of the status quo. Neither camp was easily to be dissuaded — Both tsar and president were stymied. It was for another emperor and president, in another day, to tackle the problem of serfdom and slavery in their respective countries.

By the time Alexander II gained the Russian throne, the frequency of serf revolts had increased dramatically. In the first six years and two months of the tsar's reign, there were 474 uprisings, or 32 percent of all recorded rebellions. It was obvious that the peace and good order of the realm was in jeopardy. In vain did the young monarch argue with the landlords that they had to embrace emancipation voluntarily. Within a year of his coronation, Alexander II addressed the representatives of the nobility:

> It is rumored that I wish to emancipate the peasants. This is untrue and you may tell that to everyone everywhere. But unfortunately a feeling of hostility does exist between the peasants and the landlords and, as a result, there have already been some cases of disobedience to the landlords.
>
> I am convinced therefore, that sooner or later we shall have to grant emancipation. I think that you will, consequently, agree with me that it would be very much better if it were to come from above rather than from below.[3]

Alexander II.

Library of Congress.

The tsar went on to offer a structure by which serfdom would be eliminated over a twelve-year period, but the nobles and landed gentry fought him tooth and nail; they would have nothing of emancipation. Exasperated by the recalcitrant nobility, Alexander, on March 3, 1861, finally issued an autocratic manifesto by which all serfs were set free. Thus, with a simple stroke of his pen, serfdom was abolished.

Americans received news of this dramatic development with predictable division. The southern states stood aghast at the apostasy, while the northern abolitionists applauded the measure. Impetus and new courage had now been given to the abolitionist leaders to press on in their fight to liberate the country's four million slaves. How could the United States, the professed beacon of freedom and liberty, continue to stand alone among the great powers justifying slavery? Alexander's manifesto was hailed as "perhaps the greatest single legislative act in the history of the world." The *New York Times* called the initiative "a grand act of enfranchisement."

Cassius Clay, the United States minister to Russia at the time of emancipation, spoke of the decree: "I think that I can say without implication of profanity or want of reverence that since the days of Christ Himself, such a happy and glorious privilege has not been reserved to any other man to do that amount of good, and no man has ever more gallantly or nobly done it than Alexander II of Russia."

Alexander had his way in Russia simply because he was an autocrat. We are reminded of Pososhkov's words: "The Tsar is master of his country. In the domain assigned to him, he can create, like God, everything he wants." Furthermore, he was fortunate in having a well-ordered bureaucracy that permeated every nook and cranny of the vast empire, a bureaucracy backed by a reliable army and police force. It might be added that Alexander II's conservative landowning opponents, however strident, were bound to him by an oath of allegiance. They were obliged to do as he ordered.

Abraham Lincoln hated slavery with a passion, and his determination to abolish the iniquitous practice in America was unfaltering:

> After freeing ourselves from King George, we announced
> the principle of equality for all. But now, when we are

fully fed and have no fear of being made slaves again ourselves, we have become so greedy to be masters that we declare the very reverse of this doctrine to be true.... The Tsar of Russia would be readier to take off his crown and declare all his subjects free, than our American gentlemen would be to set the slaves at liberty.[4]

As a junior congressman, Lincoln had moved a bill to outlaw slavery in the District of Columbia, but his opponents were successful in burying it in committee, and it did not come to a vote. As president, however, Lincoln's dedication to abolition was equally matched by his passion for constitutional rights. At his inaugural swearing in, he vowed to obey the

Anthony Berger, 1864. Library of Congress.

Abraham Lincoln.

provisions of the constitution and to uphold the union and its laws. And slavery was entrenched in the nation's laws, sanctioned by its courts. His conundrum, therefore was this: abolish slavery or uphold the Constitution.

President Lincoln was not vested with the autocratic power held by the tsar, and he lacked the backing of a strong army and centralized bureaucracy. He was the elected head of a "government of the people, by the people, for the people," in a nation of federated states, each carrying powers. The president had to reckon with these states and he was answerable to the electorate. An orderly outcome to a decree of emancipation, therefore, was infinitely more likely in Russia than in the United States.

The vociferous abolitionists of the northern states continued to agitate for their cause with little regard for the constitutional rights of the slave owners in the southern states. And in the American South, bitter resentment of the North swelled in intensity. With Lincoln's election in November 1860, the bubble burst. On December 20, South Carolina adopted the Ordinance of Secession in protest of the election, and in so doing created an impetus for others — within two months, six other states had followed South Carolina's example. The seven gathered together in a meeting held in Montgomery, Alabama, to form a provisional government. There, they adopted the name Confederate States of America and elected Jefferson Davis as president. The eighty-year-old United States of America was on the brink of a sensational collapse.

Russia viewed with alarm the prospect of a divided America. "The fall of the great American republic," wrote Russia's minister to Washington, Eduard de Stoeckl, "will be of no less importance for our era than the first American revolution, and it would prevent these once isolated States which are bound in federal pact from becoming a Power of the first rank." A divided America would spell an end to the Monroe Doctrine. European powers would most certainly re-engage in the U.S. arena, and chief among them was Britain. Russia's place in the continental balance of power would be seriously jeopardized. De Stoeckl therefore successfully urged his government not to recognize the newly formed Confederacy.

On April 12, 1861, Confederate troops bombarded Fort Sumter in Charleston Harbor, starting the war that was to claim over a half million lives. Lincoln's overriding mission now was to save the union. Confederate forces initially took the upper hand in the struggle and made significant advances north, but on September 17, 1862, at the Battle of Antietam they were checked. Encouraged by the growing strength and success of the Union armies, Lincoln determined now to press ahead with abolition — emancipation would strike at the heart of southern rebellion. "Slavery must die that the Union might live," he declared. As commander-in-chief of the armed forces, in a time of rebellion against the legitimate government, it was within his constitutional power to take whatever action he deemed necessary for the defence of the union. Five days after Antietam, he summoned his cabinet and informed the gathering of the critical decision he had taken: he was issuing a military edict outlawing slavery. In a calm, crisp manner, he read to those assembled from what he had written:

> I, Abraham Lincoln, President of the United States of America, do proclaim on this first day of January 1863, that all persons held as slaves within any State, or designated part of a State, the people whereof shall then be in rebellion against the United States, shall then be, thenceforth and forever free; and the executive government of the United States, including military and naval authorities thereof, will recognize and maintain the freedom of such persons, and will do no act, or acts, to repress such persons, or any of them, in any efforts they make for their actual freedom.[5]

A military measure, dictated in time of war — this was a document second only in importance to the Declaration of Independence from the viewpoint of American freedoms. After the Civil War, the legitimacy of the measure would have to be confirmed by a vote of Congress. And so it was: the Thirteenth Amendment was ratified on December 16, 1864, and the president's cherished dream became law. All men were now free throughout the land. "This amendment is a king's cure for all evils," gushed the president. "It winds up the whole thing."

Four months later, during a performance at Washington's Ford's Theatre, Lincoln was assassinated by the villainous John Wilkes Booth.

The accomplishments Alexander and Lincoln achieved were just and noble — freedom now came to all human beings in both countries. But did it really? In Russia, the serfs gained full civil rights, but the land remained with the proprietor — yearly dues or labour was required of the peasant. The serf no longer was the property of another human, but for decades following emancipation, most continued to live in abject poverty and economic bondage. As Andrew White, one-time first secretary of the United States delegation in St. Petersburg, observes in his 1905 autobiography:

> I do not deny the greatness and nobleness of Alexander II ... but thus far [the emancipation] in its main purpose has been so thwarted by reactionaries that there is, as yet, little, if any, practical difference between the condition of the Russian peasant before and since obtaining freedom.[6]

And likewise it was in America. During Reconstruction and thereafter, southern states enacted stringent laws concerning the liberated slave masses, the so-called *black codes*. Despite whatever freedom blacks had gained, they were successfully kept in a subservient, inferior position. The reaction in Russia to slave emancipation in America was double-edged. On the one hand, there was profound sympathy and understanding for the plight of slaves. But on the other hand, there was perplexity as to how the vast illiterate mass of the newly liberated would ever cope with their freedom.

At a St. Petersburg reception, Alexander II engaged in conversation with Wharton Barker — the Pennsylvania banker who was Russia's financial agent in the United States. After reviewing his own successes in emancipation, the tsar said prophetically,

> I am at a loss to understand how you Americans could have been so blind as to leave the Negro slave without tools for his salvation. In giving him personal liberty, you gave him an obligation to perform to the state which

he must be unable to fulfill. Without property of any kind he cannot educate his children. I believe that the time must come when many will question the manner of American emancipation of the Negro slaves in 1863. The vote, in the hands of ignorant men, without either property or self-respect, will be used to the damage of the people at large; for the rich man, without honor or any kind of patriotism, will purchase it, and with it will swamp the rights of free people.[7]

Barker concludes his 1904 reminiscences with the following observation:

The hopes and dreams of Emperor Alexander and of the great men who helped free the Russian serfs, and the hopes and expectations of Lincoln, Garrison and thousands of Americans who gave their lives and fortunes to the cause of Negro emancipation, have not been realized. The Emperor was right in thinking the solution of the Negro slave question would debauch our people and bring serious trouble to America.[8]

In 1864, at a formal dinner given by the Russian fleet in Kronstadt in honour of Cassius Clay, Rear Admiral Lisovski proposed a toast to the president of the United States. He raised his glass to "a name, which the possessor has already rendered immortal by the exercise of high moral courage in opposition to erroneous popular prejudice, and by the practice of a sublime humanity in the emancipation of the slave." The American minister responded with a toast to the tsar of Russia — to "Alexander, not Emperor but Liberator," whose achievement belonged not to "Russia but to the world." The exhilarated minister went on to declare that the American emancipation was "a new bond of union with Russia."

It is curious to note that Alexander "the Liberator" and Lincoln "the Emancipator" — the men who had brought freedom to *all* their people — both met their ends by violent assassination.

CHAPTER 13

THE CIVIL WAR AND THE POLES

On April 12, 1861, Confederate forces massed at Charleston and established a semicircle of guns around the harbour, each one trained on Fort Sumter. The secessionists by then had grown strong through a string of successes — a number of fortresses and arsenals had fallen effortlessly into their hands. Demands were made of Major Robert Anderson, Fort Sumter's commanding officer, that he surrender the fortification. Despite a dangerously dwindled stock of ammunition and food, Anderson refused and the southern forces retaliated by lobbing a shell over the ramparts into Sumter's interior. The Union guns returned fire. The resounding volleys that echoed over the harbour's still waters on that spring morning were the first of the Civil War.

Four years later, almost to the day, General Robert E. Lee of the Confederacy surrendered what was left of his ragged forces to General Ulysses S. Grant. By the end of the war, 620,000 soldiers had lost their lives, a figure greater than the losses incurred in all the wars America has ever fought, from the American Revolution to the present. Human passion had truly subverted democracy — the war proved to be its single greatest failure. Chattel slavery, however, had been abolished, and it was now established that no single state had the power to end the union. Before the end of the decade, Grant had become the eighteenth president of a truly *United States*. The nation had been preserved and strengthened — a new day had dawned. In the truest sense of the words, it was "the birth of the nation."

The crisis that culminated in the bombardment of Fort Sumter had been long coming. Russians had viewed the unfolding events with chagrin — it wished for nothing more than a preservation of the union. The emotional bond with the United States was robust, made so by decades of peaceful interaction and friendship. Additionally, it was in the country's strategic interest to have a strong America, one that would help check British hegemonic interests. Ambassador de Stoeckl had warned, "Great Britain seems about to enjoy a stroke of fortune rare in history. She alone will profit by the destruction of the United States, for it will be fatal to the rest of the world." The United States, in the tsar's words, was "the only commercial counterpoise in the world to Great Britain."

British hostility toward America had grown particularly firm in the years immediately before Fort Sumter, and London observed the situation developing in the United States with no small degree of satisfaction. Reflective of main-street attitudes, here is an 1856 commentary by the *Edinburgh Review*:

> We have long been smarting under the conceit of America — we are tired of hearing her boast that she is the freest and most enlightened country that the world has ever seen. Our clergy hate her voluntary system, our Tories hate her democrats, our Whigs hate her parvenus, our Radicals hate her litigiousness, her insolence, her ambition.[1]

Britain was not the only nation satisfied with the perilous condition of American affairs. A significant segment of European society, from Scandinavia to the Mediterranean, felt the same way — particularly such diverse groups as monarchists, revolutionaries, and anarchists. In France, the vainglorious Napoleon III took gleeful satisfaction in the developing war. He was, after all, the nephew of the illustrious Napoleon Bonaparte, and he felt himself destined for great things. A breakup of the union would certainly afford a possibility of re-engagement in North America — an opportunity to regain something for the loss of the Louisiana Territory — all to the glory of France. The French minister to Washington made no secret of his pleasure at the prospect of the union's breakup. "For my part, I am delighted with all this mischief."

Russia, however, continued in her exasperation with the situation, as evidenced by Ambassador de Stoeckl's words:

> During my long stay in the United States I have had the occasion to study the depth of the character of America, and … it is impossible to believe that a people so practical, so devoted to its interests and so prosperous could let their passions go to a point of sacrificing everything and precipitating themselves into an abyss that no one could foresee the depth [of].... We can view only with regret the fall of a great nation with which our relations have always been friendly and intimate.[2]

Stoeckl also said, "The fall of the great American republic will not be of less importance for our era than the first American revolution, and it would prevent these once isolated states which are bound in federal pact from forming a power of the first rank." Should the union break up, de Stoeckl reasoned, the North could endure on its own and would continue to prosper. The South, on the other hand, was insufficiently strong to survive as an independent entity, and it would undoubtedly attract foreign intervention. Essentially, that would mean an end to the Monroe Doctrine and a re-emergence of European presence in North America. Little good would come of such a scenario and would be the cause of conflict in Europe. Nothing should be done to exacerbate the developing crisis. De Stoeckl had urged St. Petersburg to withhold diplomatic recognition of the newly proclaimed Confederate States of America, and the tsar concurred.

A year later, with the war well under way, Russian exasperation with developments only increased "The Administration and the Congress have entirely lost their heads," reports Robert Osten-Saken, the imperial consul in New York. Everything is "confusion and stupidity. Mr. Lincoln's government is essentially a government of parties, while it throws up the pretense of being an independent power." And later, as the war intensified, he writes about "the revolution we are now witnessing," and suggests that the chaos enveloping the nation "be a salutary lesson for the anarchists and visionaries of Europe."

At the same time in St. Petersburg, the American ambassador, Simon Cameron, reported to Secretary of State Seward that the tsar "was very anxious that the United States, as a nation, should suffer no diminution of power or influence; our interests and those of Russia were in many respects identical."

During the Crimean War, American interest in the conflict was sufficiently aroused to prompt a number of its citizens to volunteer for service with the Russian forces. During the Civil War, however, the record of Russians arriving in America to serve in the Union cause is sparse indeed.

The most striking exception was Ivan Vasilievich Turchaninov, who, like Prince Gallitzen, was among the first of Russia's notable immigrants to the United States. Turchaninov graduated from the Imperial Military School as an artillery officer, rapidly rose through the ranks, and soon found himself as a full colonel and helping to suppress the 1848 Hungarian Revolution. He served in the Crimea and in the latter part of the war was responsible for the engineering of Finnish coastal defences.

At the war's end, Ivan married his commanding officer's daughter, Nadezhda, and immediately thereafter, the couple announced its intention to quit Russia, in protest of the shameful peace treaty signed by the emperor. Despite powerful pressure from horrified parents and family, they embarked for the United States and settled in Chicago. Ivan Vasilevich, having Americanized his name to John Basil Turchin, took up employment as an engineer with the Illinois Central Railroad Company. With the outbreak of the Civil War, John volunteered his services to the Union army and was commissioned as a colonel, commanding the Nineteenth Regiment Illinois Volunteer Infantry.

In short order, he disciplined the unit into a well-trained fighting force, and in the process he put together a concise training manual, *Drill Brigade*, which came to be adopted throughout the Union army. He also brought his knowledge of signalization into play, which proved remarkably advantageous in engagement with the Confederates.

The Nineteenth Illinois Volunteers saw active service in Kentucky, Alabama, and Missouri. Through it all, Nadezhda rarely left Turchin's side, even in the heat of battle — an irregularity that raised many a puritanical eye. Within six months of his appointment to the nineteenth

Illinois, John was given command of the Eighth Brigade in the Army of the Ohio, under General Don Carlos Buell. He fought with such daring that he came to be known as the "Russian Thunderbolt."

In May 1862, Turchin's troops successfully besieged and captured Athens, Georgia. The anguished population, however, did not stand by idly, and an underground group plotted and successfully derailed a Union supply train. The locomotive crushed to death one soldier and badly burned others. Sniggering locals at the crash site looked on impassively, refusing to offer emergency assistance. A half dozen slaves ran to the rescue of soldiers pinned under the debris, but the white spectators beat them off. So enraged was Turchin at the overall spectacle — accustomed as he was to European ways in addressing such matters — that he gathered his men together and announced that he was prepared to "shut mine eyes for von half hour" to permit his troops to loot the area.

When General Buell learned of the incident, he became so infuriated with Turchin that he ordered a court martial, and had him dishonourably discharged from the army. Nadezhda, however, would have none of that — a strong-willed, daring woman she was. (She reportedly once assumed command of her husband's forces when the colonel fell ill for a brief period.) With a disgraceful discharge at stake, she took it upon herself to travel to Washington to appeal personally to the president. So impressed was Lincoln with John's advocate that he rescinded Buell's orders and annulled the court martial's verdict. Furthermore, Lincoln reinstated Turchin to the army and promoted him to the rank of brigadier-general. John took command of the XV Corps and served with distinction in the continuing war.

After the war, Turchin resigned his commission and returned to Chicago, where with passing years his mind gradually faded. He died on June 19, 1901, at age seventy-nine in an insane asylum near Anna, Illinois.

An interesting historical parallel emerges from the story of this heroic figure: General Ivan Vasilevich Turchaninov was in the service of President Lincoln and the United States of America; some eighty years earlier, Kontradmiral John Paul Jones was employed by Empress Catherine and Russia.

* * *

The goodwill and moral support Russia showed America in those dreadful days was at the time amply reciprocated. In January 1863, the Poles rose in revolt as they had some thirty years earlier in a futile attempt to regain their independence from Russia — originally lost in 1815. The insurrection was put down harshly, and retaliatory measures were imposed. Britain and France protested the action and sought a multi-power condemnation of Russia. Napoleon III instructed his minister in Washington to invite the American government to join the initiative. (The order was no more than a mischievous machination, designed not so much to help correct a perceived wrong in Eastern Europe as to drive a wedge into Russian-American entente.)

"This is a request to which we can never accede," Secretary of State Seward informed Ambassador de Stoeckl. And, as an afterthought, he added, "especially when our own affairs are so embarrassing." Whatever little interest war-torn America had in developments in Poland was mixed. On the one hand, there was a real concern for the plight of the Polish people, "the gallant nation whose wrongs, whose misfortunes and whose valor have so deeply excited universal sympathy in Europe." On the other hand, anti-Catholic sentiment prevailed in many parts of the United States, with large numbers supporting Orthodox Russia against "the anti-Christ Poles." Minister Cassius Clay reflected that view in a personal note from St. Petersburg: "My sympathies are all on her [Russia's] side — for Poland is Catholic and of course anti-liberal, and it would be the tool of France in European wars; and as Napoleon has avowed himself our enemy — his enemies are our friends and the reverse." As one contemporary observer had it, "The interests of America and Russia [are] identical, and the reports which reach us of an *entente cordiale* between the Cabinets of St. Petersburg and Washington are felt to be both natural and credible."

Just as he had opposed foreign intervention in American affairs, so President Lincoln now refused to join the proposed collective condemnation of Russia. After all, his own country was at that very moment engaged in a life-and-death struggle with secessionist states. Like Poland, these states were insisting on the right of national independence. There was a certain commonality between the two situations. Tsar Alexander II received news of Seward's assurance with delight, and a one-word outcry: "Bravo!"

With or without American support, Britain, France, and now Austria, persisted in their "pursuit of justice" as a coalition for Poland. Alexander steadfastly contended that it was a domestic matter and foreign interference would not be tolerated. The coalition, however, pressed its case with equal determination — in its view, the Polish revolution was an international concern according to the terms of the Congress of Vienna. At one time, the dispute became so grave that the threat of a fresh European war loomed real. The tsar ordered his army to stand on full alert and to prepare for defensive action while elements of the fleet were ordered to sail out into open waters. (The painful lesson of the Crimean War had been learned, when the navy was bottled up in the Baltic and in the Black Sea by a stronger Anglo-French fleet, effectively incapacitating it for the duration.)

Secret negotiations had been concluded with Lincoln, and the tsar was assured that his ships would be welcome in the ice-free harbours of the United States. It wasn't an entirely an altruistic act — a firm show of Russian strength in American waters would be to the Union's advantage. Not only would Britain and France be less likely to launch an armed intervention in the war, but also they might be forced to think twice about extending diplomatic recognition to the Confederacy.

On September 11, 1863, the *Oslyaba*, a thirty-three-gun steam frigate, made its grand entrance into New York's inner harbour, anchoring amid visiting British and French warships. Great excitement was generated by the appearance of the elegant vessel with the cross of St. George, the naval ensign, from its jackstaff. When word got out that this arrival was but one of others imminently to come, speculation became rife as to the purpose of the visit. The Russians, many declared with certitude, were coming to reinforce the Union cause — not unlike the French had in support of the colonies during the revolutionary war. Secretary of the Navy Gideon Welles, surprised by Lincoln's secret agreement, wrote enthusiastically to Ambassador de Stoeckl on September 23:

> The Department is much gratified to learn that a squadron of Russian war vessels is at present off the harbor of New York, with the intention, it is supposed, of visiting that city. The presence in our waters of a squadron

g to His Imperial Majesty's navy cannot be but

ᵼf pleasure and happiness to our countrymen.

‗‗‗‗ʌat you will make known to the Admiral in command that the facilities of the Brooklyn navy yard are at his disposal for any repairs that the vessels of the squadron need, and that any other required assistance will be gladly extended.[3]

Welles noted in his diary, "In sending them [the warships] to this country there is something significant. What will be its effect on France and the French policy we shall learn in due time. It may be moderate; it may exasperate. God bless the Russians."

One Russian vessel had already arrived at the Brooklyn naval yard to undergo minor repairs, and the rest of the group was about to anchor off Manhattan. Speculation reached a crescendo when news was had that Mrs. Lincoln was planning a visit to the *Oslyaba*, the first such call by any first lady to any foreign warship. The Russians pulled out all the stops — amid much pomp and bonhomie, the president's wife was saluted on board and wined and dined. Toasts were raised for the health of the tsar and of the president, "toasts that will be heard with dismay in the palaces and aristocratic halls of Europe," noted the *New York Herald*.

The Confederates received news of these developments with consternation. Might this be an indication of a possible armed intervention by Russia in the continuing war? The *Richmond Examiner*, however, poured scorn on the matter and reported with unfettered sarcasm:

A health being drunk by the wife of an Illinois lawyer should convulse with fear the people of Europe! Plain Mrs. Lincoln … appendant to that extraordinary freak of nature, the President of the United States, she can not only distinguish herself by the resplendent tints of her silks and possession of jewels, but she can frighten the world!… The Tsar emancipates the serfs from their bondage of centuries and puts forth the whole strength of his Empire to enslave the Poles. Lincoln proclaims

freedom to the Africans, and strives at the same time
to subjugate freeborn Americans. In this striking coin-
cidence a similarity of character and feeling is denoted![4]

New York's excitement became palpable when reports came in that
"two large steam frigates, probably Russian" were lying off Stonington,
Connecticut. (This in fact had been so — Admiral Stepan Lesovsky,
flag officer of the Russian fleet, did anchor briefly in order to ascertain
whether war had been declared. It had not.) It was said that the fleet was
due in the city on the following day. And sure enough, as predicted, at
midday of the twenty-fourth the *Variag* and the *Vitiaz*, both seventeen-
gun corvettes, did appear, sailing smartly in line past Governor's Island,
with the Stars and Stripes flying from the masts and white-capped crews
neatly lining the rails. Loud hurrahs were cheered. The ships' guns fired
in salute — the guns of Fort Columbus (now Fort Jay) reciprocated. On
the following day, two more Russian vessels followed the corvettes —
the *Peresviet* and the flagship, the *Alexandre Nevsky*, a sparkling, new
fifty-one-gun steam frigate of forty-five hundred tons. Rumour spread
that Admiral Lesovsky bore sealed orders that were to be opened in the
event of a direct military intervention by any foreign power. The admiral
himself is reported to have told Admiral Farragut, the ranking American
naval officer in New York, "I am here under sealed orders. They can be
opened only in a contingency which has not yet occurred."

Additional excitement was generated when word was had that
another Russian squadron had arrived in San Francisco, and that its flag
officer, Admiral Andrei Popov, was in telegraphic contact with the Russian
embassy in Washington. The arrival of the fleets, concluded the *New
York Post*, is "evidence of the friendly feeling of the Tsar and the people
of Russia at a moment when other Governments of Europe have been in
accord with a desperate band of traitors and rebels seeking to destroy our
Union." It was clear that the Russian presence in American waters was a
substantiation of the long-standing amity between the two countries; the
tsar's concern that the United States remain strong and united was evident.
Few seemed to appreciate that the squadrons were there not exclusively
for reasons of friendship. Strategically, the arrivals suited both countries

equally. If the Russian fleet threatened to disrupt French and British commerce, the two would think twice in offering armed intervention on behalf of the Poles.

The Russians were overwhelmed by the receptions accorded them in New York and San Francisco, by the visible enthusiasm and the lavishness. The two cities were aflutter with Russian and American flags for the next two months as one celebratory event followed another. Parades, dinners, and balls were held; receptions and soirées followed one another; sounds of thousands of champagne bottles popping echoed in many an elegant hall and home. Shortly after the squadron's arrival in New York, a grand parade assembled at the foot of Twenty-Third Street, featuring the officers and sailors of the Russian ships and fifteen Union regiments, with three hundred to eight hundred crew members in each. With guns firing in salute and marching bands playing "Yankee Doodle" and "God Save the Tsar," the parade made its way down Fifth Avenue and Broadway to City Hall. *Harper's Weekly* describes it:

> After the procession had passed Union Square, and wheeling fairly into the vast current of Broadway, the scene became splendidly animated. The moving pageant rolled into a glittering stream down the broad thoroughfare between banks of upturned human face, the trappings of the equipages, the gold and silver epaulets of the Muscovite guests and the sabres, helmets and bayonets of the escort reflecting back unnumbered dazzling lines the glory of the evening sun. The sidewalks were packed with human beings and the balcony and windows — nay, in some instances, the very roofs of the buildings above them — were beset with eager multitudes.[5]

The civic reception at City Hall was spectacular, more of a demonstration than anything else. Mayor George Opdyke gushed geniality as he greeted Admiral Lesovsky and his crews. The extravagance of this reception was deliberately staged in an over-the-top way, its purpose not entirely a mark of friendship and appreciation. The civic fathers wished to demonstrate to the British that more fuss was being made over a Russian admiral than had been earlier made over the Prince of Wales. *Harper's Weekly* said,

> The ceremony was intended to have, and had, a political significance.... Every citizen felt bound to do what in him lay to testify to the Russians our sense of gratitude for the friendly manner in which Russia has stood by us in our present struggle, while the Western powers have done not a little to work our ruin.[6]

One event from the days that followed deserves special mention: a ball held on November 5 at the Academy of Music on 14th Street. Attended by twenty-five hundred guests, it was perhaps the most glittering of any during those halcyon days. The vast hall was decorated with white tapestry and golden tassels and at either end huge coats-of-arms offered blazes of colour, the Russian double-headed eagle and the American eagle. The decor included not only a spectacular bronze statue holding a flaming torch, but also gas-powered candelabra that offered both light and much-welcomed warmth. To one side was a "quiet little temple where guests could partake of the cup that cheers." The music was provided by two bands of fifty musicians each, and for the most part it was a continuum of waltzes and polkas. The ball's chairman, Theodore Roosevelt — father of the future president (who in his day denounced the Russian-American entente) — personally selected the program. Dazzling uniforms and stunning gowns crowded the hall. Matrons and maidens vied with one another for more attention. One buxom dowager sported a headdress of white roses on conspicuous black stems in the centre of which reposed a huge green bug. The correspondent from New Orleans's *Daily Picayune* viewed the event with sour grapes — "a vulgar display." The reporter wrote that "there were many beautiful and some refined ladies, but a great number who were neither, and some in respect to whom it was asked how they got there, or being there, why they remained, as their faces were well known to the police."

Dinner was served in an adjacent building, temporarily connected to the Academy of Music by an elaborate 125-foot canopy. Delmonico's attended to the catering, and it was served at elaborately decorated tables, the centrepieces of which featured clusters of Russian and American flags interspersed by portraits of Washington, Lincoln, Peter the Great, and Alexander II. The *New York World* reported on aspects of the menu:

> As the ovation and ball is one which may leave its traces on centuries to come, we give, for the sake of history, an account of the principle edibles used, viz:
>
> *Twelve thousand oysters (10,000 poulette and 2,000 pickled)*
> *Twelve monster salmon — 30 lbs each*
> *Twelve hundred game birds*
> *Two hundred chickens*
> *One thousand pound of tenderloin*
> *One hundred pyramids of pastry*
> *One thousand large loaves*
> *Three thousand five hundred bottles of wine*[7]

Not everyone was pleased with the proceedings and many New Yorkers criticized the lavishness showered upon the visiting Russians. The *Journal of Commerce* was especially embittered by the event:

> About the same time that people honored the Russians with music and dancing, men, women and children perished under the sharp hand of despotism in Poland, because they had dreams of liberty. So the world rolls. While the sun shines on one side it is dark on the other. We hope that the people who were guilty of the folly of last night's affair will now permit the Russian bear to gnaw his paws in peace.[8]

And another protest: "Such extravagant festivities were out of place when the Boys in Blue were dying in the trenches and when the government was having hard work to raise money for munitions.... The million spent on the 'Ovation, Volation and Ball' should instead have been given to the Sanitary Commission."

In San Francisco, the Russians were welcomed with equal lavishness. Learning of the Academy of Music Ball, the natives rallied together to outdo the New Yorkers and on November 17, an even more sparkling event was organized, attended by twenty-five hundred guests. The *Daily Alta California* reported on the event the following day:

> The ovation to our Russian naval officers, which proved to be so triumphant a success, was the theme of universal conversation in the streets, yesterday, in social gatherings, and in the passing complements of the day. Many loyal citizens who failed to receive invitations, instead of feeling chagrined, rejoiced that our Muscovite visitors had so superb an entertainment given them, and the more, that the guests were pleased with the civilities extended to them. Such persons considered that this entertainment was given not only out of compliment to our Russian visitors, but for the purpose of cementing still stronger those bonds of good will, amity and sympathy now existing between our Government and people and the Government and subjects of the Emperor Alexander.[9]

Balls and receptions eventually came to an end, but the fleets lingered on another eight months — the last ship didn't return home until late summer 1864. By that time, the threat of an Anglo-French intervention in Poland had dissipated, and there was little doubt as to the outcome of the Civil War. A couple of weeks following the famous New York ball, parts of the fleet travelled briefly to Cuba, while other ships sailed to Philadelphia, Baltimore, and Washington. Admiral Lesovsky held formal meetings with members of cabinet and with Secretary of the Navy Welles. An elegant reception was tendered on board the *Alexandre Nevsky* attended by members of cabinet and congress. President Lincoln, ill at the time, was unable to attend but Secretary of State Seward represented him. The ships' crews engaged in extensive sightseeing, visiting such places as Annapolis, Norfolk, and Niagara Falls. (Among the midshipmen who made the excursion to that spectacular marvel of nature was the composer Nikolai Rimsky-Korsakov, then a twenty-year-old on board the *Almaz*.)

The visits of the two Russian fleets had been arranged in strict secrecy; few officials on either side knew anything about them until their actual appearance in American ports. In its report to the tsar, the Ministry of Marine reported that "this sudden appearance of Russia's Naval squadrons in the ports of the American Union was even more impressive because no one expected anything of the kind, coming at the very moment when an alliance was on the eve of being concluded between two of the greatest maritime Powers." Were the visits first and foremost in reaction to the Polish crisis, or did they constitute a magnanimous reach of a helping hand by one friend to another? Historians continue to debate this. In Admiral Lesovsky's secret orders the following paragraph appears:

> The aim of the undertaking of the squadron entrusted under your leadership in the event of a war at present foreseen with the western powers is to act with all the possible means available to you against the opponents, inflicting by means of separate cruisers the most powerful damage and loss to commerce of the enemy, or making attacks with the entire squadron on the weak and poorly protected places of the colonies of the enemy.[10]

The arrival of the Russian fleet in September was timely. The evacuation of Atlanta by the Confederates had taken place. The battles of Gettysburg and Vicksburg had been fought some eight weeks earlier. The tide of the war had changed significantly in favour of the Union. If the French and British were prepared to involve themselves on the side of the Confederacy, it had to be done quickly. With the Russian fleets in Union ports, however, there was pause for reflection, and ultimately intervention did not take place

The truth of the matter most likely lies with Professor F.A. Golder's assessment, writing in 1915:

> Russia had not in mind to help us but did render us dis-
> tinct service; the United States was not conscious that it
> was contributing in any way to Russia's welfare and yet
> it seems to have saved her from humiliation and per-
> haps war.[11]

The Civil War came to an end with the capitulation of Robert E. Lee on April 9, 1865, at the Appomattox Court House. Within a fortnight, General Joseph Johnston surrendered the last of the Confederate forces to General William Sherman at Shreveport, Louisiana, and shortly thereafter, Confederate president Jefferson Davis was captured and imprisoned.

The nation set about the task of reconstruction and healing of deep-torn wounds. In the four-year struggle, not only had the aforementioned 620,000 soldiers perished, but also twice as many had been wounded. The fiscal costs of the conflict were staggering. Over a six-year period, the national debt had swelled by 4,300 percent — from $64,842,287 in 1860 to a phenomenal $2,773,236,173 by the end of the war. And this did not include the costs suffered by states and municipalities.

The financial and manufacturing establishments of New York and New England, however, had prospered during the war, and now, with its conclusion, these sectors gave impetus to the nation's reconstruction. Investment opportunities became abundant, with communications being particularly attractive.

And this brings us to the next chapter and the little-known story of the Russian–American Telegraph Company. It is a tale of entrepreneurship gone wild, of an astonishingly ambitious international construction project. The story highlights one man's fortitude and positive outlook on life — a brilliant example for young people everywhere of determination, initiative, and courage.

CHAPTER 14

SIBERIAN TELEGRAPH

Early on the morning of July 8, 1865, a motley armada of vessels sailed out of San Francisco harbour bound on a bold venture. The lead ship was the *Golden Gate*, an aging schooner in whose wake an unlikely collection of vessels followed — steamboats, sailing barks, and even a tugboat that once plied the Columbia River. The only armament in the fleet were four guns mounted on the forecastle and quarterdeck of the *Golden Gate* — placed there in the unlikely event of an encounter with a rogue Confederate privateer. These were the ships of the Russian–American Telegraph Company (RATC).

It had long been a cherished dream to connect North America and Europe by telegraph, and in October 1861, the first such attempt was made. Engineers, oceanographers, and technicians of every ilk came together to execute the ambitious plan of laying a sixteen-hundred-mile-long cable on the ocean floor from Newfoundland to Ireland. But they were stymied by the seemingly invincible Atlantic Ocean. Three additional attempts were made at enormous cost, but all for naught — the technical challenges appeared insurmountable.

In desperation, the Western Union Telegraph Company (WUTC) turned its gaze west. A connection with Europe, it was proposed, could be made by stringing telegraphic wires from San Francisco to the mouth of the Amur River in Siberia — via Oregon, Washington, British Columbia, and the Bering Strait. Working in tandem with the Russians, the existing connection from Moscow to Irkutsk might be extended further east to Nikolaevsk on the Amur River, where the two ends would be spliced.

A continuous girdle of wire circling nearly half the globe would thus connect the capitals of Europe with the cities of North America. Conceptually, the prodigious undertaking appeared sound and certainly the advantage of the scheme was plain. It did not require one, continuous cable in the Atlantic depths. To repair and maintain a land line, furthermore, is infinitely easier than to work on a deep-sea cable. The underwater sector of the shallow Bering Strait would be entirely manageable. An added advantage of the proposed overland route was that connection could be had relatively simply with the Asiatic coast cities on the Pacific. For North American business people, the rich Chinese markets would then become easier to reach.

And that is why the diverse fleet set sail from San Francisco on that hot summer day. Its mission was to put the telegraphic scheme into operation. However unimpressive the sight may have been of the ragtag armada departing the harbour, the enterprise was well financed. The Russian–American Telegraph Company, created by Western Union, raised the required capital, $10 million, within two months — at the hefty price of $75 per share, the largest stock offering to date.

A half million of those dollars were allocated to outfitting this initial expedition. A contract was concluded with St. Petersburg by which Russia committed to doing its part. The agreement also awarded the company generous privileges within its territory. The British government reluctantly made similar concessions insofar as the territory of British Columbia was concerned — it preferred the Atlantic route. President Lincoln was supportive of the scheme, as was Congress. As early as December 1863, the president announced to Congress, "Satisfactory arrangements have been made with the Emperor of Russia, which it is believed will result in effecting a continuous telegraphic line through that empire from our Pacific coast."

The imaginative undertaking was Yankee entrepreneurial spirit at its best. The sole threatening cloud was the remote possibility that the next attempt to lay a cable across the Atlantic would be successful — such development would prove fatal to the aspirations of the RATC. The odds of that happening, however, were deemed improbable and the risk seemed negligible. The company was prepared to assume it.

Colonel Charles Bulkley was named director of construction and was put in charge of the entire project. He had recently retired as superintendent of military telegraphs for the Union armies. Captain Charles Scammon was the second in charge, bearing the title of chief of marine. The expedition was run principally by newly discharged officers and soldiers of the Union army. The Smithsonian Institution grasped the opportunity of sending a sizable group of naturalists — this was also to be a scientific expedition.

Major Sergei Abaza of the Russian army joined the group and proved to be one of its most influential members — a telegraphic expert and thoroughly familiar with Siberia. George Kennan, a Western Union employee, volunteered for the expedition. In time, he became one of America's most accomplished and trusted journalists, as well as one of its foremost experts on Russia.[1] A number of personal accounts of the expedition's progress have survived, but none is more vivid and readable than Kennan's.[2]

Painstaking planning had taken place in San Francisco prior to the sailing. From his headquarters on Montgomery Street, Bulkley and his staff worked out the master plan — all quite straightforward. The first phase called for an expedition to convey exploratory parties to three points of the Pacific coastline: one in British Columbia near the mouth of the Fraser River, another at Norton's Sound in central Alaska, and the third on the Asiatic side of the Bering Strait, near the mouth of the Anadyr River. These parties were "to push back into the interior, following as far as practicable the courses of the rivers upon which they landed; to obtain all possible information with regard to the climate, soil, timber and inhabitants of the regions traversed; and to locate in a general way a route for the proposed line."

It was recognized that the first two groups would have the advantage of operating out of well-defined settlements: Victoria, British Columbia, and Fort St. Michael, Alaska. The Bering Strait group would find itself on "the edge of a barren, desolate region, nearly a thousand miles from any known settlement. Thus thrown upon its own resources, in an unknown country and among nomadic tribes of hostile natives, without any means of interior transportation except canoes, the safety and success of this party were by no means assured." The dangers were varied and conspicuous. To expose people to such conditions, it was heatedly argued by some, was simply a death sentence. The Russian consul in San Francisco urged Colonel Bulkley to forego a Bering Strait landing. Instead, he argued, send the party to one of the Russian ports on the Sea of Okhotsk where the expedition "could establish a base of supplies, obtain information with regard to the interior and procure horses or dogsleds for overland explorations in any desired direction." But despite "the wisdom and good sense of this advice," Bulkley would have none of it. He pressed on with his original plan, arguing that his vessels were coastal ships and none was sufficiently sturdy to make an ocean crossing.

The second phase called for follow-up expedition. With the exploration parties landed and hard at work charting the interior of British Columbia, Alaska, and Siberia, the delivering ships were to return to San Francisco. They would then load the building materials, equipment, and the personnel required to string the telegraph. It was anticipated that construction would begin within a year of the *Golden Gate*'s initial departure from San Francisco.

As the exploratory fleet was about to set sail, word was received that a small Russian trading vessel, the *Olga*, was about to leave San Francisco for Kamchatka. Bulkley grabbed this fresh opportunity of planting his crew on the Okhotsk and persuaded the ship's owner to take along four of his company. Major Abaz was appointed to lead that small group. The other three were James Mahood, a civil engineer from California; R.J. Bush, a recently retired army officer; and Kennan. "Not a very formidable force in point of numbers," Kennan observes, "nor a very remarkable one in point of experience, but strong in hope, self-reliance and enthusiasm." The plan was to have this advance party establish itself at Petropavlovsk, gather up work crews from among the Natives and then move northeast along the interior of the coast. Bulkley himself would proceed to the Bering Strait and then follow the coastline southwest, eventually to join up with Abaza's group.

Excitement on board the *Olga* was palpable as the four passengers made ready to sail. For Kennan, it was the start of a rousing adventure, a heroic passage for "the conquest of Kamchatka." Little did this naive enthusiast understand what lay before them, or even come close to appreciate the incredibly arduous path they were about to tread.

Confusion reigned over the hastily arranged departure:

> Dress coats, linen shirts and fine boots were recklessly thrown or given away as blankets, heavy shoes and over-shirts of flannel were purchased in large quantities. Ballard & Sharpes' rifles, revolvers and bowie knives of formidable dimensions gave our room the appearance of a disorganized arsenal. Pots of arsenic, jars of alcohol, butterfly-nets, snake bags, pillboxes and a dozen other implements and appliances of science about which we knew nothing were given to us by our enthusiastic naturalists and packed away in big boxes. Wrangell's *Travels*, Gray's *Botany* and a few scientific works were added to our small library. And before night we were able to report ourselves ready — armed and equipped for any adventure, from the capture of a new species of bug to the conquest of Kamchatka![3]

On July 3, five days before the main fleet set sail, the *Olga* put out to sea. A joyous party had assembled at the pier to wave them all off:

> Many hearty wishes for our health and success; laughing invitations to "come and see us" were extended to our less fortunate comrades who were left behind; requests to send back specimens of the North Pole and the Aurora Borealis were intermingled with directions of preserving birds and collecting bugs, and amid a general confusion of congratulations, good wishes, cautions, bantering challenges and tearful farewells, the steamer's bell rang.[4]

Within six weeks of the *Olga*'s departure from San Francisco, the three exploratory parties of the telegraph company were penetrating the inland wilds of the north Pacific Rim, charting the path of the future telegraph line. The largest such group was led by Robert Kennicott, a veteran explorer of Alaska and the Canadian North. Three years earlier, he had led an ambitious scientific expedition into the region, a journey of discovery supported jointly by the Smithsonian Institution and the Hudson's Bay Company. By March 1866, he had reached Fort St. Michael and made his way up the Yukon River into the Alaskan interior. The expedition stalled in May when Kennicott suddenly died — he was just thirty-one years old.

Major Abaza together with Kennedy had successfully mustered a willing group in Petropavlovsk and had set off, up through the interior of the Kamchatka peninsula for the rendezvous with Bulkley.

With the exploratory parties hard at work, all the company's vessels returned to San Francisco and the preparatory work of the second phase got under way. It took all of seven months to get fully organized. By May 1866, the fleet was fully loaded with crew and equipment and it made ready to sail to the various points where the construction would begin.

An immense amount of equipment had been loaded onto the vessels. To give an idea of the scale of things, the *Nighting* bore 432 tons of coal, 356 packages of telegraphic instruments, and hundreds of rolls of wire, in addition to copious quantities of food, tents, bedding, clothing and other provisions. Along with other items, two of the smaller ships carried between them twelve hundred miles of wire, thirty-five thousand insulators, and portable transmission stations.

Engineers, telegraph technicians, and administrators embarked on these same vessels. The bulk of the work crews, it was planned, would come from locally hired Natives, and by the time it was all over, more than eight hundred Natives had become involved, working side by side with a hundred Americans and Russians. The RATC was one of the world's largest binational joint ventures at that time.

All four exploratory parties suffered hardships and overcame severe challenges. The groups that penetrated British Columbia and Yukon perhaps fared a little better than the other two. Bulkley's force that landed at the Bering Strait saw the worst of it. We shall focus here on the Abaza-Kennan group that landed on Kamchatka. It was this group, after all, that penetrated most deeply the desolate regions of eastern Siberia, spending a full two years living among the indigenous tribes and some Russians. Kamchatka "is little known to the reading world," Kennan writes, "and its nomadic inhabitants have rarely been visited by civilized man. Only a few adventurous traders and fur traders have ever penetrated its almost unbroken solitudes.... The country holds out to the ordinary traveler no inducement commensurate with the risk and hardship which its exploration involves."

Ten days at sea shattered all the romantic illusions Kennan had of life on the ocean waves. "My ideas of sea life had been derived principally from glowing descriptions of poetical sunsets of 'summer isles of Eden, lying in dark purple spheres of sea,' and of the 'moonlight nights on lonely waters.'" There was none of that — it was all fog, storm, seasickness, and miserable weather. "The weather has been cold, damp, foggy with light headwinds and a heavy swell. We have been confined closely to our seven by nine after cabin and its stifling atmosphere, redolent of bilge water, lamp oil, and tobacco smoke has had a most depressing influence upon our spirits."

On August 19, after six weeks at sea, the *Olga* at last arrived at Petropavlovsk, capital of Kamchatka and Russia's easternmost settlement. The village was "a little cluster of red-roofed and bark-thatched log houses." Kennan continues:

> [Also visible were] a Greek church of curious architecture with a green painted dome; a strip of beach, a half-ruined wharf, two whale-boats and the dismantled wreck of a half-sunken vessel. High green hills swept in a great semicircle of foliage around the little village ... dark-haired natives and Russian peasants in blue shirts and leather pants gathered in a group at the landing. Seventy-five or a hundred half-wild dogs broke out suddenly into a terrific chorus of howls in honor of our arrival.[5]

The settlement numbered some three hundred Russians and Natives in addition to the tiny handful of German and American traders.

On the edge of a cliff overlooking the harbour there remained traces of the fortifications that had been erected a decade earlier. The horrors of the Crimean War did not leave the Pacific shores unscathed. In August 1854, a British squadron of five ships commanded by Rear Admiral David Price attacked Petropavlovsk. A small landing party managed to get ashore, but the fifty-six guns of the Russian ships *Aurora* and *Dvina* together with the shore batteries, repulsed the invaders. Price committed suicide and the attack was suspended. "No traces now remain of the bloody struggle that took place upon the brink of this precipice," writes our diarist. "Moss covers with its green carpet the ground which was torn up in the death grapple, and the nodding bluebell, as it bends to the fresh sea breeze, tells no story of the last desperate rally, the hand-to-hand conflict and the shrieks of the overpowered as they were thrown from the Russian bayonets upon the rocky beach a few hundred feet below."

"Our reception at Petropavlovsk by both Russians and Americans was most cordial and enthusiastic and the first three or four days were spent in one continuous round of visits and dinners." Within eight brief days, however, the *Olga* once more put to sea, this time bearing only two of the party: Mahood and Bush. They were to be landed at the mouth of the Amur where they would establish a base of operations and explore the inland mountainous region west of the Okhotsk. In the meanwhile, Abaza and Kennan would travel northward with a party of Natives, through the length of the Kamchatka peninsula to a point midway between the Bering Strait and the Okhotsk. Here, the two men would part company, one moving southwest to meet Mahood and Bush and the other northeast to meet Bulkley.

These arrangements really meant that Abaza and Kennan would each eventually find himself alone in the Siberian wilds for the duration of the winter, Native crew members aside. Of significant concern was Kennan's inability to communicate in Russian — without a command of the language, how effective would his work be? But fortune favoured the explorers. A certain James Dodd appeared on the scene, an American fur trader who had lived in Petropavlovsk for seven years. Not only was he fluent in Russian, but he was also familiar with the ways of the Kamchatka Natives and knew something of its climate and topography.

Most importantly, Dodd was eager to join the expedition:

With this addition our whole force numbered five men and was to be divided into three parties; one for the west coast of the Okhotsk Sea, one for the north coast and one for the country between the Sea and the Arctic Circle. All minor details such as transportation and subsistence were left to the direction of the several parties. We were to live on the country, travel with the natives and avail ourselves of any means of transportation and subsistence which the country afforded.[6]

Kennan then adds drolly, "It was no pleasure excursion upon which we were about to enter."

On September 4, Abaza, Kennan, and Dodd set out on their journey. The days previous had been given over to hectic preparations.

Boxes covered with sealskins and intended to be hung from pack horses were prepared for the transportation of our stores. Tents, bear skins, and camp equipage were bought and packed away in ingeniously contrived bundles; and everything which native experience could suggest for lessening the hardships for two months' journey. Horses were then ordered from all the adjacent villages and a special courier was sent throughout the peninsula by the route which we intended to follow, with orders to appraise the natives everywhere of our coming, and to direct them to remain at home with all their horses until our party should pass.[7]

Kamchatka is a peninsula that juts south from the easternmost tip of Siberia. It divides the Sea of Okhotsk from the Bering Sea, and from end to end it spans over seven hundred miles. Its northern extremity nearly touches the Arctic Circle. A massive chain of active volcanic mountains divides the peninsula longitudinally. Because of the underground heat, the climate is comparatively mild and the vegetation is luxuriant, near tropical. At the peninsula's northern extremity, where it blends into the Arctic's tundra, the climate changes accordingly.

In Kennan's time, an estimated five thousand inhabitants populated the peninsula. They were mostly Kamchadals, Natives who lived in small, scattered villages at the mouths of rivers. To the far north were the wandering Koraks, a wild, independently minded people who subsisted on their vast herds of domesticated reindeer. In addition to the Natives, there was a scattering of Russians, mostly fur traders and the occasional Orthodox missionary.

The peninsula's widely separated settlements were connected by narrow trails or by rivers. Transport was by packhorses and dog sledges or by boat and canoe:

> Through this wild, sparsely populated region, we proposed to travel by hiring the natives along our route to carry us with their horses from one settlement to another until we should reach the territory of the wandering Koraks. North of that point we could not depend upon any regular means of transportation, but would be obliged to trust to "luck" and the tender mercies of the Arctic nomads.[8]

The three men faced a daunting passage of no small difficulty. The unresolved mystery is *why* were they there? What was their purpose? The telegraph line was projected to run southwest from the Bering Strait along the Pacific coastline. Since Kamchatka jutted out to sea into a dead end, it could have easily have been bypassed. There was no earthly reason to have expended time and resources on the Kamchatka venture. But be that as it may, Bulkley's plans provided for such an exploration, and that was that. It took all of two months for Abaza's group to reach Kamchatka's northernmost latitudes, where the projected line would pass.

The start of the journey was inauspicious. The whaleboat engaged to carry them on the first leg nearly capsized before hitting a sandbar not far from Petropavlovsk. On the previous night, there had been much celebratory drinking in the town and "copious libations were poured out to the titular saint of Kamchatkan explorers." The Kamchadal crew "wholly unaccustomed to such reckless drinking were reduced to a comical state of happy imbecility, in which they sang gurgling Kamchadal songs, blessed the Americans, and fell overboard alternately, without contributing in any marked degree to the successful navigation of our heavy whaleboat." Eventually, all was brought under control with the stalwart Natives proving to be no worse for wear, despite throbbing headaches.

The days following went smoothly, with everyone marvelling at the startling beauty of the unfolding countryside. Day upon day was full of warmth and Indian summer glory — "a peculiar stillness and Sabbath-like quiet seemed to pervade all nature." Snow-covered peaks, spectacular sunsets, lush vegetation, melodious trumpets of swans, and cries of geese. "Shreds of fleecy mist here and there floated up the mountainsides and vanished like the spirits of the night dews rising from earth to heaven in bright resurrection." Isolated Kamchadal villages came and went — the roofs of low log cabins made of coarse grass or strips of tamarack bark. The window frames were "covered with irregular patchwork of translucent fish bladders, sewn together with thread made of dried and pounded sinews of reindeer."

Then they transferred from whaleboat to horseback. As the party progressed north, Natives invariably greeted them with warmth and enthusiasm. Kamchadal hospitality was overwhelming. Excellent suppers of cold roast duck and broiled reindeer tongues were offered together with black bread and butter. Blueberries and cream and wild rose petals crushed with white sugar. "We had come to Kamchatka with minds and mouths heroically made up for an unvarying diet of blubber, tallow candles and train oil. Imagine our surprise and delight at being treated instead to such Sybaritic luxuries ... preserved rose petals, a celestial ambrosia."

As they progressed north moving inland, idyllic nature soured. They entered mosquito country, where the "relentless persecution became almost unendurable." The weather turned — it was becoming colder, heavy clouds and overcast with colourful sunsets, a rarity. Settlements became few and far between and the daily distances required long, fatiguing hours in the saddle. One day "we had made sixty miles since daybreak; but the road had been good." After another day's ride, "every separate bone and tendon in my body asserted its individual existence by a distinct and independent ache, and my back in twenty minutes was as inflexible as an iron ramrod."

By the time the onerous transversal of Kamchatka was completed, they had travelled in whaleboats, rafts, canoes, dog sleds, reindeer sledges, and snowshoes.

Two months after departing from Petropavlovsk, they at last reached the point where of the would-be path most directly connected the Bering Strait with Nikolaevsk. En route adventures of every sort were had. An earthquake, a near-disastrous encounter with a colossal bear, a land-slide in which the packhorses were carried away topsy-turvy down an embankment, and a serious bout of an undiagnosed illness suffered by Major Abaza.

The first snow fell in late September and it never left them. "We were met by a hurricane of wind from the northeast, which swept blinding, suffocating clouds of snow down the slopes of our faces until earth and sky seemed mingled and lost in a great white whirling mist."

Autumn advanced and it was all snow and intense cold. Daily temperatures hovered around minus twenty-five degrees. Everything seemed forever covered by clouds of frozen mist:

> Our eyelids froze together while we were drinking tea; our soup, taken hot from the kettle, froze in our tin plates before we could possibly finish eating it; and the breasts of our fur coats were covered with a white rime, while we sat only a few feet from a huge blazing campfire. Tin plates, knives, spoons burned the bare hand when touched almost exactly as if they were red hot; and water, spilled on a little piece of board only fourteen inches from the fire, froze solid in less than two minutes.... The greatest cause of suffering in Siberia is wind.[9]

The passage was made by dogsled; fifteen were required to transport the party. On the November 25, they arrived at Gizhiga, a remote settle-ment centred about an Orthodox church:

No one who has not traveled for three long months through wilderness like Kamchatka, camped out in storms among desolate mountains, slept for three weeks in the smoky tents and yet smokier and dirtier yourts of the Koraks, and lived together like a perfect savage or barbarian — no one who has not experienced this can possibly understand with what joyful hearts we welcomed that red church steeple and the civilization of which it was a sign.[10]

The party drew up to a charming house in the best Russian style. With its double-glazed glass windows, it stood incongruously amid the low, primitive cabins of the Natives with their tamarack-bark roofs and windows of translucent fish bladders — the home of the *ispravnik,* Gizhiga's administrator.

The new arrivals were greeted warmly. The official wished to know everything at once: "When did you leave Petropavlovsk? Are you just from America? I was expecting you … sent a Cossack to look for you. Did you meet him? How did you cross the tundra — with the Koraks? What news of St. Petersburg? You must come over and dine with me. How long will you stay in town?" The animated *ispravnik* (district police chief) had had no communication with Russia for nearly a year and his delight with receiving such rare guests was abundantly obvious. The exhausted trio cheerfully accepted the invitation to dine with him … and to soak in a hot bath beforehand:

For almost a month we had slept every night on the ground or the snow; had never seen a chair, table, a bed or a mirror; had never been undressed night or day; and had washed our faces only three or four times in an equal number of weeks! We were grimy and smoky from climbing up and down Korak chimneys; our hair was long and matted around our ears; the skin had peeled from our noses and cheekbones where they had been frozen; our coats and pantaloons were gray with

reindeer hairs from our fur *kookhlankas* [a type of parka]
and we presented, generally, as wild and neglected an
appearance as men could present.[11]

That evening, "in all the splendor of blue coats, brass buttons and
shoulder straps with shaven faces, starched shirts and polished leather
boots, the 'First Siberian Exploring Party'" revelled in delight with the
"luxuries of a civilized home," and readily gave themselves over to the generous banquet laid before them. After copious vodka, smoked fish, and
caviar, "we took seats at the table and spent an hour and a half in getting
through the numerous courses of cabbage soup, salmon pie, venison cut-
lets, game, small meat pies, pudding and pastry." A happy time was had,
with the *ispravnik* eagerly devouring every tidbit of news the travellers were
able to share. He was delighted to learn of the conclusion of the U.S. Civil
War, and equally distressed at the news of Lincoln's assassination. Mostly,
however, he was interested in gossip of the imperial court — which, one
might suspect, the guests were not in the best position to deliver.

The table cleared, delicate flutes were set before the company, and to
the travellers' astonishment, a bottle of Veuve Clicquot champagne was
brought out. Imagine the incredible scene at this gathering: a foursome
— two Russians and two Americans — in the frozen wilds of remot-
est Siberia. A couple of hours earlier, the explorers had come in from
the minus-thirty-degree cold, dirty and unkempt, having suffered every
sort of privation. Now they were revelling in the warm confines of the
ispravnik's quarters and sipping vintage champagne. From the verdant
vineyards of Reims, the bottle had journeyed halfway around the world
to the edge of the Arctic Circle — and, all this was happening in 1865.

Ten days were spent in Gizhiga, most of it in intelligence gathering and in fine-tuning plans for the next leg of their exploration. The
focus had at last turned to the mechanics of the cherished telegraph line.
They had spent over two months journeying through Kamchatka and
no mention had yet been made of the telegraph line. It was as though
the Russian–American Telegraph Company had no purpose in the long
weeks spent on the peninsula — and, indeed, it had not. At last the real
work would begin.

The proposed line stretching from the Bering Strait to the Amur River had to pass through the villages of Gizhiga and Okhotsk. The two settlements neatly divided the entire distance into three equal sections. Mahood and Bush had landed at Nikolaevsk on the Amur and were making their way northeast toward Okhotsk. On the opposite end, Colonel Bulkley had arrived at the Anadyr River and was moving southwest in the direction of Gizhiga, toward Anadyrsk. The segment that remained to be covered was the Okhotsk-Anadyrsk section.

The decision was now taken by Major Abaza that he would set out on his own to the southwest to chart the section from Gizhiga to Okhotsk, a journey of approximately one month. The route would take him through rugged mountainous country where ample forests would provide telegraph poles. In the meanwhile, Kennan and Dodd would head northeast from Gizhiga to Anadyrsk to meet up with Colonel Bulkley. This four-hundred-mile passage would be mostly through desolate, uninhabited tundra that was void of the timber required for telegraph poles. It was estimated that the completion of this journey would require from twenty to thirty days, depending on the weather. If all went well, Abaza would successfully hook up with Mahood/Bush and Kennan/Dodd would meet Bulkley, thus completing the entire Russian connection. "I realized for the first time," Kennan now naively admitted, "the magnitude of the task that the Russo–American Telegraph Company had undertaken. We were 'in it,' however, and our first duty was obviously to go through the country ... and find out what facilities, if any, it afforded for the construction of our line."

Preparations for the passage were well thought out:

> The provisions we had brought from Petropavlovsk had all been used up with the exception of some tea, sugar and a few cans of preserved beef. But we obtained at Gizhiga some 120 pounds of black rye bread, four or five frozen reindeer, some salt and an abundant supply of *yookala* or dried fish. These with some tea and sugar and a few cakes of frozen milk, made up our store of provisions. We provided ourselves also with some 300

pounds of Circassian leaf tobacco to be used instead of
money; divided equally our little store of beads, pipes,
knives and trading goods. We purchased new suits of
furs throughout and made every preparation for three
or four months of camp-life in an Arctic climate.[12]

At noon on December 13, the two Americans departed Gizhiga on
the start of their odyssey. "It was just mid-day, but the sun although at its
greatest altitude, glowed like a red ball of fire low down in the southern
horizon, and a peculiar gloomy twilight hung over the wintry landscape."
One day passed like the other and with the few exceptional overnights in
isolated yourts, the group lived quite literally under the stars:

> White, cold and silent, it [the steppe] lay before us like a
> vast frozen ocean lighted up faintly by the slender cres-
> cent of the waning moon in the east, and the weird blue
> streamers of the Aurora, which went racing swiftly back
> and forth along the northern horizon. Even when the
> sun rose, huge and fiery, in a haze of frozen moisture
> at the south, it did not seem to infuse any warmth or
> life into the bleak, wintry landscape. It only drowned
> in a dull red glare the blue tremulous streamers of the
> Aurora, and the radiance of the moon and stars tinged
> the snow with a faint color like a stormy sunset, and
> lighted up a splendid image in the northwest which
> startled us with its solemn mockery of familiar scenes.[13]

The thermometer showed noonday temperatures hovering at –35°F and
–38°F at sunset. One day, it recorded –53°F.

The days passed and a brief stopover was made in the tiny settlement
of Shestakova before the journey continued:

> The bleak and dreary landscape could have been
> described in two words — snow and sky. I had come to
> Siberia with full confidence in the ultimate success of

the Russo-American Telegraph line, but as I penetrated deeper and deeper into the country and saw the utter desolation I grew less sanguine. Since leaving Gizhiga we had traveled nearly 200 miles, had found only four places where we could obtain poles, and had passed only three settlements.[14]

On January 5, they reached the Arctic Circle at the tiny settlement of Markova, where a record low to that time had been recorded of minus sixty-eight degrees.

On February 18, the two Americans reached Anadyrsk, which, despite the climate, "is as pleasant a place to live as are nine-tenths of the Russian settlements in northeastern Siberia, and we enjoyed the novelty of our life there in the winter of 1866 as much as we had enjoyed any part of our Siberian experience."

Ten days later, Kennan and Dodd finally met up with two of the exploratory party that had landed two weeks earlier on the Bering Strait as part of Bulkley's group. The colonel at the last moment did not join the expedition, putting it under the joint leadership of two of his colleagues. "For sixty-four days they had been living with the wandering Chukchi, and making their way slowly and by a circuitous route toward Anadyrsk.... They had experienced great hardships, had lived upon reindeer's entrails and tallow for weeks at a time. They had been alive almost constantly with vermin, had spent the greater part of two long months in a smoky Chukchi hut." When Kennan and Dodd met up with the haggard pair, "the sum total of their baggage was a quart bottle of whiskey wrapped in an American flag! As soon as we were all together, we raised the flag on a pole over our little log house, made a whiskey punch out of the liquor ... and drank it [in honour of the couple] who carried the Stars and Stripes through the wildest, least known region on the face of the globe."

In late March word Kennan got word that the seemingly impossible had been achieved eight months earlier — an underwater cable had been successfully laid across the Atlantic, and it was operational. The entire Pacific project was cancelled and the activities of the Russian–American Telegraph Company were ordered halted. All personnel were recalled home. The disappointed Kennan and Dodd remained behind to dispose of the company's stock of food, clothing, and other easily disposable goods. Telegraphic equipment, wire, insulators, and portable stations were returned home.

Kennan concludes his account somewhat bitterly:

> We had explored and located the whole route of the line from the Amur River to the Bering Strait. We had prepared altogether about 15,000 telegraph poles, built between forty and fifty station houses and magazines, cut nearly fifty miles of road through the forests.... The success of the Atlantic cable, however, rendered all our preparations unavailing.

Work completed, Kennan journeyed across Siberia to St. Petersburg. En route, he made notes of his experiences and impressions of all he saw — material for a future book on the condition of the country. "On January 3 [1867], after ten weeks of incessant travel we caught sight of the glittering domes of Moscow, and forever closed the book of our Siberian experience."

Today, along isolated Alaskan and Siberian shores, one can still find the occasional telegraph pole standing forlornly — a moving reminder of an aborted attempt to physically knit Russia and America together.

CHAPTER 15

SEWARD'S FOLLY

On the evening of March 29, 1867, an exhilarated Ambassador Eduard de Stoeckl paid a surprising call at the Washington, D.C., home of Secretary of State William Seward. He apologized to the family for having interrupted their quality time together, and particularly for disturbing their enthusiastic game of whist. A coded message had just been received via the recently laid trans-Atlantic telegraph cable. Its contents were simply too exciting to delay sharing until the morning. The tsar had at last consented to the sale of Alaska. For four arduous months, the two men had been meeting, discussing, and negotiating for precisely that outcome and now it had come to be.

De Stoeckl went on to suggest that he come to the state department in the morning to formalize the arrangement. But the excited Seward would have none of that — he wanted the deed done immediately. Poor Mrs. Seward. She surrendered her winning hand, the cards were put away, and with apologies the two men parted the house to gather their respective staffs. The assembled advisors worked hard into the night and by four o' clock in the morning, the treaty was on the desk of the secretary of state, ready for approval by Congress.

"At a strange midnight conference," one historian comments, "the two incredible international bedfellows, Russia and the United States, became close territorial neighbours. How close, no one was to realize until the dawn of the air age."

To this day, Americans and Russians continue to look upon the sale of Alaska with question. What on earth prompted the tsar to transfer to the

United States some six hundred thousand square miles of territory rich in furs, timber, fisheries, and mineral resources for a paltry sum — truly an unbelievable bargain price? Some view the sale as a dazzling example of Yankee ingenuity … a hoodwinking of naive Russians. But what's not appreciated is that Russia was motivated to sell Alaska more than the United States was wishing to buy it. At the start of negotiations, there was dismay in many corners of Washington, and when the talks became serious, that dismay turned into anger. One congressman bitterly summed up the feeling of others by declaring "that Alaska was created for *some* purpose I have little doubt. But our information is so limited that conjectures can assign *no* use to it, unless it is to demonstrate the folly which those in authority are capable of in the acquisition of useless territory." It was only through the energies of expansionist-minded Seward that the talks on the purchase of Alaska were revived in the months just before de Stoeckl's precipitous return to St. Petersburg.

William Henry Seward.

William H. Seward was admired for his powers of persuasion and his political talents — one of the country's brightest political lights. A one-time governor of New York, Seward won a seat in the U.S. Senate, a position held for twelve years. In 1860, he vied for the leadership of the Republican Party in anticipation of the forthcoming presidential election. The convention rejected him, as his stance against slavery was too liberal. Abraham Lincoln became the Republican standard-bearer and was duly elected president.

On assuming the presidency, Lincoln offered Seward, and Seward accepted, the primary cabinet position of secretary of state, a post he held for four years, in the process becoming one of the president's most trusted advisors. On April 14, 1865, Lincoln was assassinated by John Wilkes Booth at Ford's Theatre. Seward later narrowly escaped the same fate at the hands of Booth's fellow conspirators. Citing health reasons, he retired from cabinet in the early months of President Andrew Johnson's time in office.

Years before becoming secretary of state, Seward had openly argued that it was American destiny "to roll its restless waves to the icy barriers of the North, and to encounter oriental civilization on the Pacific." In his campaign speeches, he pressed unreservedly not only for Alaska's annexation but for a political union with Canada. In St. Paul he declared, "I see the Russians establishing seaports and towns and fortifications on the verge of this continent, and I can say, 'Go build your outposts all along the coast, even to the Atlantic Ocean. They will yet become the outposts of my own country.'" Little wonder that Seward was called "the greatest of American expansionists." So it's not surprising, then, that when Stoeckl unexpectedly appeared at his home that March evening bearing news of the tsar's decision, he wished instantly to act on it.

Five months prior to de Stoeckl's visit to the Sewards, the ambassador had returned to St. Petersburg after a twelve-year stint in Washington. No sooner had he reached home than Grand Duke Konstantin, Tsar Alexander II's younger brother, persuaded him to go back to America in order to negotiate a possible sale of Alaska.

Konstantin was keenly minded, ambitious, and attuned to geopolitics, above all issues affecting the Pacific. In matters of foreign policy, his voice was heard, particularly on issues pertaining to the navy. He was anxious to have the country's fleet increase in size and become more visible in the Far East. Vladivostok, Russia's major naval base on the Pacific, he argued, had to be fortified and made stronger. The complexities of the Chinese-Korean-Japanese nexus were simply too threatening.

Talk in St. Petersburg of Alaska's sale predated the Crimean War. At the time that Seward spoke of American waves rolling north in 1846, Nikolai Nikolaievich Muraviev, governor general of Eastern Siberia, wrote, "The United States are bound to spread over the whole of North America.... Sooner or later we shall have to surrender our North American possessions." As the Crimean War unfolded, it was feared that Alaska might become threatened by Britain. Might its fleet invade? Such a threat, however, was partially obviated by the friendly agreement of neutrality concluded by the Russian-American Company and the Hudson's Bay Company.

Following the war, St. Petersburg renewed debate on the territory's sale as a means of defraying the cost of accumulated war debt. Konstantin favoured such a course for financial reasons as well as strategic ones. "Russia must endeavor as far as possible to become stronger in the center, in those fundamentally Russian regions which constitute her main power in population and in faith, and Russia must develop the strength of this center in order to be able to hold those extremities which bring her real benefit."

He penned a long letter to Minister of Foreign Affairs Alexander Gorchakov in which he argued forcefully for the sale of Alaska. "Our interests are on the Asiatic coast, and that is where we must direct our energy. There we are in our own territory and have the possibility of exploiting a large, rich region.... We must not lose the opportunity to develop on this ocean a preeminent standing worthy of Russia."

By 1860, the state of the Russian-American Company was in lamentable decline. Trade, particularly in furs, was no longer its principal activity, and the merchants for whom the firm was originally set up were barely in evidence. It had evolved into a sort of mini-state that drained millions from the imperial treasury, offering little in return. A couple of decades earlier, there was uncertainty about whether to grant the company a second renewal of its twenty-year charter. It was recognized that the enterprise had evolved into "a certain form of governmental power, and its privilege includes not only a right but also an obligation." Now with a third renewal coming up, Konstantin mustered all his forces to persuade the government to close down the company and withdraw completely from the North American continent. Alaska was a drain on Russia's resources, he contended, and the country could ill afford maintaining it at the expense of more strategically pressing Pacific objectives.

By 1866, the grand duke's concerns appeared to have materialized, and the arguments for Alaska's sale became compelling. It seemed prudent to "gracefully yield" the territory, which would encourage the United States into even closer alliance. Furthermore, the arrangement would provide Russia with a sympathetic guardian to its Siberian back door.

The sale of Alaska came about when it did for varied reasons. It was not exclusively on account of Seward's ambitions or through Konstantin's tactical arguments. By 1867, the world market for furs had substantially declined. The Alaskan coastline had been hunted out, as it were — stocks of fur-bearing animals had shrunk alarmingly. The Crimean War caused the Russian-American Company to develop a dependency on the United States for supply and shipping needs — an unfavourable balance had been created, much to St. Petersburg's chagrin. To add to the company's woes, the issue of defence became real. Over the decades, not much thought had been given to the matter. After all, who would the Russians be guarding against? Relations with the Hudson's Bay Company had been amicable, and they enjoyed a businesslike and neighbourly relationship with the Americans.

By the middle of the century, however, global perspectives had changed, and if the Russians were to continue as they had in the past, defence expenditures would have to be incurred. British Columbia had grown in strategic importance, territorially wedged in between two unfriendly powers. Three nations actively shared the same North American Pacific coastline. Sooner or later, a territorial conflict between them seemed inevitable — either with Britain or with a burgeoning United States to the south.

For his part, de Stoeckl argued that Alaska should be surrendered to the United States for "political expediency." In his long years in

Washington, the minister had developed a profound affection for America, and he was determined that a positive, balanced relationship between the two countries be maintained. Alaska was "a breeder of trouble"; and whatever the pros and cons of a sale, Russia's distant possession was destined to drive a wedge between the two countries. The manifest destiny of the United States, de Stoeckl urged, was to control North America. On the eve of his departure for St. Petersburg in 1866, he wrote to Gorchakov, "Our role is to dominate the East. The one of the United States is to exercise an absolute control over the American continent. In the march of progress that destiny has bequeathed to Russia and the United States, the two nations will advance without their paths being blocked, without exciting jealousies, without their interests conflicting."

American expansionism was indeed a fear for Russia. Over the decades, the Russians had observed with interest the surging population growth in the western United States. "Go west, young man, go west," Horace Greeley had urged young people in the 1840s.[1] And they did, spreading throughout the far-flung regions. By the late 1860s, such divergent territories as California, Oregon, Texas, and Nevada had achieved statehood. San Francisco sported a thriving metropolis of nearly one hundred and fifty thousand. (Fort Ross had been abandoned by Russians some twenty years earlier and it was now in the hands of a private developer.) The population growth was spectacular, and St. Petersburg justly wondered how it might all end.

As for Stoeckl, it's clear that he foresaw an aggressive American push into the northwest, one that someday might conceivably involve Alaska. What then of Russia? Evidencing the legitimacy of such concern was the plight of the fifty thousand Mormons who had settled in what later became Utah. The relationship between the sect's members and those not belonging to it was one of sorrowful conflict. The Mormons rebelled against most governmental authority and agitated for greater independence — their own private space. Within all this, there was talk in their communities of a mass migration to British Columbia, or perhaps even to Alaska. If a large Mormon population moved to Alaska, de Stoeckl reasoned, it would quickly develop into the dominating influence which then would either have to be forcefully suppressed or permitted to expand. Either way, it was bad news. Apprehension of a Mormon migration was one thing. The gold strikes of 1858 in British Columbia drew some thirty thousand American prospectors to the fields. Down the line, might not the same thing happen in Alaska? By the late 1860s, the case for America's manifest destiny was clear to St. Petersburg. There was now a political expediency for the sale. Alaska *was* indeed "a breeder of trouble."

Russia was anxious to sell Alaska, but was the United States keen to buy? In those years, American enthusiasm for Alaska was negligible at best. It was considered by politicos to be a perfectly useless bit of territory, quite unnecessary for the already land-rich country. "A dreary waste of glaciers, icebergs, white bears and walrus fit only for Esquimaux," one said. As early as 1857, in President James Buchanan's time, de Stoeckl had put out feelers for the sale. Senator William Gwin of California initially rebuffed him, declaring that he had no interest in Alaska — it was simply too far away to be of any value to his state and to the country. Vocal lobbies in his state, however, and others in the Washington Territory later gave him pause to reflect. The rich fishery potential of the Alaska coast, it was argued, should not to be overlooked, and neither were the equally promising resources of inland furs.

"Even if you doubt the value of these possessions," declared Massachusetts senator Charles Sumner during the debate on the purchase, "the treaty is a sign of amity. It is a new expression of that *entente cordiale* between the two powers which is a phenomenon of history."

Gwin eventually came on side and indifferently proposed that $5 million be allocated for the purchase. President Johnson's Cabinet went along with the idea and the State Department was authorized to enter negotiations with Russia. St. Petersburg, of course, readily agreed to meet, but the Russians made it clear that Gwin's paltry figure was unworthy of consideration.

Russia was prepared to sell, and the United States now stood by to purchase — the two sides needed to settle the matter of price only. President Johnson, with Cabinet approval, authorized Seward to offer the proposed $5 million, which is what he did. (The figure, incidentally, matched the minimum amount de Stoeckl was authorized by St. Petersburg to accept.) In December 1866, Seward formally presented the American offer. It was clear to de Stoeckl that the secretary was not only enthusiastic about the deal, but was anxious to conclude it expeditiously. So the wily Russian diplomat decided to protract discussions, and there was meeting after meeting. Agreement was finally reached on the figure of $7 million — not without Seward's bitter complaint that he was exceeding all authorization.

But de Stoeckl, encouraged with the favourable outcome of bargaining, held out for even more. He now insisted that the Americans would need to add additional sums to the agreed-upon total to cover related expenses. Ostensibly, these included covering the debt of the Russian-American Company plus anticipated gold-exchange fees of London's banking houses. As we will see, there was more to this than met the eye.

"I consider the price too high as it is," countered Seward. "I have gone far beyond the wishes of my Government in order to prevent unnecessary bickering. But I will not for one moment entertain any suggestion of taking over the obligations incurred by a chartered company. And my Government will not clear the transaction in London. We had our bellyful of London in the late war." Yet more meetings and bargaining took place. The bottom-line figure finally agreed upon was $7,200,000. Alaska would then become American, "free and unencumbered by any reservations, privileges, franchises, grants, etc." That's the deal the two friends wrote into a treaty in the middle of that March night when the Sewards' game of whist was abruptly halted.

Regardless of de Stoeckl's success at the time, the purchase price for Alaska was a virtual giveaway. It cost the tsar twice that amount merely to operate the imperial navy for one year. A gift it was: American territory had expanded by 369,529,600 acres — at less than two cents an acre. (Sixty years later, the United States purchased from Denmark three Caribbean islands for $25 million at $249 per acre.)

Steward's anxiety to rush through the deal was based on his concern with the developments unfolding in Canada. For years, American economic pressure had been exerted on Upper Canada (Ontario), Lower Canada (Quebec), Nova Scotia, New Brunswick, and Prince Edward Island to join the United States and shed the British yoke. (The confederation forming Canada as we know it today came in 1867. Until then, those territories were separate colonies of Britain.) The staunch colonies not only rebuffed the United States, but they also acted to form a union of their own, free of the king's dictates. At the start of the Alaska negotiations, the Canadian territories had already begun to move in that direction.

American expectations of the colonies joining the United States were shattered. It was clear that the manifest destiny to reign over the entire continent was an elusive dream. Furthermore, with the formation of a federated Canada, it became more than likely that the lands of the Hudson's Bay Company and British Columbia would one day become part of the Dominion of Canada.

Seward understood that the dream of making Alaska part of a contiguous territory to the United States was unrealistic. He also appreciated that the country's developing mood did not favour territorial expansion, above all by purchase, especially in the hard times of Reconstruction. "The greatest of American expansionists," however, was in no mood to forsake the acquisition of the Alaskan territory. Such would be an indelible mark on the nation's development and much to his credit. If the territory was to be had, it should happen immediately — before anti-expansionist sentiment solidified, before the full impact of Canada's Confederation was realized, and particularly before Congress adjourned.

Sent to the Senate, the bill was passed thanks largely to the guiding efforts of Senator Sumner. Resistance was encountered and complaints were had that the country was taking on a "worthless territory" and acquiring Russia's problems. How could a non-contiguous land mass be effectively defended when it was accessible only by sea, particularly with Britain "ruling the waves"? The initial vote in the Senate was thirty-two for and twelve opposed — one vote more than the two-thirds required for the treaty's passage. Upon further debate and a passionate plea by Sumner for unanimity, a second vote was taken and this time the vote was forty-seven to two.

In all, it took the Senate a mere four days to pass the Alaska Bill, which was then sent to the House of Representatives. And here it bogged down, languishing for a staggering fifteen months. First, a convention of the Republican Party preoccupied members of Congress. But the main reason for the inordinate dawdling was the impeachment proceedings against President Johnson — he ultimately avoided impeachment by a single vote. Seward made no bones about expressing his exasperation with the delays being encountered in the final step of the bill's passage. But so confident was he of a favourable outcome, that he authorized the go-ahead with the territory's formal takeover.

On October 18, 1867, the territory's transfer took place in New Archangel (renamed Sitka). The Russian and American commissioners charged with the responsibility of overseeing the actual takeover — Captain Alexei Peschchurov and Brigadier-General Lovell Rousseau — had sailed together from New York on board the U.S.S. *Ossippee* on the lengthy passage around Cape Horn. The territory's future governor, Jefferson Davis (no relation to the old Confederate leader), sailed from San Francisco, also on board a warship, accompanied by a force of 250 marines and his young family — two gunboats with baggage and supplies had preceded them. All four ships were now riding at anchor in the town's tranquil harbour.

At three o'clock on that afternoon, amid the beat of drums, 250 Russian soldiers and sailors marched onto the parade ground in front of Baranov's residence. They were brought to smart halt at the base of a ninety-foot flagstaff from which flew the imperial colours. More drum rolls, and the American contingent came onto the square to assume its assigned position. Morning mist had dissipated and sunshine now warmed the gathering — all appeared in order. But then, at the critical moment when the Russian flag was to be brought down, a severe gust of wind whipped it about the staff. The harder the men sought to free the banner, the more tightly it became entangled, as though it was resisting being removed. So badly was it ensnared that a seaman had to be sent aloft in a bosun's chair to free it. As he did so, the flag slipped out of his hands and fluttered down on the bayoneted assembly below. With this, Princess Maksutova, wife of the Russian governor, "collapsed in a faint," thus offering an unmistakeably anti-climactic moment.

The guns of the *Ossippe* and the fort in turn fired salutes, however, and with further drum rolls the American flag was solemnly raised. "We now stood on American territory," recorded one witness.

All the while, the unratified Alaska Bill continued to languish in the House of Representatives. When debate was finally had, one member of Congress blithely suggested that Russia be given the money and be permitted to retain the territory. But at last, on July 14, 1868, nine months *after* the New Archangel handover ceremony, the bill was given assent and the president signed it.

Congress had been confronted with a *fait accompli*. "Seward's Folly" was approved by the House not without skulduggery. Records show that of the agreed price, only $7,035,000 was actually sent abroad. The remaining $165,000 was deposited in Riggs Bank, in de Stoeckl's name. Why? Because de Stoeckl's lobbyist, R.J. Walker, pressured the minister "to manipulate some members" of Congress and the press. Simply put, the unaccounted funds went to paying off a number of leading members of Congress and editors whose support was deemed necessary to assure the bill's passage — sums ranging from ten thousand to $30,000. The funds came from the additional $200,000 de Stoeckl had persuaded Seward at the last moment to tack onto the agreed $7 million price tag. (One wonders how it was that the secretary readily consented to tack on an additional $200,000 *after* a deal had been concluded.)

President Johnson records in his own handwriting a discussion with Seward. One sunny autumn afternoon, the two travelled together into the Maryland countryside for a leisurely outing. "We drove out into a shady grove of oak trees. While there taking refreshments, in the current of conversation on various subjects, the Secretary asked the question if it had ever occurred to me how few members there were in Congress whose actions were entirely above and beyond pecuniary influence." Johnson replied that there were probably more than he ever supposed. Seward then went on to reveal that during the time the House was deadlocked over the Alaska Bill, a number of parties had been paid to help expedite the matter — members of Congress, journalists, and others. "There was no chance of appropriation passing the House of Reps without certain influence being brought to bear in its favor." Seward went on to tell how de Stoeckl had informed him that he was accosted by John W. Forney, editor of the *Chronicle*, who "stated that he needed $30,000; that he had lost $40,000, by a faithless friend, and that he wanted the $30,000 in gold." The sum was paid and the prominent newspaper threw its support behind the bill.

"He [Seward] also stated that $20,000 was paid to R.J. Walker and F.P. Stanton for their services; N.P. Banks, chairman of the committee on foreign relations, $8,000 and that the incorruptible Thaddeus Stevens [the former secretary of the Treasury turned lobbyist for the Russians] received as his 'sop' the moderate sum of $10,000. All these sums were paid by the Russian minister directly and indirectly to the respective parties." Johnson returned to the city so shaken by Seward's revelations that he felt obliged to record the afternoon's exchanges in a memorandum, which came to light only after he died.

The deal concluded, de Stoeckl clamoured to return to Russia. "I urgently need a rest," he complained to Gorchakov. "Do not tell me to stay here in Washington because there is no other post to give me. Give me a chance to breathe for a while an atmosphere purer than that of Washington — and after that do whatever you wish with me."

The bribes he had distributed certainly did little to better the fetid atmosphere of which he now complained. The ambassador did return home and was greeted cordially by the tsar, who was delighted with the outcome of things. He ordered that de Stoeckl be given a reward of twenty-five thousand rubles (approximately $17,000) for exceptional service to the country. De Stoeckl received the sum with displeasure. It was a stingy reward, he thought, considering that he had gained for Russia 30 percent more than the authorized minimal figure, and that he had squeezed out an additional $200,000 for expenses.

The deal seemed to satisfy all parties. Russia had liquidated a financial and strategic headache, and the United States acquired a promising territory at a bargain price. The two who drove the sale, Seward and de Stoeckl, gained pages in history. Most significantly, the power triangle of Russia, Britain, and United States had been broken. With Russia departed from eastern Pacific shores and the British wedged in between its territories, America had now realized full ascendancy in that sector of the globe — certainly for the moment.

That this remarkable territory fell into American hands was due to the vision and persuasiveness of Secretary of State Seward, who in effect bullied the administration and Congress to push through the measure. (It's unfortunate, perhaps, that Seward is remembered only for the controversial Alaska purchase. Little is said of his brilliant leadership of American foreign policy during the Civil War.) A degree of credit for the move, however, might be given to George Kennan. Without the young man's colourful account of his work in Siberia, Seward might not have had the support he eventually received for the purchase.

CHAPTER 16

A FRACTURED FRIENDSHIP

With the Alaska deal completed, a much-relieved de Stoeckl returned home, once and for all. Recall that this perceptive and jovial diplomat succeeded the talented and likeable Alexander Bodisko as Russian minister to the United States. For thirty-one years, Washington had been well served by these two popular individuals, who did much to enhance harmonious ties between the two countries. But with de Stoeckl's departure from Washington, St. Petersburg now made a singularly unfortunate appointment by way of replacement: Konstantin Katacazy, a flamboyant and petulant Greek in the Russian diplomatic service.

Twenty years earlier, Katacazy had served as first secretary to the Russian legation in Washington and, therefore, when he returned to the capital, he felt himself quite at home. During that first tour of duty, he had become involved in a romantic scandal, the unhappy result of which was his sudden recall and an eventual assignment to Rio de Janeiro. During his tenure in Brazil, the diplomatic corps suffered news of an apparent kidnapping from within its ranks. The young wife of the King of Naples's representative had mysteriously disappeared without a trace. Her elderly and aristocratic husband, a Neapolitan prince, was beside himself with grief and worry, and for days there was no word of her. Some dogged work by the local police soon revealed, however, that the feared victim of crime was in fact comfortably ensconced in a romantic seaside cottage, happily living in Katacazy's embrace.

As one may imagine, the sensational turn of events proved to be the grossest of scandals, and St. Petersburg reacted to it by withdrawing the errant diplomat. He was reassigned to Washington, and that is where he found himself in October 1869 — together with his Neapolitan paramour, now his wife. Washington society greeted "Madame la Princesse" with an askance look. Invitations to social functions for the Katacazys were few and far between — the couple was ostracized. To sidestep problems of protocol, Russia's troubled representative took a house far from the city centre.

In surrendering his post to Katacazy, de Stoeckl left on his desk one important item of unfinished business: the Perkins claim, an affair that had been brewing for over a decade. In 1856, toward the end of the Crimean War, a certain Captain Benjamin Perkins had apparently agreed to supply Russia with five tons of gunpowder, and subsequently to provide thirty-five thousand muskets. In the case of the gunpowder, the Russians allegedly withdrew the order on the grounds that the explosive was no longer required. As for the guns, this order also was nullified inasmuch as the war had ended.

Unfortunately, no written records of the deals existed; both transactions were entered into without contract. The aggrieved Perkins persisted in his claim that recompense be made to the tune of $400,000. The Russians were equally adamant that in the absence of documentation, no deals had been concluded, and, furthermore, no goods had been received — no payment would be made.

The matter dragged on and on, and it continued to fester even after Perkins's death in 1860. During the Alaskan treaty negotiations, the issue lay suspended, although at one point certain members of Congress argued that the stated sum should be deducted from the purchase price (the claim had by then become an irritating political issue). After the signing of the Alaska treaty, the claimant's heirs took up the case with renewed vigour. To spearhead the work, they engaged a powerful coalition of influential Washington lawyers and lobbyists, including two of the first lady's brothers, one a lawyer and the other a judge. In time, it all filtered to the top and President Ulysses Grant instructed Secretary of State Hamilton Fish to pursue the matter.

Little purpose would be served here to detail all of the sordid events that followed, not only with respect to the Perkins claim but also about other minor issues. Suffice to say that Katacazy and Washington were at odds with one another, and they became immersed in a morass of bitter accusation and character assassination. As one journalist observed, the behaviour they displayed was "most unwise, impolitic and indecorous." This unseemly time was rife with bribes, forgeries, leaked documents, and slander. A scurrilous article, for example, appeared in the *Cincinnati Inquirer* under a pseudonym, in which President Grant was accused of harbouring a secret bias toward Britain, an allegation with severely harmful political repercussions. Fish accused Katacazy of authoring the piece, which the controversial Russian denied in an intemperate, undiplomatic letter.

Subsequently, a detective hired by the State Department to tail Katacazy reported that the minister was "a frequenter of common saloons and tippling shops," and given to profanity. This titillating goodie found its way into the press, much to the delight of Washington's gossip mill and to the fury of the Russian legation. More damaging, however, was the allegation that Katacazy had cheated his own government. He had acquired a parcel of land in downtown New York for the construction of a Russian Orthodox Church. The purchase price was $17,000, but it was charged that the minister had submitted falsified documentation to St. Petersburg claiming the cost as $20,000, and that the $3,000 difference he himself pocketed.

And so it went. Finally, with the president's blessing, Fish requested St. Petersburg to recall Katacazy. The minister had, he wrote in a formal note on June 16, 1871, "through the press and in conversation endeavored to give [the Perkins claim] undue importance and *to make it the cause of trouble between the governments and of annoyance.* He has made himself personally offensive in conversation, and by publications *abusive of the President* and it is for this cause that *his recall is asked.*"

It was early summer and for the balance of the season, exchanges on the request for recall flowed between St. Petersburg and Washington. Fish's demand was, in the words of Katacazy himself, "without precedent in the annals of diplomacy." The diplomat was beside himself, and so angry that he travelled to Grant's summer home on Long Island, and quite literally burst in unannounced. He railed that the whole business was "a triple intrigue" and he denounced the American move. The slow-boiling president, barely able to contain himself, heard him out saying little, and then furiously sent him on his way.

It was a matter of timing — the request for recall could not have come at more awkward moment. That early autumn, Grand Duke Alexis, Alexander II's third son, was due to arrive to American shores for an extended goodwill visit, an event to which both countries looked forward with enthusiasm. The tour was shaping up to be something of a state occasion, but now the diplomatic brouhaha threatened to scuttle the whole thing. After much soul searching, Fish recommended to Grant that Katacazy be allowed to remain at his post until the arrival of the distinguished visitor. "The course you recommend is no doubt right," replied the president, "but I feel very much like sending Mr. K. out of the country summarily.... No Minister of any pride of character would consent to remain in the Capital after such an interview as Mr. K. had with me [on Long Island]. How he is to be received now at any entertainment given the Prince I do not exactly see."[1] And this was the course that was followed.

On November 20, a small squadron of Russian ships sailed into New York's harbour, arriving a few weeks later than originally expected. It was led by the flagship *Svetlana*, and on board was His Imperial Highness Grand Duke Alexis Alexandrovich, a twenty-one-year-old lieutenant in the imperial navy. The pilot sent out to bring the vessel to its anchorage was severely disappointed to learn that the unassuming young officer in plain uniform stationed on duty near the wheelhouse was none other than the imperial personage himself. "Heck, if he ain't no different than other folks," he is said to have remarked, "... he ain't got a bodyguard and a special cabin and all that. What's he a Grand Duke for?" Once at anchor, a greeting party of high dignitaries came on board to welcome formally the distinguished visitor, but because of the foul weather, it was not until the following day that the Russians came ashore.

By early morning, the weather had cleared and amid playing bands and cheering throngs, Alexis stepped ashore, dressed in parade uniform complete with cocked hat, decorations, and sword. Escorted by marching bands and national guards, the procession moved its way up Broadway. As the carriages passed Trinity Church, its bells chimed out Russia's national anthem, "God Save the Tsar." Farther down the parade route, a huge sign stood starkly: "Grand Duke Alexis, son of a noble father, representative of the nation's cherished ally." Later that day, Alexis remarked at how taken he was by the warmth and enthusiasm of the thousands who lined the streets. The cheering crowd of republican-hearted Americans, he declared, was clear evidence of the country's penchant for monarchy. That day was to be one of relaxation — on the following morning, he was to travel to Baltimore and Washington. He would return to New York in due course.

Arriving in Washington, the imperial visitor was welcomed by the Russian legation. On the following day, he was received briefly by President Grant. The president appeared gruff and lacking in warmth, which was not altogether surprising given his ignorance of protocol and lack of interest in the matter. Deep down his anger at Katacazy continued to ferment.

The grand duke remained in the United States for three months, travelling across the country. By the time of his departure — embarking from Pensacola on February 23, 1872 — he had visited scores of American cities and toured sites of national interest. Earlier, the young man had received a cable from his father instructing him not to return home at the conclusion of the scheduled tour. He was now being ordered to continue the journey to Cuba and then to Asia — to Japan and China. The poor fellow raged in bitterness and frustration — it was clear to him what lay behind these unexpected instructions.

Before departing Russia, he had fallen passionately in love with the daughter of his mother's commoner lady-in-waiting and he declared his intention to marry her. Quite impossible that was — just out of the question. The tsar forbade such a match, and Alexis was now being ordered to extend his absence from St. Petersburg by continuing around the world. The imperial family no doubt reasoned that in time, heartfelt passion might fade. It was an emotionally worded cable that the grand duke received. Plead as he did with his father to be permitted to return home, the tsar stood firm. "To China the squadron must go and fulfill my wish," he cabled back.

Aside from an endless round of dinners, receptions, and balls, Alexis engaged in a wide variety of activities during his exhaustive tour.

In Chicago, he toured large parts of the city that lay in the blackened ruins caused by the Great Fire. In Kentucky, he visited Mammoth Cave; in Springfield, the Smith & Wesson revolver plant; and in Denver, the silver mines. He attended Mardi Gras festivities in New Orleans and while there, happily ate chicken gumbo, hominy, and coconut custard pie. He viewed the sights of Montreal, skated Ottawa's Rideau Canal, and travelled by sidewheeler in St. Louis. He viewed the battlefields of Vicksburg, the grain elevators of Buffalo, the waterworks of Dodge City, and the frozen splendour of Niagara Falls. In Memphis, he purposefully mingled with the black population (and was puzzled by the bewilderment and fear some had of their newly granted liberty).

The grand duke's most memorable adventure was an elaborate buffalo hunt near North Platte, Nebraska. The notorious "Buffalo Bill" Cody and General George Custer were his hosts and together they spent a week in the rough and tumble of the mid-winter "Wild West." On a cold January day, the group set out on horseback for a thirty-mile trek across the open prairie (supply carriages accompanied them), and on arrival to their first camp an elaborate welcome awaited them, staged by the U.S. Cavalry and six hundred Sioux.

On the first day of hunting, Alexis brought down a large bull and was so pleased with his success that he ordered the champagne brought out. "I was in hopes," later wrote Buffalo Bill, "that he would kill four to six more buffaloes before we reached camp, especially if a basket of champagne was to be opened every time he dropped one."

The next day, the hunt continued and fifty of the gigantic animals were brought down, two by Alexis. For their assistance in the hunt, the Sioux were permitted to retain the game. The more imposing buffalo heads, however, were kept as trophies and subsequently mounted.

One evening, a tense moment was avoided when the grand duke successfully intervened in a clash between Custer and an angry Sioux chief, with whose young daughter the inebriated general had became overly familiar. Alexis produced an assortment of blankets, hunting knives, and silver dollars, which the chief gratefully accepted, and all became calm once more.

During the week, the imperial visitor was invited to take a stagecoach drive, to which the young man enthusiastically agreed, little realizing what lay in store for him. As the party set off in the closed carriage drawn by six horses, the driver told the visitor, "Now just imagine that fifty Indians are after us." And with that he whipped the horses and gave them full reign — the vehicle took off at breathtaking speed along the primitive prairie road. Ten minutes and three miles later, it jerked to an abrupt halt.

When asked how he liked the ride, Alexis replied he would not have missed the experience for anything. But, he said with a grin, "rather than repeating it, I would return to Russia via Alaska, swim the Bering Strait, and finish my journey on one of your government mules."

All the adventures, misadventures, and anecdotes of Alexis's exhaustive tour and are simply too numerous to detail here. One tale, however, deserves recounting. In anticipation of Alexis's visit to Harvard, university president Charles W. Eliot issued strict orders that classes were to continue as usual; there would be no student welcoming of the distinguished visitor. The undergraduates were decidedly disappointed — it wasn't every day that such a colourful imperial visitor could be seen. They took their revenge. Carriages were hired to call at Eliot's residence at frequent intervals throughout the morning, and the drivers were instructed to knock at the door to announce the grand duke's arrival. As a good host, the smiling Eliot went out to welcome an empty vehicle — not once, not twice, but half a dozen times. By late morning, the exasperated man was distraught. At this point, a caterer knocked to announce the delivery of tables and settings for the 125-person lunch — food would follow shortly. The dumbfounded Eliot barked furiously that no food had been ordered and no guests were expected. The bogus caterer was summarily sent on his way, and the door slammed.

When the genuine honoured guest arrived at last in a modest carriage and in equally unassuming dress, Eliot, now on the verge of apoplexy, ordered the young man off the grounds "before I call the police." The imperial aides, who until then had remained in the carriage, protested vehemently holding out a copy of *Harper's Weekly*. Only when Eliot saw the photograph of the grand duke did the appalled academic realize his gaff. That's how the red-faced, apologetic president of Harvard University received His Imperial Highness. The visitor thought the whole thing to have been "an amusing lark."

The press fawned all over Grand Duke Alexis and reported on every detail of the tour. The *Memphis Daily Appeal* observed that Alexis "loves to talk, and talks well. His English is more accurate than copious, but unlike many Americans he uses good English." A vignette from a Baltimore paper: "A young lady from Norfolk was so agitated while dancing with the Grand Duke that she fainted in his arms. The scion of nobility merely passed her over to one of the old ladies." The *New York Herald* reporter wrote that in Milwaukee "the whole day and evening has been a continued ovation in honor of the grand duke." And the *New Orleans Daily Picayune* gushed, "What a glorious visit it has been."

And as for Alexis himself, once arrived in Cuba, he shared his impressions of America with a New York reporter. "My stay was so pleasant and the people were so kind that I can only regret that I could not have stayed longer. If I did not have a path in my life laid out for me, I should like to live in America altogether, dividing my time from May to January between New York and the prairies and spending the remainder in New Orleans."

The lamentable Katacazy affair earlier had darkened Russian-American relations. Now, however, with the young grand duke's brilliant successes in America's hinterland, a fresh glow surfaced over the traditional friendship. *The Nation* claimed that "it has plainly ended in a rupture of the *entente cordiale* between this country and Russia,.

Alas the glow was not to last.

Ten years after Alexis's brilliant round-the-world tour, on the morning of March 1, 1881, his father Alexander II inspected one of the capital's riding schools. En route home, he stopped by to call on his ailing cousin, Grand Duchess Ekaterina. Following the brief visit, he continued on his way to the Winter Palace. (His carriage was a bomb-proof vehicle thoughtfully presented by Napoleon III after a failed assassination attempt on the Frenchman, one that involved dynamite.)

As the heavy coach turned down Catherine Embankment, three stalwarts of a nihilist group, *Narodnaia Volia* (People's Freedom), awaited in breathless anticipation of fulfilling their long-cherished ambition of doing away with the hated Autocrat of All the Russias. Months before, they had condemned Alexander to death "for crimes against the people."

As the carriage passed, one of the conspirators stepped forward and hurled a homemade grenade at it. The explosion made a terrible noise, but apart from injuries to a number of bystanders, little damage was suffered. The momentarily stunned but unharmed tsar emerged from the vehicle in order to help attend the injured. At this point, another terrorist, a Pole by the name of Hryniewicki, moved forward from an adjacent position, approached the emperor and exploded a second grenade at the tsar's feet. The deafening blast far exceeded that of the first, and when the smoke cleared, some twenty wounded onlookers were scattered about in the blood-drenched snow. Alexander lay on the pavement, mortally wounded — both his legs had been ripped away. Nearby lay Hryniewicki, also mortally wounded, a victim of his own suicidal attack.

"I'm cold, very cold," the tsar whispered to an aide. "Take me to the palace to die." And within the hour, he was dead.

It wasn't long before the police ferreted out *Narodnaia Volia*, and within weeks six of the principals had been arrested and tried — five were executed. One twenty-six-year-old pregnant woman received life imprisonment. More than one hundred thousand spectators turned out to witness the executions, which were grotesquely botched by an inexperienced and partially inebriated hangman. The American legation's secretary, Joseph Hoffman, was in attendance — he came away appalled at the "stupidity and brutality of the chief executioners."

The nihilists dangling at the end of the rope had yearned for the fall of the established order. What precisely they had in mind by way of replacement was undefined, other than a determination "to give the people the decisive say" in the formation of government. Their appalling assassination succeeded, but in carrying it out the plotters defeated much of their purpose. One of history's ironies is that on that very day Alexander had signed a decree granting a limited form of representative government, a first step to precisely what the assassins had sought. As the *New York Times* observed, "It is Nihilism which retarded the growth of Russian liberty in its very infancy, and which has now perhaps dealt it a blow from which it will not recover in a generation."

Americans had little difficulty in relating to that terrible event. Sixteen years earlier, the nation had passed through a similar trauma with President

Lincoln's assassination. The country generally reacted with an outpouring of sympathy. A unanimous resolution was passed in the U.S. Senate condemning the tsar's assassination. The New York State Assembly ordered all flags to be flown at half mast. Cassius Clay vigorously condemned the act, warning that "the Nihilists are sowing dragon's teeth that soon will spring up into legions of armed men. This is the fatal disease, under various systems and many names, which comes at last to every nation, and which, if not sternly and heroically resisted, ends in death."[2]

Until that infamous day in 1881, Russian-American relations had been marked by mutual esteem. But Hryniewicki's bomb precipitated conditions that caused grave fractures in that relationship. Within the year, the United States attitude toward its friend and ally underwent change. By February 1882 the New York Times was asking "whether the Russian Government means to show itself savage or civilized."

Hours after the assassination, the fallen tsar's son and successor, Alexander III, issued a proclamation:

> It has please the Almighty, in His inscrutable will to visit Russia with heavy blows of fate.... The Emperor fell by the hands of impious murderers who ... saw in him the protector of Russia, the foundation of her greatness, and the promoter of the welfare of the Russian people.... We ascend the throne which we inherit from our forefathers, the throne of the Russian empire, the tsardom of Poland and the grand dukedom of Finland, inseparable connected with it.... May He bless our work for the welfare of our beloved fatherland, and may He guide our strength for the happiness of all our faithful subjects."[3]

As a first step, Alexander III declared "a state of emergency" and nullified the liberal document signed by his father a few hours before his death. The thirty-six-year-old successor to the throne had no intention of diluting God-given autocratic power. It wasn't long before the country found itself plunged in a period of reaction and repression, much of which lasted until 1905. A vast and efficient political police was established, the *Okhrana*, and given unprecedented authority to maintain law and order. Premises could now be searched without warrants and suspects detained without trial. The police had license to ban periodicals, close down publishing houses, and to dismiss officials or impose administrative exile. The father's liberalism was seen as the potential ruin of the country. The son would have none of that. There was to be a single absolute ruler over the nation: one nationality, one church, one language. "Autocracy, Orthodoxy and the Fatherland."

At the time of Alexander III's succession, the Russian Empire was an amalgam of some 170 nationalities and ethnic groups. The so-called "great Russians" —the likes of Moscow and St. Petersburg Slavs — made up less than half the population, but when coupled with the Orthodox of the Ukraine and Belorussia, they were the clear majority. The minorities were Poles, Balts, Germans, Georgians, Armenians, and an assortment of Turko nationalities, plus peoples in Asia and the Arctic. The tsar set about imposing a policy of Russification. Although administrative centralization had already come to all the regions, non-Slavic territories were to be deliberately colonized by great Russians. Ethnic populations would be expected to acquire the Russian language, adopt Russian customs and traditions, and integrate their cultures with the Slav population. Strong encouragement would be given for conversion to Orthodoxy.

Few people in Russia doubted that the tsar's assassination was but part of a greater Jewish revolutionary conspiracy. When it was confirmed that Gesia Gelfman, the pregnant conspirator who narrowly escaped hanging, was Jewish and a principal organizer of the dastardly deed, public ire against her people was further inflamed. "It is time to beat the Jews, or we shall all have to clean their boots," declared one functionary. *No more insidious plots*, was the feeling.

Anti-Semitism has been a deplorable fact of Russian life from earliest times. With the annexation of Polish and Ukrainian territories in the seventeenth century, the country's Jewish population increased dramatically; by 1880, it numbered among the country's larger ethnic groups. For the "true Russian" in the street, Jews were quintessential outsiders ... all subject to hostility and suspicion, to prejudice and persecution. As for the antagonism harboured by the governing classes, it's best illustrated

by a memorandum sent by Minister of the Interior Count N.P. Ignatieff
to the emperor early in his reign to Alexander II:

> In St. Petersburg there exists a powerful group of Poles
> and Yids which has direct control of banks, the stock
> exchange, the bar, a great part of the press, and other
> areas of public life. Through many legal and illegal ways
> it exerts an enormous influence over the bureaucracy
> and the general course of affairs. Parts of this group are
> implicated in growing plunder of the exchequer and in
> seditious activity.... Every honest voice is silenced by the
> shouts of Jews and Poles who insist that one must listen
> only to the "intelligent" class and that Russian demands
> must be rejected as backward and unenlightened.[4]

Although pockets of Jewish population were scattered throughout
the empire, mostly in urban areas, the majority found themselves in the
"Pale of Settlement," a selected region near the Russian Empire's southwestern boundaries. Catherine II decreed this arrangement in 1791 as
a means of checking the spread of Jewry in other parts of her realm.
Within the Pale of Settlement, the Jews had the right to form their own
societies, unhindered by authorities. These communities were free to set
up their own administrative and judicial systems and to establish their
own governing councils.

It was to the Pale that violence came on a terrifying scale in the after-
math of the assassination. The country's anger over the bombing, festering
anti-Semitism, and the program of Russification all blended to kick-start
a wave of pogroms, with intensity unlike ever before. Farms and crops
were destroyed by angry mobs; synagogues were desecrated or torn down;
residences were demolished and shops were pillaged and torched. The loss
of life was enormous, with exact numbers impossible to tally. These devastating acts of violence, sometimes spontaneous and other times carefully
planned, were the work of the resentful non-Jewish peasants living in, or
on the borders of the Pale. Local authorities habitually turned a blind eye
to the comings and goings of attackers. Reactionary Russification made it

easy to blame the empires ills on minorities, particularly on the most visible, such as those in the Pale. Religious bigotry and resentment of Jewish business acumen further served to inflame resentment and anger.

The intolerable conditions were devastating enough to cause Jews by the thousands to forsake the Pale — to abandon the pitiful remains of their property and to migrate to cities such as Odessa, Warsaw, and Minsk. In their desperation, even greater numbers left the country to relocate to central Europe and Britain.

But it was the New World that beckoned most heartily — the United States and Canada in particular. From 1882 to 1890, over two hundred thousand Russian Jews sailed into American harbours, mainly to New York where the Statue of Liberty beckoned in welcome. "Give me your tired, your poor, your huddled masses yearning to breathe free.... I lift my lamp beside the golden door!" In the decade that followed, another one and half million people flooded through those golden portals to the safety of America.

The sudden rush of enormous numbers of destitute, poorly educated, and broken individuals — virtually none speaking English — caused significant problems for the authorities. Diverse health requirements had to be met, adults needed training and jobs, and the children had to be educated. As charitable organizations and sympathetic philanthropists strained to cope with the challenge, American public opinion began to turn against Russia. Immigration quotas did not exist in those days and according to constitutional rights, nobody could be denied the right of entry into the country. The flow was so great that Washington exerted pressure on St. Petersburg to change its policy toward its Jewish population — unsuccessfully.

The press railed against Russia — practical considerations aside, the Jewish persecution was unacceptable on humanitarian grounds. *Harper's Weekly* of February 11, 1882, put the issue this way: "Honorable and humane men here and everywhere join in the indignation which the present spectacle arouses." The tsar's empire began to be referred to as a "cesspool of inequity."

A new irritant soon exacerbated the tense situation. Many of the newly arrived acquired United States citizenships, and with fresh passports in hand a few returned to their homeland, claiming the full protection of American law. "It was the same old story," wrote Andrew White, the United States minister in St. Petersburg. "Emigrants from the Russian Empire to the United States stayed just long enough to secure naturalization, had indeed in some cases secured it fraudulently before they stayed their full time; and then, having returned to Russia, were trying to exercise the rights and evade the obligations of both countries."

As with many nations, Russia at the time did not recognize the right of its citizens to foreswear allegiance to the tsar without official sanction; any such person automatically forfeited the country's citizenship. Early in the trickle of returning Jews, St. Petersburg put a clamp on the issuance of visas, particularly not wishing to receive back army deserters and suspected revolutionaries. American reaction to these measures was an explosive cry of anti-Semitism. Acting Secretary of State Alvey Adee viewed the matter dimly: "In the light of an invidious discrimination [Russians were] tending to discredit and humiliate American Jews in the eyes of their fellow-citizens." Clifton Breckinridge, Washington's minister in St. Petersburg, at the conclusion of a report on the situation, wrote, "At the risk of repetition, I will say that Russia is *semi*-Asiatic, the blemish of which is self adulation, and the weakness of which is to underestimate both its friends and its foes." There was no question about it: Russian-American relations were faltering badly.

On Passover in 1903, a day that coincided with Orthodox Easter, anti-Jewish riots broke out at Kishenev, a town within the Pale of Settlement. It was a particularly savage pogrom, with the ransacking and carnage lasting two days. At the end of it all, forty-seven Jews were killed, hundreds were wounded, and the town's Jewish section lay in rubble. By the time of the massacre, the one million Jews in America had become firmly settled, financially secure, and organized. Already angry with the visa controversy, they now rallied in protest against the outrage of Kishenev and lobbied the country's decision-makers.

A wave of condemnation swept the nation. In April alone, seventy-seven cities held public meetings of protest against Russia. The press howled and, Tarsaidze records, in that same month, "80 newspapers wrote 165 editorials on the subject and President Roosevelt received 363 addresses,

107 letters and 24 petitions." The White House was persuaded to protest Russia, but to no avail. The president's note, however, was circulated publicly and reprinted in many parts of the world. A year later, Secretary of State John Hay sent a complaint to Secretary of War Elihu Root:

> In the Kisheneff matter ... we did succeed, in spite the refusal of the Russian Government to consider the prayer of American Jews, in getting that prayer before the world.... [Roosevelt's protest] was reprinted all over the world and had a certain influence and effect.... The passport matter is another affair.... We have absolutely refused to accept their action as satisfactory, have protested against it time and again.... Short of war or a dissolution of diplomatic relations, we cannot do more than we have done and are doing, and yet it is not enough to alleviate the sense of wrong under which our Jewish friends in this country labor.[5]

The two issues — visa discrimination and Russian militant belligerency toward Jews — were the combined genesis for the dissolution of the century-old friendship that had been shared between the two countries.

More was yet to come.

CHAPTER 17

THE RISING SUN

On February 15, 1898, the battleship USS *Main* at anchor in Havana Harbor was mysteriously blown up, killing 260 men American outcry was instant and vociferous, growing so belligerent, that President William McKinley felt compelled to declare war on Spain.

The short-lived, lopsided conflict came to a rapid close with the signing of the Treaty of Paris, and soundly vanquished Spain was forced into a number of concessions. Puerto Rico was ceded to the United States, as was Guam in the Pacific. Sovereignty was given to Cuba, and the Philippines were acquired for the sum of $20 million.

The outcome of these developments firmly positioned the United States in the Pacific — the eastern edge, western shores, and in between. The vast ocean became, in one journalist's words, "our American lake." Had Secretary Seward lived long enough, he no doubt would have been delighted with these developments. The Pacific, he once remarked, "was the chief theatre of events in the world's great hereafter." Prophetic words.

Hark back now to Grand Duke Konstantin's words of 1859 arguing for Alaska's sale: "Our interests are on the Asiatic coast and that is where we must direct our energies. There we are in our own territory and have the possibility of exploiting a large, rich region."

The three decades that followed saw Russia inexorably pushing deeper and deeper into Asia — to the frontiers of Persia, India, and China. By 1895, it had gained an economic preponderance in Mongolia, Korea, and parts of China. Vladivostok as a base of operations was strengthened. The Kuril Islands and Sakhalin just north of Japan were brought into the Russian orbit. On March 27, 1898, a large Russian naval squadron anchored off Port Arthur (Lushun), and the dragon banner of China flying over the governor's residence was hauled down. The imperial flag of Russia was raised in its stead — long-cherished dreams of a warm-water port on the Pacific Ocean had been realized.

At the time, the United States and Russia were firming up their positions on the Pacific — and coping with a fractured relationship — they were faced with the common "problem of the rising sun." Japan had by then fully emerged from the shogunate. Centralized imperial power had been restored, and the island nation had passed through a dynamic period of westernization. It now possessed all the trappings of a modern world power, one that was militaristic and imperialistic.

By the turn of the twentieth century, Japan had involved itself robustly on the mainland, having successfully fought a war with China over political control of Korea. Tokyo viewed Russia's push into East Asia with alarm. It felt that the tsar's empire was transgressing its own rightful sphere of influence. The chilling prospect of Russia becoming predominant in eastern Asia was threatening. The Russian occupation of Manchuria and the acquisition of Port Arthur's warm-water harbour was already too much.

On the dark of night of February 5, 1904, Japan launched a surprise attack on Port Arthur and the Russian fleet stationed there — an aggression not unlike that of Pearl Harbor in 1941. War broke out and when it ended a year and a half later, Russia had been thoroughly beaten. Defeated at Port Arthur, driven back from the Korean frontier and with its Pacific fleet destroyed, the tsar had all along stubbornly refused to sign any form of peace treaty with the *makaki* ("little monkeys"). Additionally, its substantial Baltic fleet, sent halfway around the world in a fruitless effort to bolster the beleaguered Pacific forces, had been lost.

Japan prevailed through the use of well-organized, disciplined forces plus geographic proximity to the front and an enthusiastic support of its people. The Russians lost the war because of their cumbersome, inefficient war machine plus their vast distance from the front and the indifference of the population.

An additional factor in the country's dreadful loss was the tsar's enervation. Nicholas II, as one diplomat observed, displayed "a lack of decision in every act which had become the tragedy of his entire existence." In directing the war, he appeared not so much concerned with loss of lives and the horrendous financial costs involved as he was with the maintenance of the country's dignity and divinely inspired autocracy. Count Witte, the prime minister dismissed by Nicholas, said of the tsar, "A soft haze of mysticism refracts everything he beholds and magnifies his own functions and person." Count Vladimir Lamsdorff, Witte's successor, made a more damning indictment: "Nicholas II had no minister, Russia no leader."

Nicholas himself was no leader, but he did have a strong-willed person at his side: Alexandra, his German-born wife. The empress held a commanding influence over him. She sustained in him the conviction of his divine responsibility to preserve the country's dignity and honour. And since there could be no honour in an empty withdrawal from the struggle, the Russo-Japanese War dragged on and on. It was concluded only by the intervention of President "Teddy" Roosevelt.

Roosevelt had come to the presidency following William McKinley's assassination in 1901 — at age forty-two, he was the youngest person to hold the office. Vigorous and forceful, Teddy was a man of action who in dealing with problems of foreign affairs, abided by his well-known maxim, "Speak softly, and carry a big stick!" And the Russo-Japanese War was a problem for the United States, one to which he eventually carried his big stick.

Early in his presidency, Roosevelt oversaw a dramatic turn in foreign policy — the rapprochement with Great Britain, one which eventually cemented into the unshakable relationship prevailing today. For over a century, the mortar bonding positive Russian-American relations was their shared animosity toward Britain. The situation had now become much changed. Russia now found itself an outsider to the two Anglo-Saxon nations. The country's encroachment into the Far East had been the catalyst.

"The throne of the future of the Orient," one senator wrote bitterly in the *Saturday Evening Post* in 1902, "appears now to be planted upon the eminence that lifts above the waters of Port Arthur, and above that it already floats the Russian flag." As for Russia's audacity in taking over

Harris & Ewing, 1906. Library of Congress.

Theodore Roosevelt.

Manchuria, Roosevelt wrote, "I have not the slightest objection to the Russians knowing that I feel thoroughly aroused and irritated at their conduct in Manchuria; that I don't intend to give way and that I am year by year growing more confident that this country would back me up in going to an extreme in the matter." Additionally, Roosevelt, the fervent democrat, simply had no use for Russian autocracy — and even less for Nicholas. "A preposterous little creature," he called him.

Roosevelt viewed the gains from the war with Spain as stepping stones to further expansion, "The inevitable march of events," he declared, "gave us control of the Philippines.... We must go on with the work we have begun." The evident concern over Russian ambitions was real — the butting of heads seemed unavoidable. "Shall Russia Dominate the World?" asked one paper. Another bannered, "We Do Not Trust the Russians."

In the Russo-Japanese War, the United States had declared neutrality, but it was no secret that its sympathies lay with Japan. "Japan is playing our game," Roosevelt wrote to his son following that country's treacherous attack. The *New York Times* editorialized, "It seems hardly to become the dignity of the ruler of a great nation to complain that he has been struck before he was quite ready! To impute treachery to the Japanese."

Russian attitudes toward America were no less strident as the country began to face facts: the age-old friendship was on the rocks. It was evident that Americans were successfully sabotaging St. Petersburg's efforts to borrow money from European bankers, while giving preferential treatment to the Japanese. As tensions mounted, the city's *Novoye Vrema* complained, "The whole activity of the United States is directed toward making China an industrial power ruled by American directors and viceroys in the form of trusts.... The policy of Washington is to push Japan on to make war." Another paper, *Novy Krai*, was more vociferous: "Japan is not the real opponent ... her whole strength lies in the support of the United States." When war finally did break out, the same paper accused the United States of being the instigator — it was carrying out "the well-known policy of President Roosevelt, who has repeatedly claimed that the Pacific Ocean, with all its islands and coasts, is the proper sphere of American domination."

As developments were unfolding, anti-Semitism in Russia continued to rage; waves of pogroms kept coming, with forty-three happening in 1904. Stoking the fires was the accusation that Jews bore responsibility for the disastrous war with Japan that they not only started it, but were actively supporting it. (A degree of truth lay in the latter allegation, for many Jewish-controlled banks in United States, disgusted with persistent Russian failure to curb pogroms, did financially support the Japanese. Over $180 million in loans were extended to them.)

Roosevelt's antipathy for autocratic Russia was so strong, that he did not negate the possibility of "going to an extreme in the matter." His attitude was best reflected by an editorial in the *Arena*: "In this war Russia stands for reaction and Japan for progress.... The organization and control of the millions in China by Russia is far more dangerous to the rest of the world than would be by their control by the Japanese." As the war progressed, with Russia suffering one crushing blow after another, the international community stood in awe on the sidelines, observing it all. How could this Asiatic parvenu, so lately westernized, have possibly achieved such notable successes over one of Europe's major powers?

American awe soon turned into apprehension as the country slowly began to realize that the greater long-term peril to its Pacific interests might ultimately come not from Russia, but from Japan. Should the Japanese prevail against the Russians, would they respect American interests in Manchuria and elsewhere in Asia? Japanese imperialism could prove more poisonous than Russian imperialism. "As 1904 gave way to 1905," writes John Foster Dulles, "we were perhaps not loving Russia more, but we were decidedly beginning to love Japan less…. If Russia were crushed and completely expelled from the Far East, there would be no effective restraints upon future Japanese expansion." Roosevelt came around to the idea that his country's best interest lay in the prevention of decisive defeat for Russia. In the ideal, a peace treaty should be implemented, one that would assure a balance of power between the two belligerents.

Through dexterous diplomatic manoeuvring, Roosevelt persuaded the warring parties to work toward a settlement of differences, and he offered to mediate the process. The tsar at first balked at the suggestion — his hopes for a decisive victory were pinned on the Baltic fleet, which at the time was rounding the Cape of Good Hope en route to the Far East. With the debacle of its destruction, however, and with the opening volleys of the Revolution of 1905 that required attention at home, he agreed reluctantly to mediation.

As for the Japan, it was simply at the end of its financial ability to continue the war. It would face, furthermore, the daunting prospect of broadening the front with all the complicated problems of logistics. As with the allied armies in the Crimea a half century earlier, the question was, where does one stop? Russia is an awesomely enormous country — how far inland might an army fight its way?

In short, the belligerents agreed to come to Roosevelt's table.

On the morning of August 5, 1905, peace delegations from both countries assembled in New York.[1] They travelled separately to the 23rd Street pier to board ships for the brief trip to Oyster Bay, site of Roosevelt's spacious home on Long Island. The diplomats were introduced to the president and then shown into separate rooms — the

Japanese to the library, the Russians to the salon. Prevailing tensions reached a crescendo when Assistant Secretary of State Herbert Pierce opened the doors dividing the two rooms, and for the first time the antagonists came face to face. Witte spoke of the moment as "morally very painful."

Pierce made the formal introductions, muddling his way through the exotically spelled foreign names. Roosevelt "with his energetic good spirit, his jovial fellow sort of personality" encouraged everyone into the dining room. To avoid problems of protocol in seating arrangements, a buffet-style of lunch had been arranged. At dessert time, the president rose with his champagne flute to propose a carefully crafted toast to the tsar and the mikado — may there be lasting peace between the two.

Photographs were taken after lunch, and with much bowing and handshaking, the two delegations made their separate ways to the harbour, where a couple of naval frigates carried them up Long Island Sound to Portsmouth, New Hampshire, the site selected for the conference. Heavy fog caused the ships to anchor frequently and the trip took an inordinate sixty hours to complete, much to everyone's dissatisfaction — everyone, that is, except Count Witte.

The clever Russian had disembarked in Newport and completed the journey to Portsmouth on a private train, provided by J. Pierpont Morgan. He was in time to join the ceremonial party waiting to welcome the two delegations, thus propelling himself into the position of quasi-host. So pleased was Witte with the clever arrangements that before leaving Morgan's train, he kissed the engineer. (It was a sensational gesture that was reported by more than one newspaper, one that brought the count instant popularity.)

The assembly was billeted in Hotel Wentworth, in Portsmouth's suburbs. Accommodations and practical arrangements seemed pleasing enough — in time, other than meals. Russians came to complain repeatedly of the uninspired offerings. Witte: "Americans have no culinary taste and ... they can eat most anything that comes their way, even if not fresh." Ivan Korostovetz, Witte's secretary: "We nearly always get the same things, the same clams, everlasting boiled fish, and I am deadly tired of roast mutton and boiled greens." The two men tried hopelessly to have their Japanese opposites agree, but to no avail — Japanese etiquette wouldn't permit it. They remained silent, smiling inscrutably.

The start of the twenty-seven-day marathon focused on procedural matters — seating arrangements, order of speakers, operating language (French), secrecy of discussion. And then, cards on the table.

The Japanese presented twelve demands touching issues such as Manchuria, Port Arthur, Sakhalin, railway lines, rights and privileges, Russian naval power, fishing. But the most critical topic was the question of indemnity. They insisted that Russia pay $800 million. "Payment of the cost of the war by Russia is absolutely necessary," the Japanese ambassador to Washington wrote to Roosevelt before the conference's start. "Public sentiment in Japan is strongly demanding a far larger indemnity.... We can hardly manage our national finances and economy. The war has already been a great strain upon our national economy."

The day before the Oyster Bay lunch, Roosevelt had met with Foreign Minister Komura Jutarō and urged that a hard line on the issue not be taken — it was no secret that the Russian emperor had entrenched views on the subject. In the margin of the instructions being issued to the negotiating team, the tsar wrote in his own handwriting, "I do not consider that we are defeated: our armies are intact and I have implicit faith in them! Regarding Korea, in this question I am ready for concession — this is not Russia's land. But as to indemnity, Russia has never paid an indemnity and I will *never* consent to that."

In the days that followed, agreement was reached on a number of concerns, but the indemnity issue appeared dead ended. On August 12, the *New York Times* had it that Russia "will never agree, never, never" to indemnity. In the fortnight that followed, negotiations reached a feverish pitch with discussions frequently going well into the night. Consultative telegrams were exchanged with St. Petersburg and Tokyo, British and German views were solicited, and more than once, members of the conference were dispatched to the Oyster Bay home to seek Roosevelt's advice.

By August 27, the situation appeared truly hopeless. A cable arrived from Count Lamsdorff in St. Petersburg: "Give Witte my order to end discussions tomorrow in any case. I prefer to continue the war than to await gracious concessions on the part of Japan."

Little did St. Petersburg or the Russians in Portsmouth appreciate the extent of Tokyo's anxiety for a peace treaty. The same was abundantly true of its team in Portsmouth. On the twenty-eighth, Komura messaged Tokyo: "I believe that Japan must continue fighting with full determination until another opportunity for peace arrives." As far as he was concerned, there was no point in continuing discussions. It was all over. The Japanese packed their bags, paid the hotel bill, and a gracious note of thanks was sent to the mayor of Portsmouth for warm hospitality received. Enclosed was a cheque for $20,000, a donation for municipal charities.

Tokyo, however, was adamant that peace must be signed whatever the cost, and on the twenty-ninth, the despondent Komura was instructed to do so. "Members of the Japanese delegation were profoundly shaken by the instructions from Tokyo," writes Raymond Esthus. "[They] were thrown into the abyss of pathos and they succumbed to weeping and sobbing. Some Japanese newspaper correspondents who were present discerned what had happened and they too could not hold back tears."

The sensational news of Japanese surrender in the negotiations was delivered to the startled Witte. The Russian delegation broke out in shouts, cheers, and cries of "Peace!" An exuberant telegram was sent to Nicholas II: "I have the honor to inform, your Imperial Highness that Japan accepted our demands concerning peace conditions…. Russia will remain a great power in the Far East." And another telegram was sent to President Roosevelt: "To you History will award the glory of having taken the generous initiative in bringing about the Conference, whose labors will now probably result in establishing a peace honorable to both sides." Roosevelt immediately dispatched messages of congratulations to both sides. The peace treaty was signed on September 5.

By its provisions, Korea was to remain independent, but Japanese influence over that country was recognized as being paramount. Manchuria was to be evacuated by both Russia and Japan. The southern portion of Sakhalin was given over to Japan, and Port Arthur was leased to Japan. There would be no indemnity. John Foster Dulles succinctly summarizes the Portsmouth outcome:

In view of the military and naval history of the war, it was a diplomatic triumph for Russia. And it had been won with American assistance. Nevertheless the real victory, obscured as it was at the time, was Japan's. Roosevelt had in reality failed to uphold the balance of power in the Far East. Japan had replaced Russia as the most powerful nation in eastern Asia. She had taken an immense forward stride on her destined course of imperialistic expansion. Time was to prove that she was a far more formidable rival to American interests in the Pacific than ever Czarist Russia had been.[2]

In time, Tokyo sent a message to Roosevelt: "Your advice was very powerful and convincing, by which the peace of Asia was secured. Both Russia and Japan owe to you this happy conclusion, and your name shall be remembered with the peace and prosperity of Asia." These warm words of thanks were richly deserved. Throughout the process, Roosevelt had worked tirelessly behind the scenes, pushing, encouraging, pleading, lobbying. In his meeting with George Meyer, the United States ambassador in St. Petersburg, Nicholas enthusiastically shook the diplomat's hand and said, "Say to your President I certainly hope that the old friendship which has previously existed and united the two nations for so long a period will be renewed. I realize that whatever difference has arisen is due to the press, and in no way to your government."

Hearty handshakes and flowery words notwithstanding, Russian-American relations had undergone tumultuous times. The cordial, supportive mode that prevailed since 1776 had been shaken. The Jewish question was one thing, both as to St. Petersburg's belligerency toward that minority and the visa issue. Developments in the Pacific were another matter. But a further element was in the mix, one that had no small effect on American public opinion.

The adventurous telegraph enthusiast, George Kennan, had by the close of the nineteenth century become a pre-eminent journalist with a wide following. He was much in demand on the lecture circuit, often drawing crowds as large as three thousand. Through his wide-ranging travels in Russia, he was able to tell about the country with certain authority — as expert in its affairs as any American. In 1891, he published *Siberia and the Exile System*, a two-volume compilation of his newspaper articles, and a book that further stirred American anti-Russian sentiment. He pictured the system of exile and conditions in Siberia emotionally and in the harshest terms. One of his loyal readers was Teddy Roosevelt, whose anger and indignation over the reported situation clearly affected his inimical attitude toward that country.

Here is an illustrative sample of Kennan's inflamatory style — in which he comments on the marker at the borderline of western Russia and Siberia:

> No other spot between St. Petersburg and the Pacific is more full of painful suggestions, and none has for the traveler a more melancholy interest than the little opening in the forest where stands this grief-consecrated pillar. Here hundreds of thousands of exiled human beings ... have for the last time, looked backward with love and grief at their native land, and then, with tear-filled eyes and heavy hearts, they have marched away into Siberia to meet unknown hardships and privations of a new life.[3]

"Torn from its context," observes Alexandre Tarsaidzé, "this passage could describe the hardy pioneers who were marching, undaunted, toward the frontier. It is a passage worthy of the Pilgrims on the Mayflower or the men crossing the Cumberland Gap. Mr. Kennan knew very well that relatively few of the men sent to Siberia were political exiles, that 87 percent were criminals. It cannot be sufficiently emphasized that these people had been convicted of crimes punishable by the severest penalties of law in any country in the world." (To keep things in perspective, France at the time was beheading murderers and the United States was hanging them. In Russia, capital punishment had long been outlawed, except for political murder.)

Americans decried "the barbarian penal system." The very word *tsar* took on the meaning of arbitrary dictator, and Russia came to be regarded as a "cesspool of iniquity." Such was the power of Kennan's printed word — the book proved to be for Russia as festering a wound as *Uncle Tom's Cabin* was for Confederate states. All the while, the author continued on his triumphant lecture tour of America — as one contemporary diplomat reported, "Clad in prisoner's garb and iron chains at his feet and with a magic lantern for illustration, uttering the most impossible nonsense about Russia, and hardly believing it himself." But the celebrity pressed on, meeting with one success after another. "The most prominent man in town today," reported the *Kansas City Star*, "is George Kennan, the great Siberian explorer and lecturer, who has probably seen more persecution, seen more hardship, and found more danger than any other living American in times of peace."

By the time of the Portsmouth Treaty, Russia had substantially fallen out of grace with the America public. The harmonious and mutually supportive times of the past appeared forgotten. "Russia is the most cordially friendly nation to us of any power on earth," Jefferson had once declared. Times had changed.

The narrative, however, does not ended here. A further chapter in Russian-American relations begs attention: the United States's armed involvement in the Russian Revolution, which is perhaps the least known of the country's military interventions.

CHAPTER 18

REVOLUTION AND INTERVENTION

On June 28, 1914, Archduke Franz Ferdinand of Austria was assassinated in the streets of Sarajevo. "The shot heard around the world" ignited the fuse that unleashed an explosive reaction among European powers; within weeks, the continent had become enmeshed in the First World War. In the west Anglo-French forces, in the east the Russian — all locked in battle with Austro-German armies.

Russia maladroitly entered the Great War, and eventually saw some nine million of its men drawn into the conflict, the largest army of any. Every conceivable hardship was suffered by these troops: inadequate training, lack of supply, deficient medical attention, starvation, freezing, and incompetent leadership. By the time the country had withdrawn from the conflict, estimates were that possibly 80 percent of the soldiers were killed, wounded, taken prisoner, or missing.

As the war progressed, one frontline disaster followed another. With troop morale at its lowest, Nicholas determined to take personal command of the situation. He travelled to the front with a plan to rally his men to victory — the sacred bond of soldiers and tsar required buttressing. With the ruler away, Empress Alexandra grabbed the mantle and took over the administration of government, and behind her stood not an array of wise councillors and statesmen, but the infamous Rasputin. His story is well known, and it has been well established that his interventions and machinations stoked the growing flames of revolution.

Life in the city streets was not much less grim than at the front; the transportation system had collapsed, which had a disastrous effect on distribution. The situation was exacerbated by the wholesale call-up of peasants into the military — the resulting labour shortages negatively affected agricultural production. Inflation accelerated and most ordinary townspeople were simply unable to cope with the high costs, thus resulting in hunger and suffering throughout much of the country, particularly in St. Petersburg and Moscow.

Strikes became common, not only at home but also within the army, and wholesale arrests were being made of the leaders of the strike committees. Within weeks, the confrontations grew in intensity. Massive demonstrations were common, with regular cries going out for an end to autocracy. In February 1917, the Cossacks were summoned in the capital to quell the disorders, but rather than dispelling the crowd they joined the insurgents. Workers and soldiers in St. Petersburg — renamed Petrograd — united to form the first Soviets (workers' councils), and the example was rapidly followed in provincial towns and units throughout the army.

A liberally inclined provisional government of twelve ministers was formed under Prince Georgii Lvov, a constitutional democrat, and emissaries were dispatched to the front to meet with the emperor. On March 2, the delegation found Nicholas on a stalled train heading back to the capital, stranded near Pskov and unable to advance farther because of the strikes. The tsar was persuaded to abdicate. "It has been God's will to visit upon Russia a new and grievous trial," he wrote. "The internal disturbances which have begun among the people threaten to have calamitous effect on the future conduct of a hard-fought war. The whole future of our beloved fatherland demands that the war be carried to victory.... We have judged it right to abdicate the throne of the Russian state and to lay down the supreme power." The ruler passed the throne to his younger brother, Grand Duke Michael. But it was too late. The three-hundred-year-old rule of the Romanov dynasty had effectively come to an end.

With the signing of the abdication, a critical page had been turned, but more calamitous things were yet to come. Imperial Russia was in freefall, soon to drown in the blood stemming from the veins of war and revolt. The provisional government pressed forward in planning reforms that promised to touch virtually every sector of society: freedom of assembly, Polish independence, abolition of restrictions based on race or religion, and, most importantly, the summoning of a constituent assembly. It also renewed Russia's commitment to the war.

On March 18, Ambassador David R. Francis of the United States reported exultantly from Petrograd, "The six days between last Sunday and this have witnessed the most amazing revolution ... the practical realization of the principle of government which we have championed and advocated. I mean a government by the consent of the governed." Americans received news of these developments with unabashed delight. "The most cruel and despotic government in the world" is now gone, trumpeted the *New Orleans Item*. "We can stand upright in our principles," gloated the *Springfield Republican*, "without the taint of a decadent and besotted Caesarism defiling their consciences and mocking their faith in democracy's final triumph throughout the world."

Ambassador Francis cabled Washington recommending an immediate recognition of the new provisional government, and this was granted — a mere five days following the abdication. The United States was the first country to extend recognition, and within days, Prince Lvov formally received its ambassador. The long-standing cordiality that had hallmarked relations between the two countries for over a century and a half was re-established. To this point, the United States had not yet entered into the war, but its recognition of the new government, as Francis later claimed with certain justification, "undoubtedly had a powerful influence in placing America in a position to enter the war backed by a practically unanimous opinion." the *Literary Digest* gushed, "Instead of taking the corrupt despotism of the Romanovs as an ally, we may proudly join hands with the self-governing people of Russia in a war of peoples against kings."

Germany had long announced a policy of unrestricted submarine warfare, and vessels suspected of aiding the enemy were being torpedoed. Numerous vessels were sunk, but the most dramatic was that of the *Lusitania*, an unarmed merchant liner carrying not only nineteen hundred passengers but also a small cargo of munitions. The ship left New York on May 1, 1915, and six days later it was torpedoed off the coast of Ireland. Half the passengers perished, including 114 Americans. The outcry in

America at this outrageous act against humanity reinforced the calls for the country to enter into the war. But it took two more years for that to happen. On April 2, 1917, President Woodrow Wilson appeared before Congress to ask for the declaration of war. It was readily accorded — three-quarters of the way through the four-year struggle. In addressing Congress, Wilson asked,

> Does not every American feel that assurance has been added to our hope for the future peace of the world by the wonderful and the heartening things that have happened within the last few weeks in Russia?... The autocracy that crowned the summit of her political structure, long as it had stood and terrible as was the reality of its power, was not Russian in origin, character or purpose; and now it has shaken off and the great, generous Russian people have been added in all their naïve majesty and might to the forces that are fighting for freedom in the world, for justice and for peace. Here is a fit partner ... [as opposed to an autocratic ally].[1]

It may be argued that Wilson's view of Russia was naive, penned in ignorance and confusion as to the true state of affairs unfolding in that country — framed perhaps in wishful thinking. The provisional government had all along been displaying its effectiveness. At the front, the short-supplied armies were showing themselves disorganized and confused, while at home the proliferating Soviets were gathering strength. The quandary facing Lvov and his ministers was formidable. How would they pursue the war against the central powers while concurrently attending to the demands of an unsettled population? Mobs clamoured not only for economic and political reforms, but first and foremost for peace. Aware or unaware, Wilson and Congress had bound the United States to that country; they were now allies dedicated to a common cause.

Russia's difficulties notwithstanding, allied powers were determined to have that country continue in the war. Its army, however ineffective and ill-equipped, effectively tied down German forces in the east, troops that would otherwise be directed against the allies in the west. Victory over the central powers could come only by the maintenance of the two fronts.

Russia had to be encouraged and reinforced whatever the cost. When Boris Bakhmetev, that country's newly appointed ambassador arrived in Washington, he was heartedly greeted by the president and by Congress. The $100 million loan previously granted by the United States was increased to three hundred and $25 million, more than half of which was earmarked for the purchase of munitions (this sum was never repaid). A program was initiated to help resolve Russia's broken-down transportation network. John F. Stevens, ex-chief engineer of the Panama Canal construction, was sent to oversee the project. The private sector was encouraged to involve itself in Russia, and before long the American Red Cross, the YMCA, and other non-governmental organizations had become active in the task of bolstering the country.

Bakhmetev expressed his country's profound gratitude to the United States, and he underscored that Russia had in one spectacular leap sprung from autocracy to an American-style democracy. His country, he argued, now depended on further aid in order to achieve "the slower but not impossible task to overtake her [the United States] in education, material progress, culture and respect for order."

At about the time Bakhmetev was delivering Lvov's thanks, and Stevens was tending to the needs of the Trans-Siberian Railroad, Vladimir Lenin was secretly returning to Russia in a sealed train. German high command astutely calculated that dissensions in their favour would follow the liberation of the dedicated revolutionary from his Swiss exile. Lenin's *Development of Capitalism in Russia* had been absorbed and the firebrand's aspirations were clear. An overthrow of the provisional government would undoubtedly occur, as well as a Russian withdrawal from the war.

Summer passed into autumn and through most of the country it was a reign of continuing strikes, revolts, and mutinies. The civilian population continued to suffer every conceivable shortage amid universal discouragement and confusion. The condition of the demoralized military worsened further and the front appeared in imminent danger of being overrun by the persistent Germans. The mere fear of it served to exacerbate general unrest in the country. The presidency passed from a failed Lvov to a more radical Alexander Kerensky. The new leader appeared no less determined in pursuing the war than had his predecessor — this despite prevailing popular sentiments.

But that was not to be, for Kerensky proved equally unsuccessful in consolidating his government or in meeting popular demands. On November 7, 1917, in a coup led by Lenin, the provisional government was overthrown and replaced by the "Soviet Republic." The long-cherished dream of the Bolsheviks had at last been realized. As head of government, wasting no time, Lenin set about implementing radical socialism in Russia. The country, he declared, would become a springboard for a world revolution.

Land was confiscated and turned over to the peasants; factories were taken over and given to the workers. Banks were nationalized and private accounts appropriated. All foreign debts were repudiated. God was exiled — churches were confiscated, religious instruction outlawed. The revolution had been well and truly highjacked by the Bolsheviks. "Long live the revolution of workers, soldiers and peasants! Workers of the world, unite!"

The staggering force with which the Bolsheviks grabbed power dumbfounded the world. The undying hostility of Bolsheviks to the capitalistic world was obvious, and it didn't take long for the reeling West to fully appreciate Lenin's immediate and long-term agendas. The Soviets had appropriated two million roubles for the promotion of the world revolution, and these judiciously expended funds were beginning to germinate communistic ideals in Europe and America.

It became clear that Lenin intended to withdraw Russia from the war. The additional anxiety was not only that he might sign a separate peace, but that he also could go over to the enemy. Ambassador Francis wrote from Petrograd that he was "willing to swallow pride, sacrifice dignity and with discretion do all that is necessary to prevent Russia's becoming an ally of Germany." It did not take long for allied fear to become justified, as the Bolsheviks set about engaging the Germans in peace proposals.

Preliminary discussions between the central powers and Russia opened at Brest-Litovsk. The allies were invited to join the meetings, but they would have no part of it. They not only refused participation in discussions, but they also steadfastly refused even to recognize the revolutionary government. The Bolsheviks reacted with scorn, pouring it on Woodrow Wilson, "that prophet of imperialism." This is how *Izvestia*, the party's official newspaper, described Wilson: "The American President Wilson, adopting the tone of a Quaker preacher reads to the people a sermon on the higher practical morality. The people know that America came into the war, not in the interest of right and justice, but because of the cynical interests of the New York Stock Exchange."

By February 1918, the Germans, having had their harsh demands for an armistice rejected, were pursuing the war with alarming success, so much so that Petrograd appeared in danger of capture. On March 3, the Soviets suddenly capitulated and unilaterally signed the humiliating peace. For the allies, this was a catastrophic development. American public opinion instantly gelled against Russia's new government: "A group of lewd fellows of the baser sort," the *Baltimore American* derisively labelled them, and adding that the Bolsheviks were "filthy pocket-pickers and despicable degenerates." It seemed clear to many that Bolshevik leaders were in the pay of Germany. How else might one explain such chicanery? "The signing of a formal peace treaty on Germany's terms marks the final act of betrayal on the part of the Bolsheviki," the *New York World* declared. "Trotsky and Lenin have done their best by the Kaiser whether actuated by money, or lust for power, or insanity of class hatred." The United States and its allies took the position that the Bolshevik government was illegitimate and therefore the peace treaty was not legally valid.

"As the war rose to a frightening crescendo on the western front," writes historian John W.F. Dulles, "the dark shadow of events in eastern Europe appeared to cloud even the prospects of military victory over Germany. The democratic peoples were at once fearful of German domination over prostrate Russia, and the rise of a Bolshevik tyranny defying the capitalist powers. The counsels of Washington, London, and Paris upon how the problem should be met were divided and confused." The fear was real. For nearly a year, there had been talk of an allied intervention in the affairs of Russia and perhaps now was the time to take action.

Intervention would perhaps bring to the stricken country a "sane" leader with the ability not only to guide it away from communism, but who would also re-engage the country in the war.

Division and confusion eventually morphed into action as the United States joined its allies in direct intervention. The counter-revolutionaries would receive full support, whatever the cost. Russia would be brought back into the war and triumphant democracy would prevail over communism and ultimately over the kaiser.

The Russian Revolution had turned into civil war, with communist Red armies battling anti-Bolshevik White armies in many places. In Siberia, disturbances and lawlessness had become commonplace, particularly along the border of China. Thousands of Russians had fled to that country to escape from what Winston Churchill called "the foul baboonery of Bolshevism" and these émigrés plotted their enemy's overthrow.

Of all the aid the United States sent to Russia, the most interesting historically was John Stevens's work on railway refurbishment, for herein lay the seed of American military intervention. The rail system had for years suffered from outmoded methods of operation, inefficient organization, and a lack of updated equipment. The vital line from Vladivostok on the Pacific to the Ural Mountains, a distance of some forty-seven hundred miles, was in an especially pitiful condition. Since the Germans blocked access to Russia from the west, military aid earmarked for there had to be delivered via the Pacific and Vladivostok, and then by rail to the front. The British and French, recognizing the superiority of American railroad experience and technical skills, persuaded Wilson to focus attention on this critical problem.

Stevens arrived in Vladivostok in June, established his headquarters and assumed supervisory control of the harbour's terminals. In the meanwhile, the five commissioners who had accompanied him set off on a special train to assess the precise state of trans-Siberian tracks. Recommendations were then submitted to the provisional government and at their behest, a corps of engineers was summoned from the United States to oversee the required work.

Three hundred railway engineers — the "Russian Railway Service Corps" — therefore sailed in from the States to begin supervisory work.

It was during their slow passage across the Pacific that the Bolsheviks assumed power, and those events threw Vladivostok into such turmoil, that food and accommodation simply would not be available to the arriving Americans. They therefore delayed landing in Russia and temporarily sought refuge in Japan. From Tokyo, the impatient Stevens cabled Washington: "We should go back shortly with a man-of-war and 5,000 troops. Time is coming to put the fear of God into these people."

While Stevens was supervising Vladivostok's terminals, events in Siberia were unfolding in diverse directions. Revolutionary struggle had reached the cities and settlements along the Trans-Siberian Railroad, and White Army forces were regularly engaging the Reds. Japan, which had entered the war in 1914 on the side of the allies, was offering support to the divided factions of the White forces — all the time casting a covetous eye on Manchuria and China.

The Bolsheviks had released from prison camps thousands of Germans captured on the battlefields, and they were arming them in support of the struggle against the Whites. Irkutsk was under threat of their attack. Secretary of State Robert Lansing warned President Wilson that the situation was such "that the Germans, if masters of the place, might invade Manchuria and obtain control of the Trans-Siberian Railroad." If that happened, the allies would be unable to move military supplies arriving in Vladivostok on a reconstituted eastern front.

At this stage, the spotlight focused on the plight of nearly fifty thousand Czech soldiers who in the early stages of the war had been taken prisoner and were interred in Siberian POW camps. Unlike German and Austrian prisoners, the Czechs had surrendered at the front without firing a shot (forcibly conscripted, they bore no allegiance to the central powers). They were, however, excellent fighters, disciplined and well trained. In early 1917, the allies decided to form these Czechs into a brigade and allow them to join in the fight for the liberation of their homeland. Plans called for bringing them by rail to Vladivostok, and then across the Pacific, through the Panama Canal, and east to France.

As the loaded trains made their way to Vladivostok, a vicious brawl broke out between the Czechs and some Hungarian prisoners, one of whom was killed. The Bolshevik authorities reacted intemperately, and when they sought to disarm the Czechs and arrest the suspected ringleaders, the entire brigade rose up and disarmed the arresting police — for good measure, they went on to overthrow the local Soviet government. Buoyed by these successes, the irrepressible Czechs pressed on, gaining victory after victory — control fell to them of a number of cities on the railway line. They then joined factions of the White forces and spread their offensive west toward the Urals. At one time, Ekaterinburg — the city where the tsar and his family were being held captive — appeared to be under threat. Local Bolsheviks panicked about the Czechs possibly liberating the Romanovs. They gathered the unfortunate family in the basement of the makeshift prison, and in cold blood they executed everyone.

As successful as the enterprising Czechs had been, their overall position was not reassuring — supplies were running out, and the well-provisioned Bolsheviks were closing in on them. The cry went out for help, and the plea was heard. Direct military intervention by the allies had been discussed for weeks, but now the notion found serious support — the Czechs had to be rescued. The French persuaded the Japanese to send in troops, while the British pressed the Americans to intervene. President Wilson vacillated: "I have been sweating blood over the question of what is right and feasible to do in Russia." American public opinion, however, clearly supported intervention and demands were heard not only for the rescue of the Czechs, but also for the overthrow of the Bolshevik regime and a continuation of the war. "If a force of Allied troops were sent into Siberia," declared the *New York Times*, "it would provide a supporting nucleus around which the people of Russia could rally.... Is Germany to kill democracy by the sword and the Allies by watchful waiting?" Wilson relented, but only at the persistent urging of allied governments and of his own Supreme War Council. Orders were issued for an expeditionary force to join the Japanese in Russia for the succour of the stranded Czechs. "Boots on the ground."

In late July, a contingent of seven thousand U.S. troops sailed from San Francisco to Vladivostok to join the allies, including five thousand Canadians, already there. Major General William Graves commanded the force under orders that were as ambiguous as they were contradictory. The sealed envelope was delivered to him personally by Secretary

of War Newton Baker who offered the officer gratuitous advice: "This contains the policy of the United States in Russia which you are to follow. Watch your step; you will be walking on eggs loaded with dynamite. God bless you and good-bye." Graves's double-barrelled assignment was to liberate the stranded Czechs and preserve the security of the Trans-Siberian Railroad. In pursuing this twofold goal, the major general was to remain neutral, without taking sides with any revolutionary faction. The dynamite-loaded eggs of which Baker spoke had in fact been handed to him by the secretary of war, himself.

The American contingent disembarking in Vladivostok was one of two groups the United States dispatched to Russia during that last summer of the war. At the other end of that vast country, in the extreme northwest, another American troop landing took place at Murmansk and Archangel. It had been rumoured that the Germans were planning to capture Murmansk in order to establish a submarine base on the Arctic Ocean. Even more important was the very real threat to the extensive stores of allied-provided armaments together with civic and military equipment stored in both cities — in Archangel alone, were some 162,000 tons of *matériel*. The Allied Supreme War Council was anxious for both reasons. The Americans were to reinforce the allies already there in a collective effort to thwart German designs on that part of the world. Churchill later commented on this mandate, "The reconstruction of an Eastern front against Germany and the withholding of Russian supplies from the Central Powers seemed even from the end of 1917 vital to win the war."

By summer's end, forty-five hundred American infantrymen had been transferred from France and to Murmansk, where they joined up with the British contingent and the Canadian Expeditionary Force, plus some five hundred French Foreign Legionnaires. Aside from a couple of hundred draftees from Wisconsin, the entire contingent came from Michigan — the 339th Infantry Battalion, affectionately called "Detroit's Own." Mostly, they were hastily trained raw recruits. "This was the very worst class of material to send out to Russia," one senior British commander complained bitterly. "The Regiment had received absolutely no training and the officers were, one and all, of the lowest value imaginable … inexperienced to a degree that

I have never seen before in American troops in France." Another twelve hundred American engineers and medical personnel also arrived. The land forces were supported by a small fleet of allied warships, including HMS *Nairana*, one of the world's first flight carriers equipped with seven aircraft and the French cruiser *Admiral Aube*. The entire allied force was put under British supreme command, the most notable of the commanding generals was the thirty-eight-year-old General William Ironsides, a towering six foot, five inch giant, who in every respect lived up to his name.

Just as Major General Graves in Siberia had been ordered to maintain neutrality, so it was with the Americans in Russia's arctic region — the struggle in that country was a politically internal affair, and of no concern to the allies. Only such aid was to be given "as shall be acceptable to the Russian people in their endeavour to regain control of their own affairs, their own territory and their own destiny." Strive for neutrality as they might, there was no way for the troops of either mission to succeed without pulling a trigger against one revolutionary faction or another. To maintain the security of the Trans-Siberian Railway and of the northern supply depots ipso facto involved not only outright assistance to anti-Bolshevik forces, but also an exchange of gunfire. American troops had been sucked willy-nilly into the morass of the Russian Revolution, and they quickly found themselves fighting shoulder to shoulder with the Whites.

Barely three months passed following the two American landings, when the much-heralded Armistice was signed at Compiègne, France, which brought an end to the cataclysmic war.

The Czechs had been evacuated, and there was no further need to attend to the security on the Trans-Siberian Railway. The Archangel supply depots were no longer vital — anyway, much of the material had been used up or had been stolen by the Bolsheviks. The stated rationale for allied presence in Russia dissipated.

Yet the United States and Western powers lingered on, for by then they had become actively committed to the fight against Bolshevism. In Siberia, Admiral Alexander Kolchak had emerged as perhaps the most promising hope the Whites had for reversing the Red tide. He promised the allies that on winning power in Russia, he would work for the freedom of the Russian people, and that all foreign debts would be recognized. On the basis of these assurances and upon the pressure of allied governments, Wilson reluctantly agreed to assist Kolchak economically and militarily — the president wished to avoid upsetting his allies. He subsequently declared that he had found it "harder to get out [of Russia] than it was to get in."

By late spring 1919, news of the anti-Bolshevik forces was discouraging. On June 12, Kolchak's Siberian forces suffered a decisive defeat at the hands of the Reds, which effectively stopped further advance of the White army. On the Dvina River, some two hundred miles upstream from the White Sea, the allied armies had become bogged down, and morale and confidence plummeted. The Armistice had been signed and the German threat was no more; the declared war against the central powers had now become an undeclared war against the Bolsheviks. The initial enthusiasm of the American public for intervention began rapidly to dissipate following November 11. Reports were being received at home of abysmal conditions suffered by the "doughboys" and of their frustration and incomprehension of continued battle. In Michigan especially, home of the 339th Infantry Battalion, the anger was palpable as upsetting letters of complaint poured in from sons and husbands in far-off Russia.

In Siberia, the Reds pressed their advance on the Whites and with increasing frequency allied troops came under fire — on one occasion, a particularly bloody attack saw thirty-six U.S. servicemen killed. Before it would all end, 222 soldiers from the 339th Infantry Battalion would die fighting the Reds. "Why are we in Russia?" asked one soldier. "Why are we fighting the Bolsheviks? How long are we to remain?" And a more thoughtful one complains, "We are meddling with a Russian revolution and counterrevolution.... We have been unable to reconcile this expedition with American ideals and principles instilled within us." The ordinary soldier was confused as to the point of it all and, in his frustration, impatient to return home.

It seemed that the soldiers' anger was shared by virtually everyone else in Siberia. The Bolsheviks were furious that the Americans were assisting the Whites; the Whites were unhappy that they were not doing more. The British and the French were displeased that the American objectives seemed undefined. Japan was distrusting of the United States, suspecting that its ally continued on merely to check her imperialistic aspirations (which, to some measure, was true).

And in northern Russia, the complaints were strident: "We are living worse than a bunch of hogs. You should see us. We are full of cooties [lice], dirty, ragged, no hair cut, no shave, and you should see your ragged soldier now." Conditions in the hastily constructed barracks were primitive to an extreme — inadequately insulated, minimally furnished with filthy latrines, the buildings more often than not were on grounds contaminated by raw sewage. Cesspools were cleaned periodically, but "due to the disorganisation resultant from war conditions, the labor necessary to effect this has been lacking. The cess pits had overflowed, flush latrines had become plugged and human excreta was conspicuous and abundant both inside and outside of buildings." Infestations of lice everywhere and so big were the insects that for relief of boredom, soldiers captured them and for amusement engaged them in races. Nobody was free of these pesky creatures — not even Ambassador Francis, who had withdrawn from Petrograd to Archangel. He wrote his wife requesting "two large boxes of Getz's best roach powder or the best kind. I would appreciate this very much. Also three boxes rough on rats or the best. They crawl all over me at night. None to be had in Russia."

Archangel, the centre of allied operations, was a particularly unwholesome place. "Up here in this tough town there are 269,831 inhabitants, of which 61,329 are human beings and 208,502 are dogs," wrote one soldier sardonically. "The wind whistles across the Dvina River like the Twentieth Century Limited passing Podunk." The city had no central sewage system and effluent flowed freely under the wooden sidewalks into large, uncovered cesspools. "This is some city … it can be smelled for quite a distance. Among his other crimes, Peter the Great was responsible for this place."

Military hospitals and infirmaries lacked beds at a time of rampant influenza. The sick "lay on stretchers without mattresses or pillows, lying in their O.D. [olive drab] uniforms, with only a simple blanket covering. The place was a bedlam of sinister sounds of rasping, stertorous breathing, coughings, hackings, moans and incoherent cries." In the September of their arrival, nearly four hundred Americans contracted influenza and before long, seventy-two had succumbed or died from pneumonia. The situation mostly was similar in the other allied camps. Coffin makers could not keep up with demand, and bodies were buried only in shrouds.

For the troops, it was not merely a time of suffering and privation — it was, above all, one of hard battle. On January 19, 1919, for example, some 190 miles south of Archangel, the Reds engaged a position held by American and Canadian forces fighting alongside the Whites. A heavy-artillery bombardment of over a thousand rounds pounded the entrenchment, followed by an attack of 1,300 infantry. The battle raged for three days and devastating losses were inflicted on the allies — so much so that they were forced to retreat at night in temperatures hovering around –33°F.

It was now a situation rife with abysmal conditions, intense cold and snow, wounded and dead, vermin and homesickness, and a war nobody understood. It is little wonder that general disgruntlement turned into mutiny. The first to rise up was a British unit from the Yorkshire Battalion. "Why are we in Russia? How long are we to remain?" The two ringleaders — both sergeants — were arrested and the short-lived commotion came to rest. The French were next to rebel. When ordered to relieve American troops at a certain position, they refused and demanded that Russians be assigned the task. Ironsides had 113 of the rebellious troops disarmed and arrested.

Finally, it was the turn of the Russians. Eight mutineers from the Slavo–British Regiment burst into the officers' quarters one night and killed five British and four of the sleeping Russians. "Not content with this they tore their intestines open with knives and bespattered their faces with them." The killers then persuaded some two hundred Russian troops to join them in a desertion to the Soviets. None of the guilty was apprehended, but a goodly number of the deserters were caught in the act of running away. They were arrested and General Ironsides ordered that "about twenty of them" be executed by a firing squad as an example to others.

The British War Office protested that the numbers were too high, so eight of the condemned were freed. On the day of execution, it was members of the Slavo-British Regiment who were ordered to carry out the sentences upon their comrades, while they, themselves, were put under machine-gun surveillance. A poignant description of the proceedings is offered by a witness:

> Act 1: The prisoners — all thirteen of them — were in tents and a priest went to bless them and take any messages to relatives. Each one was sprinkled with Holy water and the priest kissed each one. Act 2: The prisoners were marched under escort to the place of execution, where Russian and French troops formed three sides of a square, the other side being taken by spectators. The doomed men were placed in a row with their backs to the place of execution and their sentences read out. Two were reprieved and sentenced to imprisonment. Act 3: Those to be shot were blindfolded and the stripes of a fine looking sergeant were torn off his coat sleeves. Each man was then taken by the arm by British soldiers and led to posts where they were tied arms and feet. A disc was placed on their breast opposite their hearts as a target. Some of the cowardly ones cried hysterically but the sergeant was a real stoic.... The signal to fire was given when the Russian officer dropped his sword. There was a hush when he lifted his sword, then a strange thing happened which lengthened the lives and agony of those Bolos for about one minute. A little dog appeared from somewhere and trotted up to one of the prisoners and sniffed his leg. The dog had to be got away before the officer dropped his sword. I shall never forget the rattle of those machine-guns and the wriggling bodies as their lives went out of them. The executioner of the sergeant, either deliberately missed him or became very nervous, because when the smoke of the guns cleared away the N.C.O. had pulled off his handkerchief and was shouting, "Long live Bolshevism!"[2]

Within two weeks another mutiny took place, but this time an entire Russian battalion crossed over to the Bolshevik side.

It was clear that the will of the Whites to continue the struggle against the Bolsheviks had all but vanished. Ironsides admitted that "my efforts to consolidate the Russian National Army are definitely a failure," and recommended "as early an evacuation as possible."

In Washington, President Wilson and Congress were under intense scrutiny, and pressure to "bring home our gallant boys." In mid-February, Republican senator Hiram Johnson of California addressed his colleagues: "Under the orders of foreign nations," he blustered, "Americans wage war without declaration by the American Congress or the consent of the American people," and he tabled a motion requiring the immediate withdrawal of the 339th Infantry Battalion. To the profound embarrassment of the Wilson Administration, it proved to be a tie vote, which Vice-President Thomas Marshall had to break.

President Wilson ordered the withdrawal of the troops "as soon as practicable after the opening of navigation." Five months later, there was nothing left of American presence in Siberia or in the Arctic — all troops had returned home. After another three months, the British, French, and Canadians had also left. "None of the peoples of the allied countries had any stomach for further fighting," writes John W.F. Dulles. "There could be no rallying of a war-weary world for another crusade, however dark the picture of Bolshevism painted by conservative statesmen." A *finis* had been written to one of the more remarkable and unlikely military ventures ever launched by the United States.

By the time it was all over, allied intervention in the Russian Revolution had seen troops from eleven countries battling the communists, including Japanese, Poles, Greeks, Serbs, Romanians, and Italians. They fought not only on the Pacific coast, in Siberia, and Archangelsk, but also in Crimea and the Ukraine. (The Czecho-Slovak contingent was by far the largest: fifty-thousand men of the 145,000 allied total.)

"Wilfully or unwillingly," one American commentator concluded, "our country had engaged in an unprovoked intensive, inglorious, little armed conflict which had ended in disaster and disgrace." A much-relieved Senator Johnson welcomed the return of the troops, and eulogized them by declaring, "They served under conditions that were the most confusing and perplexing that an American army was ever asked to contend with, but they did their duty."

The military interventions were undeniably a blunder, comparable with the worst mistakes of the Crimean War. Just as Russia and the opposing nations had stumbled into that war, so did the United States and its allies flounder into the Russian Revolution. George Kennan declares succinctly, "The simple fact remains: had a world war not been in progress, there would never, under any conceivable stretch of the imagination, have been an Allied intervention."

In American corporate memory of the allied expeditionary forces is all but forgotten. And that's perhaps for the better. But not so in Russia, where anamnesis is strong — for decades, the intervention continued to be bitterly denounced. For the Soviets, it was a case of "wanton aggression and an act of sheer violence and brutal force … an attempt to curb the liberty, the political and social life of the people of another country." In 1959, Nikita Khrushchev pointedly reminded President Richard Nixon of that inglorious episode. "We remember the grim days when American soldiers went to our soil," he said. "Never have any of our soldiers been on American soil, but your soldiers were on Russian soil. These are the facts."

At the start of this book, claim was made that the United States and Russia, having at one time or another fought just about every major world power, never shed one another's blood. Might it not now be legitimately argued that the American intervention in Russia negates this assertion? Perhaps. But then, the United States was not at war *against* the Russians, but rather *with* the Russians — against the Bolsheviks and communism. Surely that's different.

AFTERWORD

In the decades following the withdrawal of the American Expeditionary Forces, Russian-American relations were severely strained, if not completely belligerent. They remained thus until the coming of a thaw in the late 1980s as perestroika and glasnost took root in the Soviet Union. Economic, political, and social contact between the two peoples had been scarce for most of the twentieth century — the two most notable exceptions were in the periods of the famines, and the alliances of World War II.

As the Russian Revolution was drawing to a close, Lenin continued as the major force in the Soviet Union. By 1923, however, he had suffered two strokes. Physically debilitated, he retired and the baton was callously grabbed by Joseph Stalin, general secretary of the Communist Party. Shortly thereafter, the "Father of the Revolution" died, and the ex-seminarian from Georgia became Soviet leader. The United States didn't officially recognize the Soviet Union until 1933, but the period between the Revolution's close and establishment of diplomatic relations wasn't entirely barren of contact between the two governments.

For over a decade, the Soviet Union suffered from the affects of famine, beginning with the famine of 1921 and culminating with an even greater one in 1932. Taken together, the period may be regarded as one of the greatest disasters in human history — eclipsing even the horror of the Holocaust. Estimates of deaths vary wildly, but certainly there were more than six million — and some figures run as high as eight million. There is no denying that the causes of the horrendous losses were manufactured, the handiwork of Leninists and Stalinists.

The strategic thrust for collectivization of farmlands by the imposition of *kolkhoz* (collectivization) was wrought in the government's determination to lay its hands on a generous portion of harvests. Grain export was a source of foreign currency — funds required for the country's program of industrialization. The state requisitioned; the peasant lost — over 30 percent of his produce was being confiscated by the state. Until the kolkhoz, the individual peasant sold up to 20 percent of his production, kept 15 for sowing, 40 percent for feeding cattle, and the balance for his family's use.

With the imposition of the new laws, conflict inevitably arose between the grower and the confiscator. As soon as the thrashing season started, peasants connived to steal or hide portions of the harvest. Resistance was ruthlessly met by the authorities with "shock troops" being sent in to make wholesale arrests. If the government-dictated allotment was not delivered on time, entire villages were declared saboteurs, and the right to buy essential goods — salt, sugar, soap, matches, and the like — was withdrawn.

Further repressive laws were promulgated in 1932, exacerbating the peasants' plight. Hundreds of thousands were killed, villages emptied, and the land left to grow wild. Professor Nicholas Werter notes in his article, "The State against Its People," that in one five-month period of 1932, 125,000 people were sentenced to ten years imprisonment, and 5,400 were executed. Mass deportations of villages became commonplace, and that year, Siberian gulags received 71,236 deportees, with the number jumping in the following year to 268,091.

Peasants sought escape to other parts of the country — a mass exodus got under way. But laws were then implemented suspending the sale of railway tickets. By March 1933, the professor notes, "219,460 people had been intercepted as part of the operation to limit the exodus of starving peasants to the cities ... 186,5888 had to be escorted back to the place of their origin." Day-to-day life in famine country is well documented. I recall very well Katya Kapinkin, a family friend, describing her firsthand experiences. As a young woman, she was on the ground managing an orphanage in the Volgodonsk region. She told of hunger so severe that people consumed not only cats and dogs, but wild birds and rats. Horse manure was scraped in search of oat seeds — soon, all the horses were gone. Fields were picked over for every last stalk of straw and blade of grass. Trees were stripped of bark for the making of soup. Bloated and cadaverous death was a commonplace fact of life. Cannibalism was not unknown, and Katya told of one skeletal mother knocking at the orphanage's door pleading to accept the emaciated boy she carried in her arms lest she eat him.

The Italian consul in Kharkiv reported,

> Every night the bodies of more than 250 people who have died from hunger or typhus are collected. Many of the bodies have had their liver removed, through a large slit in the abdomen. The police finally picked up some of these mysterious "amputators" who confessed that they were using the meat as a filling for the meat pies that they were selling in the market.[1]

Such was the terror of the time, brought about by the extortionist system of enforced collectivization. Resistance and acts of sabotage, Stalin claimed, were the work of unpatriotic and ignorant enemies of the state who were "prepared to leave workers from the Red Army without bread!" As the millions were dying of hunger, his government continued to export grain by the millions of hundredweights, all "in the interest of industrialization" — foreign currency was needed to purchase heavy equipment.

In the earliest famine years, the Soviet apparatus sought to deny the existence of any hunger. The outside world, however, did not buy this notion; it was impossible to hide the facts. Cries of the suffering for help resonated in Europe and North America. Among the organizations seeking to alleviate the woeful situation, two in particular successfully negotiated with Soviet authorities the delivery of emergency humanitarian aid: the International Red Cross and the U.S. government. For two years commencing in December 1921, some three hundred Americans worked side by side with scores of thousands of Russian personnel in the supply and distribution of food in the most stricken regions. Medical teams were dispersed throughout the region to tackle the problem of typhus outbreak.

But then the American Relief Administration, under the direction of Herbert Hoover, closed its Russian program when it discovered that the Soviets had resumed grain exports. By the time of the pullout, $20 million worth of food and medicine had been provided by United States. American medical units had been largely responsible for bringing under control the outbreak of typhus.

In June 1941, Adolf Hitler abrogated Germany's non-aggression pact with the Soviet Union by invading the country, thus drawing it into the raging war. Russia now found itself in league with the Allies of World War II: Britain, Canada, France, China, and a handful of lesser powers. (The United States at the time continued in neutrality, a half year away from its declaration of war.) President Roosevelt had, however, persuaded Congress to approve Lend-Lease as a means of delivering critically needed military equipment to the struggling Allies. The program in effect was a sale, one made affordable by the extension of non–interest-bearing loans that were to be repaid five years after the war's conclusion.

In the long months to come, American aid poured into the Soviet Union through Arctic ports. Nearly four million tons of supply arrived in the form of tanks, armoured vehicles, aircraft, armament, motorcycles, petroleum, and foodstuffs. Plus 427,284 trucks, 2,000 locomotives, 11,000 railway cars and a complete, fully equipped tire-manufacturing plant — all to attend to unimaginable transport requirements of the country's vast distances. By the time it was over, the cost of the Lend-Lease program to Russia amounted to $11.3 billion, a sum nearly the same as the post–World War II Marshall Plan. (The "loan" was only marginally repaid.)

With the war's end and the establishment of the United Nations, a new period of strained relations was ushered in by the Cold War. In Churchill's words, "From Stettin in the Baltic to Trieste in the Adriatic, an iron curtain has descended across the continent." American and Western European contact with Russia swirled around containment and confrontation: Sputnik and the space race, spying and the U-2 incident, and the Cuban Missile Crisis. The faint light of change dawned in Reykjavik in 1986 with the first Reagan-Gorbachev summit, the discussions of which formed the basis for the later non-proliferation treaty. A cautious step toward détente was taken — and then in 1989, the spectacular fall of the Berlin Wall, followed by the full bloom of glasnost and perestroika. In December 1991, Mikhail Gorbachev was replaced by Boris Yeltsin, "the flawed founder of Russian democracy," who for eight years held office. It was Yeltsin who oversaw the establishment of promising democratic structures in his country. The United States and the Western world applauded.

As a youngster I was startled by my Russian tutor who declared that the history of Russia is that of "an isolated nation."

It is clearly an uncommon country, unlike any other — a country that's neither European nor Asiatic, and one that forms a natural bridge between the two. Its flanks have constantly been menaced or assaulted, invaded from the east and west, from the north and south. But always the enemy was repelled by the unity and sheer determination of its people. Thirteenth-century Mongols alone met with success in overcoming the country, locking it up, as it were, for two hundred years. While Europe developed spectacularly as it did in that period, Russia stagnated under this yolk. "Scratch a Russian, find a Tartar" … a certain truth can be found in that saying. There's something non-European about Russians, something untamed about the fathomless, single-minded Slavic character of its peoples — fatalistic, introspective, lyrical, and emotional, with an uncanny capacity to endure suffering. The peoples' generosity — in the country's vast, unprotected spaces an individual feels lost and helpless. Only by sharing and supporting one another can goals be achieved and dangers avoided. Nationalism and defiance are deep-rooted. It's their way of life — all part of the intangible something called the "Russian soul."

Within it all, the Orthodox Church stands prominent, integral to the whole human and to the state. Its rich ceremonial, age-old traditions of chant and choral responses, its saints and icons — they colour the sombre candlelit kingdom. Russia's brand of Christianity stands apart from the rest. And the kingdom is closely coupled to the state apparatus.

Recall Churchill's view of Russia as being "a riddle wrapped in a mystery inside an enigma." As one contemplates the prevailing condition of Russian-American relations, those words seem to resonate. Try as the United States does to convey its message on the woeful state of relations, the road to St. Petersburg appears strewn with intractability.

Oh, the days of Jefferson ... "Russia is the most cordially friendly nation to us of any power on earth."

For well over a hundred years, the harmony and general optimism that prevailed between these two contrasting countries endured. "What is so surprising," historian Norman Saul points out, "is that the relationship was beneficial and friendly. Although credit must go to the two governments and their leaders, more must be given to the individuals, both Russian and American, who devoted their lives, or at least a substantial portion, to the furtherance of relationships."

Tsars and presidents aside, hark back to such figures as Francis Dana and young John Quincy Adams, to Dimitri Gallitzen of the Alleghenies, and to Ministers Henry Middleton and Alexander Bodisko; to General John Turchin and Grand Duke Alexis. Give thought also to the cheeky Tom, to the singular Nero Prince and her St. Petersburg shop. And let's not forget the intrepid Lynne Cox who in that summer of 1987 doggedly swam that shortest distance between the two countries.

In closing, I turn to Alexander Yakovlev, the stalwart Soviet ideologue and one-time secretary of the Communist Party of the Soviet Union. In the late 1980s, "the godfather of glastnost" was at the sides of Gorbachev and Eduard Shevardnadze in the remodelling of Russia. In his 2002 book *A Century of Violence in Soviet Russia*, he neatly encapsulates the tenor of the country's rulers:

> As we know, the land of Rus accepted Christianity in 988 A.D. Characteristics of Byzantine rule of that era — baseness, cowardliness, venality, treachery, over-centralization, apotheosis of the ruler's personality — dominate in Russia's social and political life to this day. In the twelfth century the various fragmented Russian principalities from the Volga to the Carpathians were conquered by the Mongols. Asian traditions and customs, with their disregard for the individual and for human rights and their cult of might, violence, despotic power, and lawlessness became part of the Russian people's way of life.

The tragedy of Russia lay first and foremost in this: that for a thousand years it was ruled by men and not by laws. The rulers were princes, tsars, various chairmen, and general secretaries. They ruled ineptly and bloodily. The people existed for the government, not the government for the people; the state was everything and the individual nothing.[2]

In speaking of his country shortly before his death in 2005, Yakovelv quipped, "we should overcome all our misfortunes if we overcome ourselves." His words echo today.

NOTES

Chapter 1: The Shortest Distance

1. Foster R. Dulles, *The Road to Tehran* (Princeton, NJ: Princeton University Press, 1971), 2.
2. Alexis de Tocqueville, Democracy in America, Bantam Classics (New York: Bantam, 2000).

Chapter 2: The Determinative Period

1. In contrast, the population of New York was 60,515; Philadelphia, 41,220; Baltimore, 26,514; Boston, 24,937; Charleston, 18,824; Providence, 7,614; Nantucket, 5,617; New Haven, 4,049. Some others: London, 960,000; Paris, 600,000; Montreal, 15,000; Halifax, 8,500 (mostly the garrison).
2. Abigail Adams, letter to her daughter, November 21, 1800, quoted in Kate Caffrey, *The Lion and the Union: The Anglo–American War, 1812–1815* (London: Andre Deutsch, 1978), 68.
3. A half-century later, the city had grown in numbers but its overall aspect remained provincial. Stratford Canning, a British diplomat, complained in 1853, "Hot! Hot! Hot! Most terribly hot! ... The Secretary of State was seen one morning at an early hour floating down the Potomac with a black cap on his head and a pair of green goggles on his eyes.... [Pennsylvania Avenue is] the only thing approximating our notion of a street ... chewing and spitting appear on the decline; indoor spitting is also less common.... The

diplomatic body at Washington ought really to be reckoned amongst the laboring classes ... life is one of privation and restraint."

4. Alfred W. Crosby, *America, Russia, Hemp, and Napoleon: American Trade with Russia and the Baltic, 1783–1812* (Columbus, OH: Ohio State University Press, 1965).

5. An amusing vignette: So quickly did she retreat from the White House, that when the first troop of British soldiers entered, they found the still warm dinner on the table. Having made short of it, they then invaded the president's bedroom and helped themselves to a fresh change of linen and stockings.

Chapter 3: The Pacific Passages

1. At his death, Astor was the country's wealthiest person, whose net worth was $20 million (in today's terms, estimated in excess of $84 billion). He, and subsequently his son, invested heavily in real estate and at one time they owned more than seven hundred New York properties. John Jacob was known for his one-liners: "You should buy Manhattan; they aren't making any more of it." Another gem: "If you want something done, hire someone; if you want something done right, do it yourself."

2. Assuming the guise of a common labourer, Peter eschewed any direct address such as "Your Majesty" or "Sire." He insisted that his fellow workers call him either "Carpenter Peter" or "Maas [Master] Peter." In time off from the shipyard, he inspected sawmills, factories, museums, paper mills, botanical gardens, surgeries, laboratories, and the workplaces of every sort of tradesman. He even spent time with a dentist and learned enough of the art to experiment on his servants. Peter was a man of insatiable curiosity.

3. One tangible result of these discussions was the tsar's removal of restrictions on the import of tobacco into Russia. Peter extended a virtual monopoly to British tobacco merchants for such imports, in the process helping to expand significantly the lucrative market for the colonies, Virginia in particular.

4. G.F. Miller, *Bering's Voyages: The Reports from Russia* (Fairbanks, AK: University of Alaska Press, 1986), 17.

5. The name stems from the adventurous Portuguese navigator, Vasco da Gama whose sixteenth-century voyages of discovery had nothing to do with the Pacific. Early on, the Portuguese had given the name to all the unknown territories of the northwest Pacific — a clever ploy to secure tenuous claim to whatever there was to be had in the *terra incognita*.

Chapter 5: The Admiral and the Prince

1. It was christened thus to honour Benjamin Franklin, at the time the U.S. ambassador to France, and derives its name from Franklin's *Poor Richard's Almanac*.
2. Samuel E. Morrison, *John Paul Jones: A Sailor's Biography* (Boston: Little, Brown and Co., 1959), 237.
3. A. Tarsaidzé, *Czars and Presidents* (New York: McDowell & Obolensky, 1958).

Chapter 6: The Pacific Frontier

1. Originally the *Resolution* was named the *Drake*. In anticipation of a possible meeting with the Spanish in California, the vessel was hastily renamed — all to avoid causing offence. One of Cook's younger officers on this voyage was William Bligh, later the captain of the *Bounty*, the ship that suffered the notorious mutiny in the South Pacific. (An island within Nootka Sound is named after Bligh.)

Chapter 7: Supply for Alaska

1. We do have precise statistics for 1833 of the total population of Russian America, a figure of 10,738. Of these, 627 were Russian (563 males, 64 females) and the balance either Métis or Natives.
2. James R. Gibson, *Imperial Russia in Frontier America* (New York: Oxford University Press, 1976), 44.
3. Ibid., 144.
4. Ibid.
5. Ibid., 122.

Chapter 8: Pacific Misadventures

1. Richard A. Pierce, *Russia's Hawaiian Adventure, 1815–1817* (Berkeley, CA: University of California Press, 1976), 93.
2. Otto von Kotzebou *A New Voyage Round the World in the Years 1823–1826* (Amsterdam: N. Israel, 1967).
3. Pierce, *Russia's Hawaiian Adventure*, 93.
4. Ibid.

Chapter 10: The Ambassadors

1. George Ticknor Curtis, *Life of James Buchanan: Fifteenth President of the United States* (New York: Harper & Brothers, 1883), I: 170.
2. *Washington Herald.*
3. *New York Herald.*
4. *National Intelligencer.*
5. Grand Duke Michael Bodisko, last will and testament.
6. James Buchanan, *The Works of James Buchanan: Comprising His Speeches, State Papers and Private Correspondence* (Charleston, SC: Nabu Press, 2012), II: 375.
7. Alexis de Tocqueville, *Democracy in America* (New York: Colonial Press, 1900).
8. Alexander Pushkin, Review of *A Narrative of the Captivity and Adventures of John Tanner during Thirty Years Residence among the Indians in the Interior of North America,*
9. Ibid.
10. Platon Chikachev, *On Shipping and Lakes in North America.*

Chapter 11: The Crimean War

1. United States Review, April 1856.
2. Michael Crichton wryly comments on the charge. Ineptitude in Crimea "culminated in Lord Cardigan's Charge of the Light Brigade, a spectacular feat of heroism which decimated three-quarters of his forces in a successful effort to capture the wrong battery of enemy guns."

Chapter 12: Serfdom and Slavery

1. Alexander H. Stephens.
2. In 1820, as debate was had on whether to admit Missouri into the union as a slave state or a free state, Jefferson firmly argued for its admission as a slave state — an abrupt reversal of his earlier views. A reflection of his attitudes is found in a comment he made that same year in a letter written to an in-law: "I consider a [slave] woman who brings a child every two years as more profitable than the best man on the farm."
3. N. Stone and D. Obolensky, eds. *The Russian Chronicles: A Thousand Years That Changed the World* (Godalming, UK: Bramley Books, 1998), 288.
4. At the time, Lincoln was unaware that Alexander was contemplating travelling down the very path of emancipation to that he himself aspired to do.
5. Lincoln.
6. Andrew White.
7. Warton Barker, "The Secret of Russian Friendship." *The Independent*, vol. 56. (March 1904).
8. Ibid.

Chapter 13: The Civil War and the Poles

1. *Edinburgh Review.*
2. Norman E. Saul, *Distant Friends: The United States and Russia, 1763–1867* (Lawrence, KS: University Press of Kansas, 1991), 322.
3. Albert A. Woldman, *Lincoln and the Russians.* (New York: The World Publishing Company, 1952), 141.
4. Tarsaidzé, *Czars and Presidents*, 194.
5. *Harper's Weekly*, vol. XII, 661.
6. Ibid.
7. Ibid.
8. *Journal of Commerce.*
9. *Daily Alta California.*
10. Admiral Lesovsky.

11. F.A. Golder, *The Russian Fleet and the Civil War* (n.p.:Isha Books, 2013).

Chapter 14: Siberian Telegraph

1. George Kennan was the great uncle of the George F. Kennan (1904–2005), arguably America's most influential twentieth-century diplomat.
2. It's from Kennan's personal writing in *Tent Life in Siberia* (twelfth edition, 1882) that I quote certain details of the grand adventure.
3. George Kennan, *Tent Life in Siberia* (New York: G.P. Putnam's Sons, 1882).
4. Ibid.
5. Ibid.
6. Ibid.
7. Ibid.
8. Ibid.
9. Ibid.
10. Ibid.
11. Ibid.
12. Ibid.
13. Ibid.
14. Ibid.

Chapter 15: Seward's Folly

1. These often-quoted words were not, in fact, his. Greeley was quoting one John Soule. Here was the actual advice offered by this noted newspaperman: "The best business you can go into you will find on your father's farm or in his workshop. If you have no family or friends to aid you, and no prospect opened to you there, turn your face to the great West, and there build up a home and fortune."

Chapter 16: A Fractured Friendship

1. To conclude the Katacazy story, following the grand duke's visit, the minister did return to St. Petersburg, where he unsuccessfully

sought to clear his name. He then went into self-imposed exile in Paris where, after some years of continuing to press his case, he died.

2. Clay's statement was prophetic. Within three decades of the tsar's violent end more than one head of state or high official shared the same fate, including American presidents Garfield and McKinley, King Umberto of Italy, President Carnot of France, Empress Elizabeth of Austria, Mahmud Shevket Pasha of Turkey.

3. Alexander III.

4. Count N.P. Ignatieff, quoted in Stone and Obolensky, eds. *The Russian Chronicles*, 313.

5. John Hay.

Chapter 17: The Rising Sun

1. One member of the Russian delegation was K.D. Nabokov, uncle to the then six-year-old Vladimir Nabokov, the future renowned author.

2. Dulles, *The Road to Tehran*, 93.

3. Kennan, *Tent Life in Siberia*,

Chapter 18: Revolution and Intervention

1. Dulles, *The Road to Tehran*, 100.

2. Benjamin D. Rhodes, *The Anglo–American Winter War with Russia, 1918–1919* (New York: Greenwood Press, 1988), 112.

Afterword

1. Stéphane Courtois and Nicolas Werth, *The Black Book of Communism: Crimes, Terror, Repression* (Harvard University Press, 1999).

2. Alexander Yakovlev, *A Century of Violence in Soviet Russia.* (New Haven, CT: Yale University Press, 2002), 235.

BIBLIOGRAPHY

Afonsky, Bishop Gregory. *A History of the Orthodox Church in Alaska, 1794-1917*. Kodiak, AK: St. Herman's Theological Seminary, 1977.

Anschel, Eugene. *The American Image of Russia, 1775-1917*. New York: Frederick Ungar, 1974.

Babey, Anna. *Americans in Russia, 1776-1917*. New York: Comet Press, 1938.

Bailey, Thomas A. "Days That Shook the World." *American Intervention in the Russian Civil War*. B.M. Untermberger, ed. Lexington, MA: D.C. Heath & Co., 1969.

Barker, Wharton. "The Secret of Russian Friendship." *Independent* 56 (March 1904).

Barratt, Glynn. *Russia in Pacific Waters, 1715-1825*. Vancouver: University of British Columbia Press, 1981.

——. *The Russian Discovery of Hawai'i*. Honolulu: Editions, 1987.

——. *Russian Shadows on the British Northwest Coast of North America, 1810-1890*. Vancouver: University of British Columbia Press, 1983.

Bolkhovitinov, N.N. *Russia and the American Revolution*. Tallahassee, FL: Diplomatic Books, 1976.

Bradley, John. *Allied Intervention in Russia*. London: Weidenfeld & Nicolson, 1968.

Caffrey, Kate. *The Lion and the Union: The Anglo-American War, 1812-1815*. London: Andre Deutch, 1978.

Cresson, W.P. *Francis Dana, a Puritan Diplomat at the Court of Catherine the Great*. Toronto: Longmans, Green & Co., 1930.

Crosby, Alfred W. *America, Russia, Hemp, and Napoleon: American Trade with Russia and the Baltic, 1783–1812*. Columbus: Ohio State University Press, 1965.

Cudahy, John. *Archangel: The American War with Russia*. Chicago: A.C. McClurg and Co., 1924.

Curtiss, J.S. *The Russian Army under Nicholas I*. Durham, NC: Duke University Press, 1965.

Dillon, E.J. *The Eclipse of Russia*. New York: G.H. Doran, 1918.

Dowty, Alan. *The Limits of American Isolation: The United States and the Crimean War*. New York: New York University Press, 1971.

Dulles, Foster R. *The Road to Tehran: The Story of Russia and America. 1781–1943*. Princeton, NJ: Princeton University Press, 1971.

Dunning, William A. "Paying for Alaska." *Political Science Quarterly* XXVII., no 3 (September 1912).

Esthus, Raymond A. *Double Eagle and Rising Sun*. Durham, NC: Duke University Press, 1988.

Fisher, H.A.L. *A History of Europe*. Vol. III. London: Eyre & Spottiswoode, 1905.

Fisher, Robin. *Approaches to Native History in Canada*. Ottawa: National Museum of Man, 1977.

Foley, J.P. *The Jefferson Cyclopedia*. New York: Russell & Russell, 1911.

Froncek, Thomas, ed. *The City of Washington*. New York: Alfred A. Knopf, 1977.

Gerus, Oleh. "The Russian Withdrawal from Alaska: The Decision to Sell." *Revista de Historia de America,* no 76 (1973).

Gibson, James R. *Imperial Russia in Frontier America*. New York: Oxford University Press, 1976.

Golder, F.A., "The American Civil War through the Eyes of a Russian Diplomat." *American Historical Review* 26, no. 3 (April 1921).

———. *Bering's Voyages*. New York: American Geographical Society, 1922.

———. "The Purchase of Alaska." *American Historical Review* 25, no. 3 (April 1920).

———. "Russian-American Relations during the Crimean War." *American Historical Review* 31, no. 3 (April 1926).

Gough, Barry M. *The Northwest Coast: British Navigation, Trade, and Discoveries to 1812*. Vancouver: University of British Columbia Press, 1992.

Goulevitch, A. *Czarism and Revolution*. Hawthorne, CA: Omni Publications, 1962.

Graves, William S. *America's Siberian Adventure, 1918–1920*. New York: J. Cape & H. Smith 1931.

Grünwald, Constantine de. *Alexandre Ier, le tsar mystique*. Paris: Amiot-Dumont, 1955.

Halliday, E.M. *Understanding Thomas Jefferson*. New York: HarperCollins, 2001.

Hans, N. "Tsar Alexander I and Jefferson: Unpublished Correspondence." *Slavonic and Eastern European Review* 32, no. 78 (1953).

Harper's New Monthly Magazine, 27.

Harper's Weekly, 7.

Hickey, Donald R. *The War of 1812*. Chicago: University of Illinois Press, 1990.

Hodge, Thomas P. "On Feodor Ivanovich Tolstoy: 'The American' and Russian Literature." M.A. thesis, Stanford University, 1987.

Hosking, Geoffrey. *Russia, People, and Empire and People, 1552–1917*. London: Fontana Press, 1998.

Kennan, George. *Tent Life in Siberia*. New York: G.P. Putnam's Sons, 1882.

Kotzebou, Otto von. *A New Voyage Round the World in the Years 1823–1826*. Amsterdam: N. Israel, 1967.

Kushnarev, E.G. *Bering's Search for the Strait*. Portland, OR: Oregon Historical Society, 1990.

Kuykendall, R.S. *The Hawaiian Kingdom*. Vol I. Honolulu: University of Hawaii Press, 1968.

Langelier, J.P., and D.B. Rosen. *El Presidio de San Francisco: A History under Spain and Mexico, 1776–1846*. Denver, CO: National Park Service, August 1992.

Laserson, Max. *The American Impact on Russia: Diplomatic and Ideological, 1784–1917*. New York: Macmillan, 1950.

Lincoln, W. Bruce. *Nicholas I, Emperor and Autocrat of All the Russias*. DeKalb, IL: Northern Illinois University Press, 1989.

Livock, G.E. *To the Ends of the Air*. London: HMSO, 1973.

Lorenz, Lincoln. *The Admiral and the Empress*. New York: Bookman Associates, 1954.

Maclaren, Roy. *Canadians in Russia, 1918–1919*. Toronto: Macmillan of Canada, 1976.

Massie, Robert K. *Peter the Great, His Life and World*. New York: Alfred A. Knopf, 1981.

McCullough, David. *John Adams*. New York: Simon & Schuster, 2001.

Miller, G.F. *Bering's Voyages: The Reports from Russia*. Fairbanks, AK: University of Alaska Press, 1986.

Montefiore, Simon S. *Prince of Princes: The Life of Potemkin*. London: Phoenix Press, 2000.

Morrison, Samuel E. *John Paul Jones: A Sailor's Biography*. Boston: Little, Brown and Co., 1959.

Murphy, Robert. *The Haunted Journey: An Account of Vitus Bering's Voyages of Discovery*. New York: Doubleday & Co., 1950.

Nikolai Mikhailovich. *Znamenitye Rossiane XVIII–XIX Vekov*. Lenizdat: St. Petersburg, 1996.

Nikoliukin, A.N. *A Russian Discovery of America*. Moscow: Progress Publishers, 1986.

Okun, S.B. *Rossiysko-Amerikanskya Kompaniya*. Moscow, 1939.

Paxton, John. *Imperial Russia: A Reference Handbook*. New York: Palgrave, 2001.

Pierce, Richard A. *Russia's Hawaiian Adventure, 1815–1817*. Berkeley, CA: University of California Press, 1976.

Rhodes, Benjamin D. *The Anglo-American Winter War with Russia, 1918–1919*. New York: Greenwood Press, 1988.

Riasanovsky, Nicholas V. *A History of Russia*. New York: Oxford University Press, 1984.

Rossya y SCHA, Obroz tserkovnyh svyazei. Vol. I. Minneapolis, MN: AARDM Press, 1991.

Russell, D. *The Lives and Legends of Buffalo Bill*. Norman, OK: University of Oklahoma Press, 1960.

Saul, Norman E. *Distant Friends: The United States and Russia, 1763–1867*. Lawrence, KS: University Press of Kansas, 1991.

————. *Concord and Conflict: The United States and Russia, 1867–1914.* Lawrence, KS: University Press of Kansas, 1996.

Smith, R.F. *The Caribbean World and the United States.* New York: Twayne Publishers, 1994.

Souvorin, A. *Russkii Kalendar na 1888 Goda.* St. Petersburg, 1888.

Srodes, James. *Franklin: The Essential Founding Father.* Washington, D.C.: Regnery Publishing, 2002.

Stone, N., and D. Obolensky, eds. *The Russian Chronicles: A Thousand Years That Changed the World.* Godalming, UK: Bramley Books, 1998.

Sweltenham, John. *Allied Intervention in Russia, 1918–1919: The Part Played by Canada.* Toronto: Ryerson Press, 1967.

Tarsaidzé, A. *Czars and Presidents.* New York: McDowell & Obolensky, 1958.

Thompson, John M. *Russia, Bolshevism and the Versailles Peace.* Princeton, NJ: Princeton University Press, 1966.

Tikhmenev, P. *Supplement of Some Historical Documents to the Historical Review of the Russian-American Company.* Seattle, WA, 1938.

Tocqueville, Alexis de. *Democracy in America,* New York: Colonial Press, 1900.

Tolstoi, Serge M. *Tolstoï et les Tolstoï.* Paris: Hermann, éditeurs des sciences et des arts, 1980.

Troubetzkoy, Alexis. *Imperial Legend: The Mysterious Disappearance of Tsar Alexander I.* New York: Arcade Publishing, 2002.

————. *The Road to Balaklava: Stumbling into War with Russia.* Toronto: Trafalgar House, 1986.

Unterberger, B.M. *America's Siberian Expedition, 1918–1920.* Westport, CT: Greenwood Press, 1969.

Werter, Nicholas. "The State against Its People: Violence, Repression, and Terror in the Soviet Union." *The Black Book of Communism,* E.S. Courtois, ed. Cambridge, MA: Harvard University Press, 1999.

Woldman, Albert A. *Lincoln and the Russians.* New York: World Publishing Company, 1952.

Yakovlev, Alexander. *A Century of Violence in Soviet Russia.* New Haven, CT: Yale University Press, 2002.

INDEX

ALSO BY ALEXIS S. TROUBETZKOY

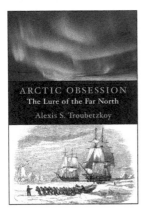

Arctic Obsession: The Lure of the Far North

More than an account of the human delusion and fortitude in penetrating one of the most inhospitable areas of the world, *Arctic Obsession* goes beyond the gripping history of northern exploration and the searches for the Northwest and Northeast Passages.

From early medieval times to the twenty-first century, what has been the beguiling attraction of the North? What manner of men were they who boldly ventured into those hostile and unpredictable regions, scores never to return home, swallowed by the merciless North.

Today's Arctic is developing into tomorrow's hot spot. *Arctic Obsession* dwells on the contemporary issues besetting the most fragile part of our planet: global warming and environmental and political concerns. The book also provides an overview of the entire Arctic region, from Canada, Russia, and Alaska, to Greenland, Iceland, and the North Sea.

ALSO FROM DUNDURN'S ARCTIC CULTURE AND SOVEREIGNTY LIBRARY

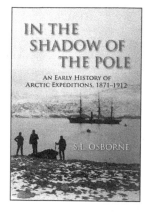

In the Shadow of the Pole: An Early History of Arctic Expeditions, 1871–1912
S.L. Osborne

How did the Arctic come to be part of Canada?

In the Shadow of the Pole explores the history of Arctic exploration and tells the story of how the Dominion government established Canada's jurisdiction there. It describes the early expeditions to Canada's North, including the little-known Dominion government expeditions to the sub-Arctic and Arctic carried out between 1884 and 1912. The men on these expeditions conducted scientific research, such as geological explorations and hydrographic surveys. They informed the people they met in the North of Canada's jurisdiction in the region and raised the Canadian flag from Hudson Bay to Ellesmere Island.

These men endured as much hardship and adventure as Peary, Nansen, Amundsen, and other famous polar explorers, yet their expeditions were not widely publicized and they received no glory for their efforts. This book attempts to correct that by showcasing the stories of the remarkable men who led these expeditions.